COMPUTER PROGRAMMING FUNDAMENTALS:

4 Books in 1:

Coding For Beginners, Coding With Python, SQL
Programming For Beginners, Coding HTML.
A Complete Guide To Become A Programmer With
A Crash Course.

Ashton Miller

Table of Contents – Coding For Beginners

Table of Contents – Coding With Python

Table of Contents – SQL Programming For Beginners

Table of Contents – Coding HTML

CODING FOR BEGINNERS:

A SIMPLIFIED GUIDE FOR BEGINNERS TO LEARN SELF-TAUGHT CODING STEP BY STEP. BECOME AN EXPERT CODER IN THE SHORTEST TIME POSSIBLE.

Ashton Miller

Introduction

C omputers are a lot different from humans.

They are not neutrally active and doesn't consist of any emotions that humans possess. Computers mostly rely on instructions.

The only reason why computers have become better than humans is that they do tasks effectively without wasting any time. However, we can consider computers as dumb machines. If they are not provided with a solution to the problem beforehand, they can't solve it. Even after twenty years of tremendous research robotics is not a successful field because it is challenging to make machines that take decisions by themselves.

In the early stages of computer development, people used to use instruction sets to complete tasks. These instructions sets are allowed to use only for scientific and military purposes.

Several multinational companies started to experiment with their employees to create a whole new way to pass instructions to computers. All dreamt of an easy way to make things work out.

After a few years with excellent research, computer scientists introduced the concept of programming to the technological world with the help of programming languages. Programming languages provide a set of defined libraries that can help you to create programs.

Programs are considered as an analytical representation of algorithms and the definite task of creating valid programs that can be understood by a machine is known as programming.

What is a Program?

Programming languages use programs to give varied instructions to the computing machines. From a mathematical perspective, the process of providing step-by-step instructions is called an algorithm.

A lot of statistical concepts in mathematics too use algorithms to solve a problem. An algorithm is not only a step-by-step procedure but a way that is proven to be effective.

In programming, we use programs to create a logical instruction that can make us solve a specific problem as quickly and effectively as possible.

Experienced programmers try to create programs that are in less code length and which consumes fewer resources. It is not only essential to create a working code, but it is also important to develop code that is feasible and which effectively understands the resources that are available to it.

What is the difference between Algorithm & program?

Algorithm and program are closely interlinked. When a programmer is solving a problem, he first finds a logical and provable way to complete it.

He monitors the inputs and outputs that are available and creates a step-by-step procedure to solve it.

This is called an algorithm from a theoretical basis.

However, computers can't understand human language. They use the binary system to follow instructions.

This is the reason why we need to represent our algorithm in a way such that computers can understand.

This process is technically known as programming. Programming uses a set of programs to make the computer understand what needs to be done.

What are the programming languages?

When the concept of programming is introduced the scientific and computing community has overwhelmed. They started developing a lot of instruction sets and began developing programs with them.

However, just after a few projects programmers and computing scientists understood that there needs to be a specific regular platform to create programs. It is not feasible to use each other's instruction sets to create meaningful software.

So, they worked hard to develop programming languages that can maintain and provide a lot of libraries for their usage. Programming languages like ABC, Pascal are developed and people started using them for developing programs. All these distinct programming libraries are enhanced and named as programming languages. They are also called as high-level languages and remember that they are only used to make it easy for humans to communicate with computers.

We always need a compiler to let computers understand the program.

To understand C programming in depth it is vital to learn about the default programming process in detail. Just like every other technological advancement, programming languages too follow a strictly adhered guideline system to make things work in the way they are intended to.

As said before, it is difficult to make computers understand the programs by themselves. So, computer scientists started to create programs that can be compiled and converted into machine language.

All the programs are compiled, interpreted before running the program.

This task is done by interpreters and compilers.

A programming language is a language that has a set of instructions that is designed to give a desired output. Programming languages are used to provide instructions to the underlying computer they run on. The computer in turn processes the information and then provides the desired output.

With a programming language, we would then develop a set of instructions known as a program. This program would be designed based on a set of requirements. Let's say we wanted to create a system that could handle the purchase orders created by a company. We could then write a program in the programming language of our choice to achieve this.

The programming language itself would be based on a set of constructs, and we would need to create the program based on these constructs. There is a broad series of programming languages available, and it's always wise to choose the right language based on the type of program we want to create. For example, let's say that we wanted to create a system that could work on the internet and be accessible through an internet browser. We would then choose a language that has the necessary capabilities we need, which also function on the web.

The very first popular high-level programming language was a language known as FORTRAN. It was invented by IBM and was made to design programs that could run on the world's fastest supercomputers of the time. It was used to develop programs in compute-intensive environments, such as numerical weather prediction, finite element analysis, computational fluid dynamics, computational physics and crystallography.

Then from the 1960's to the 1970's a great deal of low-level programming languages were developed. Some of these were:

- APL (A Programming Language), which introduced array programming and influenced functional programming.

- ALGOL which was a structured procedural language.

- Lisp, which was the first dynamically typed functional language.

- Simula, which was the first language designed to support object-oriented programming.

- C, which was developed between 1969 and 1973 as a system language for the Unix operating system and still remains a popular language to date.

Then came the age of object-oriented programming languages during the 1980's. During this time C++ was introduced as an object-oriented language and was also used for systems programming. Following this, came the growth of the Internet and the adoption of websites. Naturally there had to be programming languages that could support the applications built on the Internet. Perl was one of the first languages used for creating dynamic websites. It was initially intended for the Unix platform, but then branched out to support dynamic web applications.

The subsequent fourth generation of programming languages had additional support for database management, report generation, mathematical optimization, GUI development, and web development. Some of the general purpose fourth generation languages were Visual Foxpro, PowerBuilder and Uniface.

The fifth generation languages were based on problem solving. Here, constraints were given to the program, rather than using an algorithm written by a program. The reign of each language was dependent on how effective it was at fulfilling its purpose. Some older programming languages are still being used to this day, such as C and C++. At the same time, to keep up with the pace of technology, new programming languages had to be devised. For example with mobile devices, a programming language had to be developed to ensure that compatible programs could be created.

As time progressed, each programming language also had to be updated in order to keep up with technological trends. Java, for instance, has gone through multiple updates and is currently in version 8. Along with programming languages, application and web servers also had to be put in place to run these programs from a central point. So in addition to ensuring the programming languages were regularly updated, the application and web servers that hosted these programs also had to be continuously updated.

At present, we have the advent of Serverless programming. This is where we don't need to provide any infrastructure to run the program. All code is designed to run on a serverless cloud platform.

Chapter 1: *Popular Programming Languages*

The C Programming Language

T his was one of the earliest languages developed, and many systems were built around the C language. The features of the C programming language are:

- It has a rich set of built-in features and custom functions, which allow developers to create elaborate and complex programs.

- It has numerous functions that can be used to interact with the underlying operating system. For this reason it is used substantially in systems programming.

- Programs written in C are efficient and fast. This is mainly due to its variety of data types and powerful operators.

- It allows for the creation of various modules that can be used to logically separate bits of code.

Even though the C language had many features at the time, the advent of technology brought some pitfalls to light that necessitated a new set of programming languages. One shortcoming of the C language was that the programmer had to manage the memory allocation of the program correctly. If this were not achieved properly, it would lead to undesirable consequences such as the program crashing unexpectedly.

A significant limitation came with the need for web-enabled programs. The C language did not have the required libraries to work with web programming and hence was mostly used for system and network programming.

The C# Programming Language

This language was invented by Microsoft to have all the features of C, along with many new concepts. Some of the key elements of the C# language are:

- The ability of the environment itself to manage aspects such as memory. Now the memory allocation does not have to be governed by the programmer. Instead, the underlying environment, known as the runtime, would be responsible for allocating and deallocating the memory whenever required.

- It is an object-oriented language, which refers to its ability to create objects that represent real-life entities. The C# language does this with the help of classes and objects. So if we wanted to represent a person in a program, it could be done via the definition of the person as a class. This class would have properties that could then define the real-life features of a person, such as their name and surname. Hence each individual could then be represented by creating an object of that class.

- It has the ability to create programs for both desktop and web users. With modern technology, it is no longer realistic only to develop programs that run on the desktop. C# has gained significant popularity because it was designed to run both types of programs.

- It is regularly being maintained by Microsoft and hence there are always updates to this programming language. This means that it will be able to keep up with new technologies, and any shortcomings will likely be addressed as they crop up.

The Java Programming Language

This language was initially created by Sun Microsystems, but is now owned by the Oracle Corporation. It has key features that are similar to C#, such as the ability to have classes and objects, as well as memory management. But what makes this language even more popular, is the fact that it is an open source programming language. This allows developers to see how Java works under the hood and contribute to its growth.

Java also allows for its programs to be compatible with almost any platform, by only requiring the equivalent runtime to be installed that pertains to that operating system. While C# was meant to work primarily on the Windows operating system, the Java programs were meant to run on virtually any platform via the Java Runtime Environment.

The Java language also has different editions that focus on specific applications, such as enterprises and mobile platforms. Due to its open source framework, Java has a large support community. Hence if you encounter any problems or issues, you have the support from a large online community.

To learn about the programming versatility of Java, look out for our complete series on Java programming.

The JavaScript Programming Language

This is a client scripting language that runs mostly on the user-end in a browser. It is one of the three core technologies the web is based on, along with HTML and CSS. It is used for applications from web pages to video games. JavaScript has indeed become one of the most popular languages to date. Some of the key features of the language are:

- It is a lightweight programming language.

- It negates the need for content to be sent to a server to be processed. Usually for client-server applications that use C# or Java, the commands need to be sent to a server for processing. However with JavaScript, most of this can be done locally on the client machine itself, which saves a lot of time.

- It is also an object-oriented language, but differs slightly in the way objects are treated.

- It negates the need to compile a program before submitting the changes, which allows for faster deployment.

The Python Programming Language

This is another extremely popular programming language that is used in a variety of different applications. It is a high-level language that is quick to learn and easy to use. Python has also been around since 1991 and has built up a considerable fanbase. This makes it easy for newcomers to get support when they are stuck or their applications malfunction. Some of the essential features of this language are:

- It has a simple language. The code statements used resembles the English language, hence the programs are easier to read and understand.

- It is a free and open source language.

- The programs can be ported to a wide range of operating systems, without the need for major changes.

- It supports procedure-oriented programming and object-oriented programming.

- It has a wide variety of libraries available that can extend the available functionality.

To learn more about programming in one of the most popular languages in the community, be sure to look out for our complete series on Python.

The Angular JS Framework

This is a framework that is built around the JavaScript programming language, and is created and maintained by Google. Many popular websites use this framework to build dynamic websites. Some of the key features of Angular JS are:

- It can be used to develop rich web-based applications.

- It provides an easy way to ensure that data is integrated with business logic code.

- It uses HTML (Hyper Text Markup Language) to build user interfaces.

- It enables developers to write applications with less code.

- It is straightforward to test code, due to the Angular framework that was built with unit testing in mind.

The PHP Programming Language

This is a server-side scripting language that was designed for web development, but is also used for general programming. It is most notably used in combination with web content management systems, web template systems, and a diverse array of web frameworks. Some of the key features of this language are:

- It is straightforward and easy to use when compared to other scripting languages.

- It negates the need to compile a program beforehand. This means you don't need to prepare the program for running, you can make changes to the program whenever required and then run the changed program.

- Its programs can be ported to a wide range of operating systems, without the need for major changes.

- It is a free and open source language.

The Ruby Programming Language

Ruby is defined as a dynamic, reflective, object-oriented, general-purpose language. It is used in combination with a set of libraries known as Rails, which allows for much higher functionality. Some of the critical features of this programming language are:

- It is entirely free of charge, and can be used, copied and modified quite easily.

- It is an object-oriented programming language.

- It can be used as a server-side scripting language.

- It can be embedded into HTML.

- It has a clean and easy to understand syntax that makes it easy for new developers to learn.

- It is quite easy to write and maintain complex programs.

Chapter 2: *Getting Started With Coding*

Preparing Your Vision

T hink about why you wanted to learn to code in the first place. For a lot of people, it is because they want to make something that just doesn't exist yet. Others may want to do it because they know software developers are high-paying jobs and happen to be high in demand by tech and non-tech companies alike. Identify what drives you and then start looking for sources of inspiration that encourage you to stay focused on your goals. For a coder, an inspiration would be something like working for Apple or building the next competitor of Twitter. Identifying your vision is necessary in steering you towards the right tools. Like if you want to get involved with artificial intelligence and tinker with robots, Python is a functional starting language and has a lot of flexibility. If you're going to build the next Candy Crush addiction, you will need to focus on mobile apps and learn Swift, Objective-C, Kotlin and Java.

Preparing Your Program Structure

Building algorithms and flowcharts is essential. It is not an absolute requirement of course and you may be able to get away with making a quick piece of software without spending so much time on the planning phase but for the sake of efficiency and not wasting so much time taking multiple trips back to the drawing board, you should come up with a solid structure of your program. Rushing directly to the code editor without a plan would be like trying to build a house without a blueprint. Algorithms and flowcharts do not have to be a single night affair; you should take the time to study them and identify potential pain points or areas that may cause conflict. Depending on the size of your vision, a single mind may not be enough to run through all sorts of case scenarios. Let other people or perhaps friends take a look at your flowchart and algorithm so you can get their user perspectives. If you don't feel like the structure lacks polish, don't rush things because realizing there is a problem during the coding phase can cause a world of issues.

Preparing Your Hardware

The really cool thing about coding is the hard fact that you don't need a fancy computer to get started. Even an ancient Windows XP laptop can be capable of coding as long as you install the right software. Of course, your mileage will be significantly reduced with low-end hardware so I'm going to recommend something a bit more middle ground while keeping things budget-friendly. Coding is not by any means a huge investment! Your choice of hardware depends on where you will spend time coding for the most part.

If You Are A Home And/Or Office Dweller

Desktop computers remain as the best bang-for-the-buck coding workstations and it's pretty easy to explain why. Mobile components and chipsets tend to be more expensive and today's powerful laptops are very thin with sophisticated engineering. They also have parts that you don't find in desktops like trackpads, keyboards and batteries. Performance absolutely matters when you are compiling a program, using an interpreter or debugger, running a complicated program.

So what's the best processor to choose? Or more specifically, what's the best combination of desktop specs to consider? The answer is straightforward when it comes to coding and you don't even have to worry about the brand. For the CPU choice, the more cores, the better. The higher the clock speed (in GHz), the better. If you are stuck picking between Intel and AMD, go with the one with the lower price. If you have Windows 10, you should at least have 8 GB of RAM or else coding might not be so fun since Windows 10 tends to eat a significant chunk of your RAM with nothing running and you will probably need a browser tab or two open followed by whatever IDE or source-code editor you plan on using. More RAM means your system is less likely to bog down when you have lots of applications running at the same time.

The next key component of a coding workstation is the monitor. A modern computer screen has a screen resolution of 1366×768. You can see what that looks like below at 100% scaling.

```
long COggDecoder::Read()
{
    long i=ov_read_float(&m_vf,&m_buf,CHUNKSIZE,&m_bitstream);
    switch(i)
    {
    case OV_HOLE:
        {
            float f=ov_time_tell(&m_vf);
            swprintf(m_error,MAXERROR,L"OV_HOLE @ %dm %02ds",((int)f)/60,((int)f)%60);
        }
        return -1;
    case OV_EBADLINK:
        {
            float f=ov_time_tell(&m_vf);
            swprintf(m_error,MAXERROR,L"OV_EBADLINK @ %dm %02ds",((int)f)/60,((int)f)%60);
        }
        return -1;
    case 0:
        if(!m_vf.os.e_o_s)
        {
            wcscpy(m_error,L"TRUNCATED");
            return -1;
        }
    }
    return i;
};
```

It doesn't look too bad. With a font size of 11, you can see about 27 lines of code on a maximized screen and there is a little bit of space for a sidebar or side panel which you can find in many IDEs and coding environments. EmEditor is more on the source code editing side and is suitable for beginners but when you factor in things like testing code, you are going to wish you had a little bit more screen real estate. Having a Full HD display or 1920×1080 resolution is a significant upgrade and pretty inexpensive thanks to the advent of 4K displays. But could you go beyond 1080p? Would 4K be a wise choice? If you are a beginner, 4K is a waste unless you plan on using font scaling which will make the characters a whole lot smoother. The real winner is to use multiple displays.

A pair of 1080p displays will make a world of difference even if you are a beginner programmer. It is much better than those ultrawide displays that spreadsheet fanatics love. You do not need an ultrawide display since coders generally need more vertical screen real estate. But with a two displays and set in "extended desktop" mode, you can have a full screen dedicated to your coding environment and another screen for another coding environment if you like doing multiple projects or managing different codes or you can open up your browser for research or your flowchart or anything you just want to drag there at your leisure.

Next up is the keyboard and this is going to surprise you if you've been stuck with the same $10-$20 keyboard for the past several years. You might even be pretty comfortable mashing away at 60-70 words per minute and not thinking about "fixing what isn't broken". Try a mechanical keyboard as soon as you have the budget.

If You Are A Road Warrior

Picking a laptop geared towards coding is going to be a little bit more complicated since virtually all laptops come with each of their own compromises. It's really going to boil down to preference and what strengths of a computer you really need and even then you might still have a lot of laptops to choose from. But with this, should be able to narrow down your selection to the point that all the remaining candidates are winners. Prepare your checklist!

You obviously want to address the portability first as that should be the reason why you want to consider a laptop in the first place. A heavier laptop often means heavy-duty while a lighter laptop means more travel-friendly at the expense of flexibility in terms of handling coding and programming apps.

No matter what type of laptop you are going to get, having 8 GB worth of RAM along with an SSD and a 1080p display should be the three core essentials to consider. If you are really on a shoestring budget, the 1080p display should be your minimum. Then make sure you can upgrade your RAM and storage as there are several budget thin and light laptops that have soldered parts and are therefore non-upgradable.

Preparing Your Software

Flowcharting Software

Drawing a flowchart is easy but if you want to present a pretty complicated program flow in the cleanest way possible or just want to sort out your thoughts and algorithm in a friendly way, you should use a flowcharting software. If you have an active Internet connection, then I have some good news; you don't have to install any flowcharting software at all! Just head to http://www.draw.io and you can immediately get started with illustrating. Draw.io has a gridded interface and is pretty easy to learn as the flowcharting shapes are readily available on the sidebar. Connecting the shapes with arrows is pretty straightforward. You can save your work on Google Drive, OneDrive, Dropbox and a few code repositories or you can save it right on your computer. There is even an "Offline" option so you can switch off your Internet without fear of the web-based app interrupting your workflow.

Web Development Tools

C++ is a great programming language to play around with for understanding the basics of coding but if you want to go hands-on the fastest way possible, give HTML a shot because there is a useful and free (with ads) sandbox for placing HTML codes called https://htmlcodeeditor.com . The user interface isn't exquisite but it has a live preview so you can play around with the different codes and see the end result in real-time. You don't have to wait for anything to compile even though you are restricted to pure classic HTML code. CSS support is only available in the paid version.

If you want a free solution you can install to your Windows computer, give openElement a try. This Chromium-powered Web authoring tool has been around for several years and it is ready for the modern Web development world with support for HTML5 and CSS3. It even comes with a local server so you can test PHP scripts.

Source Code Editors

Whether you are going to take the nomadic route and do some pure raw coding or you are going to try out fancy IDEs, it always helps to have at least one source code editor installed in your computer. Source code editors are generally not heavy apps by any stretch and beginners have no reason to go for any paid software over the free ones. Just install Notepad++ and you'll see exactly what I mean. In addition to full HTML support for syntax highlighting, Notepad++ supports more than a dozen other programming languages. For a more elegant but still free alternative, you should try Sublime Text and it has Mac and Linux versions too in addition to Windows. The dark-themed interface should blend well with your dark mode themes and it has a highly customizable user interface.

IDEs

Once you are ready to move on beyond HTML, Python should be your next stop as it is one of the most accessible modern programming languages to learn. To quickly get started, consider trying PyCharm which is an IDE that even the pros use. The smart assistance feature helps with the debugging while the extensive documentation can walk you through the different features so you can run and test web apps. JavaScript, TypeScript, CoffeeScript, HTML, CSS and other technologies are supported by this IDE. If you want to expand beyond HTML and CSS and dive into JavaScript, Java and PHP, install Apache NetBeans IDE. Google even has its own IDE called Android Studio serving as the primary IDE for developing Android mobile apps with Kotlin as the primary language.

Chapter 3: <u>Functions</u>

Remember how we asked Merlin to store a set of commands in a file and later referenced that file whenever we wanted to repeat the same exact commands?

Well, we basically used what we'll call from now on, "functions". A function is effectively a block of statements that takes in inputs from other parts in the program, processes (or doesn't, in some cases) these inputs, and gives results.

So, an entire program can contain multiple functions and these functions can be invoked multiple times depending on what use we have for them. Why do we need functions though?

Well, primarily because we will need them sometimes. We will be dealing with really complex problems where we will end up using functions in order to write reusable code. Sometimes, problems are so big that we have to break our approach to solving them into steps and we can model each such step using a function. It is a very effective way of organizing both code and our thoughts.

Quick question - what function have you already seen in C++? The main function! It is a particular type of function that defines all the code that will run.

Let's see how we can define a function and run a function in C++:

```cpp
#include<iostream>

using namespace std;

int sum(int a, int b) {

int returnSum = a + b;

return returnSum;

}

int main() {
```

```
int numOne = 10;

int numTwo = 20;

int sumValue = sum(numOne, numTwo);

//sumValue will have the value 30

cout << sumValue;

}
```

The above program creates and uses a function called sum, to compute the amount of two numbers and return the result. Usually, you wouldn't make functions for

such trivial applications but we're looking at the above program to learn about functions.

Let's look at the function call first -

```
int sumValue = sum(numOne, numTwo);
```

The above statement calls the function by passing in the variables numOne and numTwo to be processed by the sum function (definition is mentioned above the main function) and the result of the computation done by the function is then assigned to the variable sumValue.

Let's look at the function definition:

```
int sum(int a, int b) {

int returnSum = a + b;

return returnSum;

}
```

The variables in the parentheses (a and b) specify the datatype and labels for the variables that will be sent to the function. Once returnSum is computed, we use the "return" keyword to specify that we want this value to be sent to back to wherever the function is being called once the necessary computation/processing/work is done. Note that the variables a and b hold the values that are sent to the function. Also, the reason the value of the variable

returnSum will be accessible outside the function is that its value is being sent out of the function. If you created any other variable for any other purposes inside the function it wouldn't be accessible outside the function. In other words, it's "scope" is limited to the function in which it is defined.

The function itself has a datatype. This data type specifies the data type of the value being returned. So, if your function returns a string its value is eventually being stored in a variable with a double datatype, C++ would raise an error. It would first try to make sense of your mistake and try to convert the string to a double but because such a conversion is not possible, it would then raise an error.

Let's look at another example of a function -

```
#include<iostream>

using namespace std;

void functionExample() {

cout << "This function does nothing!" << endl;

}

int main() {

functionExample();

}
```

In the above function, we've defined a function called functionExample. Pay attention to the syntax. The function's data type is "void" which is a keyword that indicates that the function does not return a result to from where it was called.

The statements within the curly braces following the function name specify what the function does. In order to utilize the function, you will have to use it in other functions by specifying its name and passing variables. For example, in the above program, the function is called from the primary function by the command

"functionExample();".

Pass By Value and Pass By Reference:

Remember how we passed variables to our functions? That's a widespread thing to do in any language that you will come across. However, C++ has a unique feature when it comes to this particular process.

Let's look at what this is through an example -

```cpp
#include<iostream>

#include<string>

using namespace std;

void addTwo(int input) {

input = input + 2;

}

int main() {

int a = 10;

addTwo(a);

cout << a << endl;

}
```

The program above adds 2 to whatever the input value is. One would usually expect that the output of the program would be a 12. But, it is actually a 10. This is because even though the value 10 and the variable a is passed to the function addTwo, it's value is copied to the input variable in addTwo. As a result, C++

treats the variables a and input as two separate entities even though they share the same value. The variable input effectively copies the value of the variable a.

Pass By Reference:

In order to modify this behavior, we'll make use of the ampersand operator (&) just before mentioning the label for the inputVariable. This would make C++ look

at the inputVariable's label as an alias for the variable that's being passed in. Any modifications made to this "alias" would now also affect the variable whose value was passed in. This way of passing a variable to a function is termed as passing by reference. Let's modify the function we just worked with -

```cpp
#include<iostream>

#include<string>

using namespace std;

void addTwo(int& input) {

input = input + 2;

}

int main() {

int a = 10;

addTwo(a);
```

```
cout << a << endl;

}
```

The output would be 12.

Example - Write a program that reverses any string that the user provides.

```
#include<iostream>

#include<string>

using namespace std;

string reverseString(string input) {

string reverse = "";

for (int counter = input.size() - 1;counter >= 0;counter--) {

reverse = reverse + input[counter];

}

return reverse;

}

int main() {

string str;

cout << "Enter a string: ";

cin >> str;

string reversedString = reverseString(str);
```

cout << "Reversed String: "<<reversedString<<endl; cout << "Original String: " << str << endl;

}

Example Output:

Enter a string: Library

Reversed String: yrarbiL

Original String: Library

Press any key to continue . . .

The above program takes in a string and passes it to the reverseString function which traverses the string from the last letter and adds it to an empty string until it reaches the index 0. The function then returns this newly formed string. Since we are passing by value the value of the original string (str) does not change.

Example- Check if a given string is a palindrome. Assume that every string that is sent in as input is always in lowercase. (Hint - a palindrome when reversed still matches the original string)

```
#include<iostream>
#include<string>
using namespace std; string reverseString(string input) {
string reverse = "";
for (int counter = input.size() - 1;counter >= 0;counter--) {
reverse = reverse + input[counter];
}
```

```cpp
return reverse;

}

bool isPalindrome(string input) {

string reverse = reverseString(input);

if (reverse == input) {

return true;

}

else {

return false;

}

}

int main() {

string str;

cout << "Enter a string: ";

cin >> str;

string reversedString = reverseString(str);

cout << "Reversed String: "<<reversedString<<endl; cout << "Original String: " << str << endl; if (isPalindrome(str)) {

cout << "The string you entered is a palindrome." << endl;

}

else {
```

cout << "The string you entered is not a palindrome" << endl;

}

}

In the above program, the isPalindrome function calls the reverse function and uses the reverse of the input string to determine whether the string is a palindrome or not. Notice how the function call (isPalindrome()) has been used in an if-else block as it returns a bool value. This program can be simplified and written better but it has been written in this way to show how it can be built from the former program by just adding another function.

Example Outputs -

1)

Enter a string: madam

Reversed String: madam

Original String: madam

The string you entered is a palindrome.

Press any key to continue . . .

2)

Enter a string: palindrome

Reversed String: emordnilap

Original String: palindrome

The string you entered is not a palindrome

Press any key to continue . . .

Chapter 4: <u>Containers</u>

C ontainers are precisely what their name conveys. They hold data in forms that are easily accessible for us. We will look at arrays and vectors.

Arrays:

Arrays are containers that hold data of a particular data type and are fixed in size. That is, once you initialize an array with a specific size you can't increase its size unless you create another variety of a larger size and copy over all the elements. Arrays also hold data in a linear sequence and preserve "order". Once data is put inside an array, it stays in the exact place you put it in unless you make changes to the variety.

Arrays are also not for beginner coders but when used properly, you can make far more efficient programs. If you find yourself making too many variables to store similar data, you can simplify things by creating an array that can store these values in their own dedicated cells. Think about the way apartments and condos work. Each room doesn't have its private mailbox. Instead, there is a dedicated room in the apartment containing a large mailbox with individual compartments each with their own locks to represent each room.

Let's learn how to create an array through an example:

```
#include<iostream>

using namespace std;

int main() {

int arrayOfNumbers[5] = { 10,23,45,67,12 };

}
```

The above example shows how to create an array. The array is defined by the label "arrayOfNumbers". The number within the square braces - 5 in this case establishes the number of elements the array holds. The "int" specifies that the array will contain only integers. This datatype can be changed depending on what type of array you want to create. Finally, the numbers within the curly braces represent the data that the array holds. When you initialize an array with its values, you specify the values between the curly braces.

To access a number, say 23, within the array, we do so by specifying an "index"

as follows -

cout<<arrayOfNumbers[1];

The above statement will print the number 23 on to the screen. Now you may notice I used the number 1 as my index and not 2. That's because C++ follows zero-based numbering where the first number in a collection starts at the index 0. So, in order to access the first number in arrayOfNumbers, you would use the 0 index like -

cout<<arrayOfNumbers[0];

Instead of initializing the array at the very moment you declare it, you can create it and later assign individual values to each position by indexing it. By the same logic, you can modify the values in the array as well.

So, you can do things like -

arrayOfNumbers[1] = arrayOfNumbers[1] + arrayOfNumbers[2] - 5; Now, arrayOfNumbers[1] would equal 63.

Everything looks fine and dandy until now doesn't it? Well, what would you do if your array had 200 elements and you had to go through each component and add 5 to it? You can't do something like arrayOfNumbers + 5, because arrayOfNumbers is a "container" that holds numbers. It points to a memory space in your computer that contains the numbers in the array. So, adding 5 to arrayOfNumbers doesn't make sense and will actually throw an error.

Chapter 5: Strings

S tring refers to the group of words which can be of meaningful or without meaning. String basically used to represent text and characters in programming language. It always carry multiple characters to named as string. In other words strings are array but of character datatype. An array of character is called string. Strings are one dimensional array of character which areASCII terminated by null character represented by '\0'. A-Z = 65-90 a-z = 97-122 0-9 = 48-57

Example: Physical representation of
string of size 6 which conations string "Hello" in computer memory.

Address in computer memory

600 601 602 603 604 605 H e l l o \0 A[0] A[1] A[2] A[3] A[4] A[5]

Name of array

Function of Strings

There are basically four functions in String
1. Strlen()
2. Strcpy()
3. Strcat()
4. Strcmp()

strlen() :

This function is used to find the length of a String.

For example :-
Char str[5] = {"Hello"};
int l ;
l = Strlen(str);

strcpy() : This function is used to copy String from one string variable to another string variable.

For ex :-
Char str[5] = {"Hello"} , str2[6] = {"World"} ; //Strcpy(destination , source);
Strcpy(str , str2);

strcat() :

This function is used to concat two string or to join two strings variable .

For ex :-
Char str[5] = {"Hello"} , str2[6] = {"World"} ; //Strcat(destination , source);
Strcpy(str , str2);

strcmp() :

This function is used to compare two string or to join two string variable.

For ex :-
Char str[5] = {"Hello"} , str2[6] = {"World"} ; //if (Strcmp (str , str2)==0)
Then both string variable are same
//if (Strcmp (str,str2)>0)
Then str is greater
//if (Strcmp (str,str2)<0)
Then str2 is greater

Chapter Programs

1. **A Program to read and display string without any space**

```
#include<stdio.h>
#include<conio.h>
#include<string.h>
void main()
```

```
{
char str [30];
clrcsr ();
printf ("\n Enter String : ");
scanf ("%s",str);
printf ("\n You typed = %s ",str); getch();
}
```

2 . **A program to read and display string with space**

```
#include<stdio.h>
#include<conio.h>
#include<string.h>
void main()
{
char str [30];
clrcsr ();
printf ("\n Enter String : "); gets(str);
printf ("\n You typed = %s ",str); getch();
}
```

3. **A program to find the length of the String**

```
#include<stdio.h>
#include<conio.h>
#include<string.h>
void main()
{
char str [30] , l;
clrcsr ();
printf ("\n Enter String : ");
```

gets(str);

1 = Strlen(str);

printf("\n Length of String %s is %d ", str ,1);

getch();

}

4. <u>**A program to read two string variables and concat or join them**</u>

#include<stdio.h>

#include<conio.h>

#include<string.h>

void main()

{

char str [30] , str1[30] ;

clrcsr ();

printf ("\n Enter 1st String : "); scanf ("%s",str);

printf ("\n Enter 2nd String : "); scanf("%d",str1);

strcat(str , str1);

Printf("\n Result after concatenation : %s ",str);

getch();

}

5. <u>**A program to copy a word from one string variable to another variable**</u>

#include<stdio.h>

#include<conio.h>

#include<string.h>

void main()

{

```
char str [30] , str1[30] ;
clrcsr ();
printf ("\n Enter 1st String : ");
scanf ("%s",str);
printf("\n Enter 2nd String : ");
scanf("%d",str1);
strcpy( str , str1);
Printf("\n Result after copying : %s ",str); getch();
}
```

6. A program to check which string variable is greater

```
#include<stdio.h>
#include<conio.h>
#include<string.h>
void main()
{
char str [30] , str1[30] ;
clrcsr();
printf ("\n Enter 1st String : "); scanf ("%s",str);
printf("\n Enter 2nd String : "); scanf("%d",str1);
if(strcmp (str , str1)>0)
{
printf("\n %s is greater ",str); else
{
printf("\n %s is greater ",str1); }
getch();
```

7. A program to count the number of alphabet 'a' in a sentence

```
#include<stdio.h>
#include<conio.h>
```

```
#include<string.h>
void main()
{
char str [30] ;
int count=0 , l , i ;
clrcsr ();
printf ("\n Write a sentence : "); scanf ("%s",str);
l = strlen(str);
for(i=0 ; i<l ; i++)
{
If( str[i] == 'a')

printf("\n Number of 'a' character in a sentence is : %d ",count);
getch();
}
```

8. A program to count the number of vowels in a sentence

```
#include<stdio.h>
#include<conio.h>
#include<string.h>
char str [30] ;
int count=0 , l , i ;
clrcsr ();
printf ("\n Write a sentence : ");
scanf ("%s",str);
l = strlen(str);
for(i=0 ; i<l ; i++)
{
If( str[i] == 'a' || str[i] == 'e' str[i] == 'i' || str[i] == 'o' || str[i] == 'u')
```

```
printf("\n Number of vowels in a sentence is : %d ",count);
getch();
}
```

9. A program to count the number of consonant in a sentence

```
#include<stdio.h>
#include<conio.h>
#include<string.h>
char str [30] ;
int count=0 , l , i ;
clrcsr ();
printf ("\n Write a sentence : ");
scanf ("%s",str);
l = strlen(str);
for(i=0 ; i<l ; i++)
{

If( str[i] != 'a' || str[i] != 'e' str[i] != 'i' || str[i] !='o' || str[i] != 'u')
printf("\n Number of consonant in a sentence is : %d ",count);

getch();
}
```

10. A program to reverse a string

```
#include<stdio.h>
#include<conio.h>
#include<string.h>
void main()
{
char str [30];
```

```
clrcsr ();
printf ("\n Enter String : ");
scanf ("%s",str);
strrev(str);
printf ("\n Reverse string = %s ",str); getch();
}
```

11. <u>A program to change the string in both upper and lower case</u>

```
#include<stdio.h>
#include<conio.h>
#include<string.h>
void main()
{
char str [30] , str1[30];
clrcsr();
printf ("\n String in lower case : "); gets(str);
printf ("\n String in upper case : "); gets(str1);
strupr(str);
strlwr(str1);
printf("\n Lower to upper case %s",str); printf("\n Upper to lower case %s",str1); getch() ;
}
```

12. <u>A program to compare two string variables without case comparing</u>

```
#include<stdio.h>
#include<conio.h>
#include<string.h>
void main()
{
char str [30] , str1[30];
clrcsr();
```

```
printf ("\n Enter 1st word : ");
gets(str);
printf ("\n Enter 2nd word : "); gets(str1);
if( strcmpi (str , str1)==0) {
printf("\n Same ");
}
Else
{
printf("\n Not Same ");
}
getch();
```

Chapter 6: Loops

L oops are a way for us to execute a set of statements multiple times. We can specify the number of times we want to accomplish these statements or we can also specify conditions which when are or are not satisfied with the execution of this set of statements stop.

There are three types of loops we're going to look at - for, while, do while Let's look at the for loop first -

The for loop is mostly used for executing a set of statements a set number of times. It's also used to iterate through extensive collections and do something to each element.

Let's look at an example and then see what for loop is all about.

```cpp
#include<iostream>

using namespace std;

int main() {
for (int i = 0; i < 10; i++) {
cout << "hello" << endl;
}
}
```

The output is -

hello

hello

hello

hello

hello

hello

hello

hello

hello

hello

Press any key to continue . . .

The program above basically printed hello ten times. Basically, the for loop that we just defined ran the statement below it 10 times and so "hello" was published ten times.

But why correctly did it run 10 times?

We'll know once we understand the structure of the for loop.

The for loop consists of three parts - initialization, logical comparison, and the increment or decrement statement.

Initialization (int i=0):

In the for loop, the variable i is initialized to the value 0. The variable i works as a counter and at the start of the circle, before any statements are executed, the amount of this variable is 0. That is what initialization means. Also, notice how I didn't have to define the variable outside the loop and then equate it to 0 within the loop (although I can do that as well). The fact that I declared it within the loop means that the variable i will not be accessible outside the loop. However, if I declared it outside the loop and assigned to it an initial value inside the loop, I would still be able to access the variable outside the loop.

Logical Comparison (i<10):

The logical comparison defines the condition that needs to be satisfied for the loop to keep executing the statements inside it. This condition is checked every single time the loop is run including the very first iteration. In our example, we check if the variable i is less than 10. If that is true the loop runs, otherwise, the loop is broken.

Increment (or Decrement) (i++):

Every time the loop finishes running, the increment or decrement part is executed. In our example, the value of i increases after every iteration of the loop. But this is also within our control. We could depending on our purposes, decrement the variable we defined or increase it by multiplying it by itself, etc.

How it all works together:

The loop counter is initialized, the condition is checked and if the condition holds, the statement(s) below is/are executed. Then the increment or decrement part is reached and the logical comparison part is rerun. If the condition holds, the loop runs again, if not, it breaks.

The for loop can be used in different ways apart from just as a tool to do something multiple times. We can use it to access elements in our array.

Here's how we can do that -

```
#include<iostream>

using namespace std;

int main() {

const int arraySize = 10;

int arrayValues[arraySize] = { 1,2,3,4,5,6,7,8,9,10 }; for (int counter = 0; counter < arraySize; counter++) {

cout << arrayValues[counter] << endl;
```

```
}

}
```

In the code above, we've first declared the arraySize as 10 and as a constant.

And then we've initialized our array with the numbers from 1-10. Now, instead of individually accessing each element separately, we've used a for loop to do the work for us.

Since the variable counter initially equals 0 and it grows one step at a time and stops at 9, we can use counter's value to index the array's elements at each position.

So, the output would look something like this -

1

2

3

4

5

6

7

8

9

10

Press any key to continue . . .

We can also modify the array's value depending on certain conditions.

```
#include<iostream>

using namespace std;

int main() {

const int arraySize = 10;

 int arrayValues[arraySize] = { 1,2,3,4,5,6,7,8,9,10 }; for (int counter = 0; counter < arraySize;
counter++) {

if (counter > 5) {

arrayValues[counter] = arrayValues[counter] * 2;

}

cout << arrayValues[counter] << endl;

}

}
```

In the above program, we've basically written the code such that it would double an array element's value if it's index is greater than 5. The output is as follows -

1

2

3

4

5

6

14

16

18

20

Press any key to continue . . .

Another way to loop is with while loops. Let's explore with an example:

```cpp
#include<iostream>
using namespace std;
int main() {
int arrayValues[5] = { 5,6,7,8,9 };
int counter = 0;
while (counter < 5) {
cout << arrayValues[counter] << endl; counter++;
}
}
```

The while loop executes the statements inside it 5 times in the example. The counter variable is initialized outside the loop and is incremented once all the statements in the loop are specified. If you forget to update the counter, the while loop will run forever!

A slight modification of the while loop above is the **do-while** loop. The do while loop is exactly like the while loop, except that it runs the statements inside at least once, irrespective of the condition.

Let's look at an example based off of the while loops -

```
#include<iostream>

using namespace std;

int main() {

int arrayValues[5] = { 5, 6, 7, 8, 9 }; int counter = 0;

do {

cout << arrayValues[counter] << endl; counter++;

} while (counter < 5);

}
```

In the above program, the statements within the "do" block are run at least once irrespective of the comparison being made. Subsequent iterations are however made on whether the condition is met.

Now that we know quite a bit about loops, let's move back to arrays.

Remember how I said that arrays in C++ are fixed in size? Well, that can't be changed. However, C++ has a built-in container called a vector. A vector is built on top of an array and doesn't have a fixed size. It can be added to as long as you want to.

To use vectors, you have to include the vector library.

As always, let's learn through an example --

```
#include<iostream>

#include<vector>
```

```
using namespace std;

int main() {

vector< int> vec = { 1, 2, 3, 4, 5, 6 }; cout << vec[0] << endl;

vec.push_back(7);

cout << vec[vec.size() - 1] << endl;

}
```

So, you can see that we're using the vector library. And we're initializing the vector "vec" just like we initialized an array. However, there are a couple of differences. The first one is that we're specifying the data type of the vector within angular brackets after the keyword "vector". This data type basically defines the datatype of all the elements within the vector.

Notice how indexing with vectors is just like indexing with arrays.

"vec.push_back(7)" adds the number 7 to vector. So, the vector now contains 1,2,3,4,5,6,7. The ".push_back(7)" notation may be new to you. It basically makes use of the "push_back" method to add a value to the vector. The "." basically specifies that this method applies to the vector you created. We'll look at methods in detail when we talk about Object Oriented Programming.

Just as you added integers to the vector, you can also "pop" integers from the end of the vector. For that you will use the pop_back method - vec.pop_back().

Doing so will remove the last element from the array.

Here is a list of some commonly used vector methods: Method

Purpose

push_back(<value>)

Add's <value> to the end of the vector

pop_back()

Remove the last element from the

vector

insert(<position>,<value>)

Adds <value> to the vector at the

index specified by <index>

clear()

Clears the entire vector

Alright, now let's look at a comprehensive example.

Example - Create a vector containing the scores of all students in a class (the number of students and the scores will be provided by the user).

Calculate the sum of all the scores, and the average score of the class.

```cpp
#include<iostream>
#include<vector>
using namespace std;
int main() {
vector<double> scores;
int numStudents;
cout << "How many students are in your class?"; cin >> numStudents;
```

```
cout << endl << endl;

for (int counter = 1;counter <= numStudents;counter++) {

cout << "Enter the score for student #" << counter << " : ";

double scoreValue;

cin >> scoreValue;

scores.push_back(scoreValue);

}

double classScoreSum = 0;

for (int counter = 0;counter < scores.size();counter++) {

classScoreSum += scores[counter];

}

double average = classScoreSum / numStudents;

cout << endl << "Sum of all the scores - " << classScoreSum << endl; cout << "Class Average - " << average << endl;

}
```

Sample Output:

How many students are in your class? 5

Enter the score for student #1 : 75

Enter the score for student #2 : 70

Enter the score for student #3 : 80

Enter the score for student #4 : 92.75

Enter the score for student #5 : 93.50

Sum of all the scores - 411.25

Class Average - 82.25

Press any key to continue . . .

The first for loop takes in the score for each student and puts the score in a vector. This vector is later accessed and all the scores are added to compute the net score of the class. The average is then calculated by dividing this sum by the number of students in the class.

Example - Build a calculator program that calculates the sum, the product, and the difference between the two numbers and keep doing this until the user enters the string 'STOP'. This program has to run at least once.

```cpp
#include<iostream>

#include<vector>

#include<string>

using namespace std; int main() {

string stopString;

do {

cout << "Enter the first number: "; double firstNumber;
```

```
cin >> firstNumber;

cout << endl << "Enter the second number: "; double secondNumber;

cin >> secondNumber;

cout << endl << "Sum: " << firstNumber + secondNumber << endl; cout << "Product: "
<< firstNumber*secondNumber << endl; cout << "Difference: " << firstNumber -
secondNumber << endl; cout << "Enter STOP if you want to stop otherwise enter any other
string";

cin >> stopString;

} while (stopString != "STOP");

}
```

Here's a sample output -

Enter the first number: 1

Enter the second number: 2

Sum: 3

Product: 2

Difference: -1

Enter STOP if you want to stop otherwise enter any other string continue

Enter the first number: 5

Enter the second number: 7

Sum: 12

Product: 35

Difference: -2

Enter STOP if you want to stop otherwise enter any other stringSTOP

Press any key to continue . . .

Chapter 7: *Modules*

I n Python, a module is a portion of a program (an extension file) that can be invoked through other programs without having to write them in every program used.

Besides, they can define classes and variables.

These modules contain related sentences between them and can be used at any time.

The use of the modules is based on using a code (program body, functions, variables) already stored on it called import.

With the use of the modules, it can be observed that Python allows simplifying the programs a lot because it will enable us to simplify the problems into a smaller one to make the code shorter so that programmers do not get lost when looking for something in hundreds of coding lines when making codes.

How to Create a Module?

To create a module in Python, we don't need a lot; it's straightforward.

For example: if you want to create a module that prints a city, we write our code in the editor and save it as "mycity.py".

Once this is done, we will know that this will be the name of our module (omitting the .py sentence), which will be assigned to the global variable __city__.

This is a straightforward code designed for users of Python 2.

The print function is not in parentheses, so that's the way this Python version handles that function.

But, beyond that, we can see that the file "mycity.py" is pretty simple and not complicated at all, since the only thing inside is a function called "print_city" which will have a string as a parameter, and what it will do is to print "Hello, welcome to", and this will concatenate with the string that was entered as a parameter.

Import Statement

This statement is used to import a module.

Through any Python code file, its process is as follows:

- The Python interpreter searches the file system for the current directory where it is executed.

- Then, the interpreter searches for its predefined paths in its configuration.

- When it meets the first match (the name of the module), the interpreter automatically executes it from start to finish.

When importing a module for the first time, Python will generate a compiled .pyc extension file.

This extension file will be used in the following imports of this module.

When the interpreter detects that the module has already been modified since the last time it was generated, it will create a new module.

Example:

This will print:

You must save the imported file in the same directory where Python is using the import statement so that Python can find it.

As we could see in our example, importing a module allows us to improve the functionalities of our program through external files.

Now, let's see some examples. The first one is a calculator where will create a module that performs all the mathematical functions and another program that runs the calculator itself.

The first thing we do is the module "calculator.py" that is responsible for doing all the necessary operations.

Among them are the addition, subtraction, division, and multiplication, as you can see.

We included the use of conditional statements such as if, else, and elif.

We also included the use of exceptions so that the program will not get stuck every time the user enters an erroneous value at the numbers of the calculator for the division.

After that, we will create a program that will have to import the module to so that it manages to do all the pertinent mathematical functions.

At this time, you might be thinking that the only existing modules are the ones that the programmer creates.

The answer is no since Python has modules that come integrated to it.

With them, we will make two more programs: the first one is an improvement of the one that we have just done, and the second one will be an alarm that will print on screen a string periodically.

First example:

The first thing that was done was to create the module, but at first sight, we have a surprise, which is that math was imported.

What does that mean to us?

Well, that we are acquiring the properties of the math module that comes by default in Python.

We see that the calculator function is created that has several options.

If the op value is equal to 1, the addition operation is made.

If it is equal to 2, the subtraction operation is made, and so on.

But so new is from op is equal to 5 because, if this is affirmative, then it will return the value of the square root of the values num1 and num2 through the use of math.sqrt(num1), which returns the result of the root.

Then, if op is equal to 6, using functions "math.radians()" which means that num1 or num2 will become radians since that is the type of value accepted by the functions "math.sin()", meaning that the value of the sin of num1 and num2 will return to us, which will be numbers entered by users arbitrarily who will become radians and then the value of the corresponding sin.

The final thing will be to create the main program, as it can be seen next:

Here, we can see the simple program, since it only imports the module "calculator.py", then the variables num1 and num2 are assigned the value by using an input.

Finally, an operation to do is chosen and to finish is called the calculator function of the calculator module to which we will pass three parameters.

Second example:

We are going to create a module, which has within itself a function that acts as a chronometer in such a way that it returns true in case time ends.

In this module, as you can see, another module is imported, which is called as "time", and as its name refers, functions to operate with times, and has a wide range of functions, from returning dates and times to help to create chronometers, among others.

First, create the cron() function, which starts declaring that the start Alarm variables will be equal to time time, which means that we are giving an initial value to this function o know the exact moment in which the function was initialized to then enter into an infinite cycle.

Since the restriction is always True, therefore, this cycle will never end, unless the break command is inside it.

Then, within the while cycle, there are several instructions.

The first is that the final variable is equal to time.time() to take into account the specific moment we are located and, therefore to monitor time.

After that, another variable is created called times, and this acquires the value of the final minus start Alarm.

But you will be wondering what the round function does.

It rounds up the values; we do that to work easier.

But this is not enough, therefore, we use an if since, if the subtraction between the end and the beginning is greater or equal to 60, then one minute was completed, and what happens to this?

Why 60?

This is because the time module works with a second and for a minute to elapse, 60 seconds have to be elapsed, therefore, the subtraction between the end and the beginning has to be greater than or equal to 60, in the affirmative case, True will be returned and finally, we will get out of the infinite cycle.

Once the alarm module is finished, we proceed to make the program, as we can see below:

We can see that the program imports two modules, the one we have created, the alarm and the time module.

The first thing we do is to create the variable s as an input which tells the user if he wants to start.

If the answer is affirmative, then the variable h representing the time will be equal to "time.strftime ("%H:%M:%S")", which means that we are using a function of the time module that returns the hour to use in the specified format so that it can then be printed using the print function.

The next action is to use the alarm module using the command alarm.cron(), which means that the cron() function is being called.

When this function is finished, the time will be assigned to the variable h, again, to end printing it and being able to observe its correct operation.

We can say that the modules are fundamental for the proper performance of the programmer since they allow to make the code more legible, in addition, that it enables subdividing the problems to attack them from one to one and thus to carry out the tasks efficiently.

Locate a Module

When importing a module, the interpreter automatically searches the same module for its current address, if this is not available, Python (or its interpreter) will perform a search on the PYTHONPATH environment variable that is nothing more than a list containing directory names with the same syntax as the environment variable.

If, in any particular case, these previous actions failed, Python would look for a default UNIX path (located in /user/local/lib/python on Windows).

The modules are searched in the directory list given by the variable sys.path.

This variable contains the current directory, the PYTHONPATH directory, and the entire directory that comes by default in the installation.

Syntax of **PYTHONPATH**

A PYTHONPATH syntax made in windows looks like this:

Unlike a PYTHONPATH syntax made in UNIX

Chapter 8: *Files*

P rograms are made with input and output in mind.

You input data to the program, the program processes the input, and it ultimately provides you with output.

For example, a calculator will take in numbers and operations you want.

It will then process the operation you wanted.

And then, it will display the result to you as its output.

There are multiple ways for a program to receive input and to produce output.

One of those ways is to read and write data on files.

To start learning how to work with files, you need to learn the open() function.

The open() function has one required parameter and two optional parameters.

The first and required parameter is the file name.

The second parameter is the access mode.

And the third parameter is buffering or buffer size.

The filename parameter requires string data.

The access mode requires string data, but there is a set of string values that you can use and is defaulted to "r".

The buffer size parameter requires an integer and is defaulted to 0.

To practice using the open() function, create a file with the name sampleFile.txt inside your Python directory.

Try this sample code:

```
>>> file1 = open("sampleFile.txt")

>>> _
```

Note that the file function returns a file object.

The statement in the example assigns the file object to variable file1.

The file object has multiple attributes, and three of them are:

- name: This contains the name of the file.

- mode: This includes the access mode you used to access the file.

- closed: This returns False if the file has been opened and True if the file is closed. When you use the open() function, the file is set to open.

Now, access those attributes.

```
>>> file1 = open("sampleFile.txt")

>>> file1.name

'sampleFile.txt'

>>> file1.mode

'r'

>>> file1.closed

False

>>> _
```

Whenever you are finished with a file, close them using the close() method.

```
>>> file1 = open("sampleFile.txt")

>>> file1.closed
```

False

>>> file1.close()

>>> file1.closed

True

>>> _

Remember that closing the file does not delete the variable or object.

To reopen the file, just open and reassign the file object.

For example:

>>> file1 = open("sampleFile.txt")

>>> file1.close()

>>> file1 = open(file1.name)

>>> file1.closed

False

>>> _

Reading from a File

Before proceeding, open the sampleFile.txt in your text editor.

Type "Hello World" in it and save.

Go back to Python.

To read the contents of the file, use the read() method.

For example:

```
>>> file1 = open("sampleFile.txt")
```

```
>>> file1.read()
```

'Hello World'

```
>>> _
```

File Pointer

Whenever you access a file, Python sets the file pointer.

The file pointer is like your word processor's cursor.

Any operation on the file starts at where the file pointer is.

When you open a file, and when it is set to the default access mode, which is "r" (read-only), the file pointer is set at the beginning of the file.

To know the current position of the file pointer, you can use the tell() method.

For example:

```
>>> file1 = open("sampleFile.txt")
```

```
>>> file1.tell()
```

0

```
>>> _
```

Most of the actions you perform on the file move the file pointer.

For example:

```
>>> file1 = open("sampleFile.txt")
```

```
>>> file1.tell()
```

0

```
>>> file1.read()
```

'Hello World'

```
>>> file1.tell()
```

11

```
>>> file1.read()
```

"

```
>>> _
```

To move the file pointer to a position you desire, you can use the seek() function.

For example:

```
>>> file1 = open("sampleFile.txt")
```

```
>>> file1.tell()
```

0

```
>>> file1.read()
```

'Hello World'

```
>>> file1.tell()
```

11

```
>>> file1.seek(0)
```

0

```
>>> file1.read()
```

'Hello World'

```
>>> file1.seek(1)
```

1

>>> file1.read()

'ello World'

>>> _

The seek() method has two parameters. The first is offset, which sets the pointer's position depending on the second parameter.

Also, argument for this parameter is required.

The second parameter is optional.

It is for whence, which dictates where the "seek" will start.

It is set to 0 by default.

- If set to 0, Python will set the pointer's position to the offset argument.

- If set to 1, Python will set the pointer's position relative or in addition to the current position of the pointer.

- If set to 2, Python will set the pointer's position relative or in addition to the file's end.

Note that the last two options require the access mode to have binary access.

If the access mode does not have binary access, the last two options will be useful to determine the current position of the pointer [seek(0, 1)] and the position at the end of the file [seek(0, 2)].

For example:

>>> file1 = open("sampleFile.txt")

>>> file1.tell()

0

```
>>> file1.seek(1)

1

>>> file1.seek(0, 1)

0

>>> file1.seek(0, 2)

11

>>> _
```

File Access Modes

To write to a file, you will need to know more about file access modes in Python.

There are three types of file operations: reading, writing, and appending.

Reading allows you to access and copy any part of the file's content.

Writing allows you to overwrite a file's contents and create a new one.

Appending allows you to write on the file while keeping the other content intact.

There are two types of file access modes: string and binary.

String access allows you to access a file's content as if you are opening a text file.

Binary access allows you to access a file on its rawest form: binary.

In your sample file, accessing it using string access allows you to read the line "Hello World".

Accessing the file using binary access will let you read "Hello World" in binary, which will be b'Hello World'.

For example:

```
>>> x = open("sampleFile.txt", "rb")
```

>>> x.read()

b'Hello World'

>>> _

String access is useful for editing text files.

Binary access is useful for anything else, like pictures, compressed files, and executables.

There are multiple values that you can enter in the file access mode parameter of the open() function.

But you do not need to memorize the combination.

You just need to know the letter combinations.

Each letter and symbol stands for an access mode and operation.

For example:

- r = read-only—file pointer placed at the beginning
  - r+ = read and write
- a = append—file pointer placed at the end
  - a+ = read and append
- w = overwrite/create—file pointer set to 0 since you create the file
  - w+ = read and overwrite/create
- b = binary

By default, file access mode is set to string.

You need to add b to allow binary access.

For example: "rb".

Writing to a File

When writing to a file, you must always remember that Python overwrites and not insert file.

For example:

```
>>> x = open("sampleFile.txt", "r+")
>>> x.read()
'Hello World'
>>> x.tell(0)
0
>>> x.write("text")
4
>>> x.tell()
4
>>> x.read()
'o World'
>>> x.seek(0)
0
>>> x.read()
'texto World'
>>> _
```

You might have expected that the resulting text will be "textHello World".

The write method of the file object replaces each character one by one, starting from the current position of the pointer.

Practice Exercise

For practice, you need to perform the following tasks:

- Create a new file named test.txt.

- Write the entire practice exercise instructions on the file.

- Close the file and reopen it.

- Read the file and set the cursor back to 0.

- Close the file and open it using append access mode.

- Add a rewritten version of these instructions at the end of the file.

- Create a new file and put similar content to it by copying the contents of the test.txt file.

Chapter 9: <u>Programming Paradigms</u>

W hat follows is an introduction to the three main programming paradigms based on popularity and application. You've heard me mention when describing different programming languages, whether a specific language was multi-paradigm or not. What this usually means is that with multi-paradigm languages you can code your applications following these three different "styles", even though there are more than just these three. The paradigms are:

- Procedural Programming

- Object-Oriented Programming (OOP)

- Functional Programming

Just like the programming languages themselves, these paradigms came about with the idea to solve specific problems, and then, because we're all lazy monkeys, we ended up forcing them to solve all problems. There is nothing bad about any of them, although you may not believe this from hearing me speak about them. Programming suffers from most of the same issues regular writing does and we can boil them all down to one word: clarity. How to code without repeating yourself? How to organize your code so that you don't end up adding to your workload? How to make sure other people can understand your code? How to make sure you can get back to your code months from now and still understand it? These are all worthy concerns in programming and each paradigm will try to address these problems in their own way.

I chose to introduce the paradigms with the old and tried method of coding the same thing in the three different styles. For this, I decided the game of Cluedo (or Clue depending on where on the globe you grew up in). Not unlike the way we coded the magic tricks, we'll transform a typical game of Cluedo into code. I suspect the choice for this came from the fact that procedural is a word often used to describe a type of murder mystery and because OOP has the idea of "inheritance" as one of its unique concepts and the word put me in mind of rich aunts being murdered for the sake of their millions. I fear my mind thinks in puns.

Be aware that with the exception of the first paradigm, it will feel like you're learning to program all over again. Relax. It's not true. Remember that programming is just a bunch of simple operations (store, add, multiply, compare...) built around strings, numbers, and booleans and abstracted to readable syntax and structures (collections, loops, if statements, and functions). Try to focus on these building blocks first and then take notice of the curious ways things are accomplished through each paradigm. We'll be adding new ways to add context to our code, new kinds of code blocks with their own peculiar rules, and a whole bunch of new syntax and abstractions, but at the heart of it, we're still talking about the same thing.

The paradigms also bleed into each other, the lines between them is quite blurred, and when I introduce a concept connected to one of them I do not mean that concept is not applicable to the others (remember, the languages I've shown you here are all multi-paradigm). You can code procedurally with a slight bent towards objects. You can code objects with a tendency towards functional ideas, and with some functional languages, you can use objects in your logic.

Chapter 10:   *Object-Oriented Programming*

B efore proceeding, I want you to think about what an object is. Yes, objects that you come across every day. What's common to all objects? The fact that a lot of them have specific characteristics and functions. A pen can have a color and can be used to write. So in the case of a pen, its color is one of its characteristics whereas its function is that it allows people to write with it. Now, this same framework applies to living things too. A dog has a breed, is of a certain height and can bark.

In C++, we can model such objects and work with them. Object-Oriented Programming is basically building a program around objects! Each object has attributes (the characteristics) and methods (the functions/utility). Now in order to create an object, we have to give C++ a blueprint on how to create this specific object that we're trying to make. This blueprint is termed a class. All objects are created from a class and come with a set of attributes and functions that we can use.

Now, a valid question is why? Why do we even need Object Oriented Programming?

The most significant benefit is that it lets us reuse code whenever and wherever we want.

Once I create an object, I can use it wherever I want. And once a class is designed (correctly, without any errors) every purpose that the class produces is free of errors and can be used reliably, therefore, allowing us to create more bug-free code. We don't have to know how an object works once we create it and use it.

We just need to know how to use it. This becomes an advantage when we work with extended programs.

So to recap - An object has functions (we will call these "methods") and attributes (we will call these "instance variables"). There are other types of variables called "static variables" or "class variables".

Objects are created from classes which basically act as blueprints.

```
#include<iostream>

using namespace std;

class EmptyClass {


};

int main() {


EmptyClass emptyClassObject;

}
```

The above program creates an empty class and instantiates an object.

```
class EmptyClass {

};
```

The above stub of code represents the class that we created. Notice how we've used the keyword "class" to specify that we're creating a class. "EmptyClass" is the name of the class we've created. We can change this depending upon the name we wish to give our class. All the instance variables and methods will go within the brackets, but since we created an empty class we don't have any class members.

In the primary function, we've instantiated an object.

```
EmptyClass emptyClassObject;
```

emptyClassObject in the above stub is an object that's created using the EmptyClass class and thus holds all the properties that the class defines. But because we haven't set any properties within EmptyClass, its object is practically useless.

But before we start adding stuff to the class we have to understand what access modifiers are. Now, one of the features of object-oriented programming is that it is able to abstract details of the class from parts of the program outside the class.

This is also known as data hiding. The way we enforce this in C++ is through access modifiers. There are three access modifiers in C++ - private, public, and protected. We're going to look at private and public.

When we use the private access modifier while defining a variable or a method we're basically saying that these members of the class cannot be accessed outside of the class, even by their own objects! These members can only be accessed by methods within the class. If you don't want any part of the code to access certain variables or methods, make them private!

When we use the public access modifier while defining class members, we're saying that they can be accessed from "everywhere". They can be accessed from outside the class using an object of the class.

Example:

```cpp
#include<iostream>

using namespace std;

class ExampleClass {

private:

int privateVariableOne;
```

```
public:

int publicVariableOne;

void initializePrivateVariableOne(int value) {

privateVariableOne = value;

}

int incrementPrivateVariableOne() {

privateVariableOne++;

return privateVariableOne;

}

};

int main() {

ExampleClass object;

object.publicVariableOne = 10;

//Error - object.privateVariableOne = 10;

object.initializePrivateVariableOne(20);

//OK! Now, privateVariableOne = 20

object.incrementPrivateVariableOne();

//OK! Now, privateVariableOne = 21

}
```

In ExampleClass, all variables and methods declared under the modifier "private:" are not accessible outside the class. The opposite is true for members declared under the "public:" label which can be accessed outside the class through objects (also called "instances") of the ExampleClass class.

The primary function shows how an instance is created. Akin to how the data type is used while declaring a variable, the name of the class is used while creating an example of the class.

ExampleClass object;

In the above line of code, "object" is an instance of ExampleClass and can access everything that is declared as public within the class. This access is allowed for by using the dot operator (".").

object.publicVariableOne lets us access the publicVariableOne that is tied to the instance. Keep in mind that if we create another example of this class, we'll get access to a completely separate and a brand new example which won't reflect changes made to the first instance that we created - "object" in this case.

Now, there are times when we want to instantiate an object with a set of predefined values. We can do using a constructor, which is declared within the class definition. It has no datatype, and its name is the name of the class followed by brackets that may or may not take in parameters (depending on how you wish to create this class).

Let's add a constructor to ExampleClass:

#include<iostream>

using namespace std;

class ExampleClass {

private:

int privateVariableOne;

public:

ExampleClass(int publicVariableValue) {

```
//This is the constructor

publicVariableOne = publicVariableValue;

}

int publicVariableOne;

void initializePrivateVariableOne(int value) {

privateVariableOne = value;

}

int incrementPrivateVariableOne() {

privateVariableOne++;

return privateVariableOne;

}

};

int main() {

ExampleClass object(30);

//object.publicVariableOne is now 30.

object.publicVariableOne = 10;

//Error - object.privateVariableOne = 10;

object.initializePrivateVariableOne(20);

//OK! Now, privateVariableOne = 20

objet.incrementPrivateVariableOne();
```

```
//OK! Now, privateVariableOne = 21
}
```

In the above code stub, the following code represents the constructor -

```
ExampleClass(int publicVariableValue) {
//This is the constructor
publicVariableOne = publicVariableValue;
}
```

It takes in an integer and assigns its value to publicVariableOne.

To instantiate an object of the class where the value of publicVariableOne will be 30, we do the following:

```
ExampleClass object(30);
```

Now, there's another way of instantiating values in the constructor: ExampleClass(int publicVariableValue):publicVariableOne(publicVariableValue) {

```
//This is the constructor
}
```

Example- Create a Dog class that stores a dog's age and the name and has methods called bark and eat.

```
#include<iostream>
#include<string>
using namespace std;
class Dog {
```

```cpp
private:
int age;
string name;
public:
Dog(int dogAge, string dogName) :age(dogAge), name(dogName) {}
void printDogName() {
cout << "Dog Name: " << name << endl;
}
void printDogAge() {
cout << "Dog Age: " << age << endl;
}
void bark() {
cout << "WOOOF WOOOOF!!" << endl;
}
void eat() {
cout << "I'm eating right now. Don't bother me!" << endl;
}
};
int main() {
Dog henryTheDog(2, "Henry");
henryTheDog.printDogName();
```

```
henryTheDog.printDogAge();

henryTheDog.bark();

henryTheDog.eat();

}
```

Here's the output -

Dog Name: Henry

Dog Age: 2

WOOOF WOOOOF!!

I'm eating right now. Don't bother me!

Press any key to continue . . .

Chapter 11: *Functional Programming*

F unctional programming is computing paradigm or way of thinking. It focusses on pure functions and avoids changing-state and mutable data. To explain all of this, let's have a look at the key aspects of functional programming.

Immutability

The first key aspect is that functional programming is considered to be immutable. An immutable object's state cannot be changed after it is created. To illustrate, imagine we defined a function in a program with a specific purpose. If the state of the output is the same whenever the input is the same, then that function follows the functional programming paradigm. If the function changes the state of data and gives a different output for the same input, then that function does not follow the functional programming paradigm.

No Side Effects

Another essential aspect of functional programming is not having side effects. So what exactly is a side effect? It is when a function does something that is outside the boundaries of what it is supposed to do.

Let's say we defines a function called 'GetStudentData', which takes in a student ID and then gives the student name as the result. If this function is set correctly, the student name should always be the same for the same student ID. But if the function does further internal processing, like modifying the student ID based on other parameters before retrieving the student name, then this could result in a different output. This is an unwanted side effect of the function.

Expression Based

Another trait of functional programming is that a functional program deals more with expressions than statements. To illustrate, let's look at a simple statement based program.

```
string result;

if(value>0)

result ="Greater than 0"

else

result="Less than 0"
```

In the above program we define a variable called 'result', which is a string data type. Then we state a condition for the variable called 'value'. We assign a string to the variable 'result' depending on whether the value is greater or less than 0. Now let's look at the same piece of code, but this time using expressions.

```
var result=value>0?"positive":"negative"
```

So here we are implementing the same logic, but programming languages have expressions available that can achieve the same result. In our example we have a ternary expression, which accomplishes the same as the set of statements defined earlier. One advantage of using expressions is that the code becomes more concise and manageable.

Higher-Order Functions

Next we'll look at the concept of higher-order functions. These are functions that can either take other functions as arguments or return them as results. In functional programming, functions are deemed as first class citizens. This means that they are allowed to appear anywhere in the code. They can also be used as parameters to other functions. For example, the Python code below shows that we can define functions that call other functions.

```python
def a(x)

return x+5

def b(c,x)

return c(x)*2

print(b(a,30))
```

Probably the most common place you might have seen this is when generating Fibonacci numbers. The code below is used to generate the 10 Fibonacci numbers using complete functional programming in PHP.

```php
function fib(int $n) : int {

    return ($n === 0 || $n === 1) ? $n : fib($n - 1) + fib($n - 2);

}

for ($i = 0; $i <= 10; $i++) echo fib($i) . PHP_EOL;
```

Pure Functions

A major selling point for functional programming is having pure functions. These are small functions that have been built for a specific purpose. To elaborate, assume we wanted to decide if a value is less than or greater than 0. We could define the function as shown below.

```
bool decide(int value)

{

string result;

if(value>0)

result ="Greater than 0"

else

result="Less than 0"

return result

}
```

We have seen a similar piece of code earlier. Here we pass the value to the function and then return the desired result. Now we could very well also define two pure functions instead by splitting up the above functionality. One function would determine if the value was greater than 0 and the other function would determine if the value was less than 0. This program would look something like this:

```
bool decidegreater(int value)

{

if(value>0) return true else return false;

}

bool decideless(int value)

{
```

```
if(value<0) return true else return false;

}
```

Chapter 12:   Bash

G iven the following Bash Code:

```
#!/bin/sh
cat 'testfile.txt' |
while read line ; do
  echo "Line read: $line"
  outputDirectory=${line##* }
  echo "Output directory: $outputDirectory"
  mv $outputDirectory/streamFolder/output/*.log
$outputDirectory/streamFolder/output/archive/ > /dev/null 2>&1
  mv $outputDirectory/streamFolder/output/*.txt
$outputDirectory/streamFolder/output/archive/ > /dev/null 2>&1
done
```

Let's now apply the coding metrics to the above Bash script. Here is the list of metrics.

1. Too short variable names and has no usage context

2. Code that gives no context or obvious purpose

3. Uneven spacing

4. Uneven parameter type definition

5. Incomprehensible code

6. Too long code

7. No exemption handling

8. No automatic resource management

9. External calls that are not kept in separate methods

10. Insufficient abstraction - need for higher level code

11. Code that is hard or impossible to change

Out of the metrics, I think only a few apply in the case of this Bash code. This is an important issue: In real world code, don't expect it to be all bad! If you're modifying legacy code, the original author may well have done a great job with it. If this is the case, then your task is more straightforward.

In this case, the required change may be straightforward. However, there may also arise a situation where you can make an improvement as part of another change. We'll see this in the present example.

So, in my opinion the Bash code violates metrics 7 and 10 only:

- No exception handling

- Inadequate abstraction - need for higher level code

Why is this the case? Well, the calls to mv can fail and we won't know about it. This is because the script is coded to swallow output and errors. How do I know this? The clue is in the redirect code: > /dev/null 2>&1. This has the intentional effect of not letting us see the result of the preceding mv operation.

So, as per metric 7, we need to at least record if an exception occurs in the calls to mv.

In regard to inadequate abstraction, the file name can be made into a constant. Then, the constant can be referenced in the script. This is better than embedding the name as a literal string value, mainly if the file name is used in multiple places in the script. A downstream maintainer might be tasked with changing the script and could easily forget to change the file name in all areas. Defining the file name as a constant avoids this unpleasant possibility.

So, with all of the above observations in mind, Listing 1 is the modified version of the Bash code.

Listing 1 Post-metric Bash code

```
#!/bin/sh
readonly fileName='testfile.txt'

cat $fileName |
while read line ; do
  echo "Line read: $line"
  outputDirectory=${line##* }
  echo "Output directory: $outputDirectory"
  mv $outputDirectory/streamFolder/output/*.log
$outputDirectory/streamFolder/output/archive/ > /dev/null 2>&1
  error=$?
  if [ $error -ne 0 ] ; then
    echo "First mv failed with exit code of $error"
  fi
  mv $outputDirectory/streamFolder/output/*.txt
$outputDirectory/streamFolder/output/archive/ > /dev/null 2>&1
  error=$?
  if [ $error -ne 0 ] ; then
    echo "Second mv failed with exit code of $error"
  fi
done
```

Notice in Listing 1 that we now have a constant called fileName representing the file name. This constant can now be used throughout the script instead of embedding the file name. So, if a different file name is required at some future time, then it has to be changed in just one place instead of potentially multiple places in the script.

The other major change is to store and examine the error code from each of the mv calls. This allows us to know for sure if the mv call succeeded or not. To complete the example, it would probably make sense to log the error code details to disk. But, you get the idea! Following the metrics helps to take the guesswork out of the code, mainly when errors occur.

There is still an issue with inadequate abstraction (metric 10) in Listing 1. Can you see it? The new error handling code is an improvement, but it has introduced a problem with code duplication. We should really try to fix this, and one way to do this is to abstract the error handling code itself into a function. Listing 2 illustrates the final offering for the Bash code.

Listing 2 Second iteration of the post-metric Bash code

```sh
#!/bin/sh

readonly fileName='testfile.txt'
errorHandler() {
  echo $1
  echo $2
  if [ $2 -ne 0 ] ; then
    echo "Failed in errorHandler $1 Exit code is $2"
  fi
}

cat $fileName |
while read line ; do
  echo "Line read: $line"
  outputDirectory=${line##* }
  echo "Output directory: $outputDirectory"
  mv $outputDirectory/streamFolder/output/*.log
$outputDirectory/streamFolder/output/archive/ > /dev/null 2>&1
  errorHandler "first call to mv", $?
  mv $outputDirectory/streamFolder/output/*.txt
$outputDirectory/streamFolder/output/archive/ > /dev/null 2>&1
```

errorHandler "second call to mv", $?

done

Now, any failures that occur during execution of the code in Listing 2 appear as illustrated in Listing 3. These errors can be logged to disk if required by adding more code to the errorHandler function.

Listing 3 - Running the modified Bash code

Line read: mydirectory

Output directory: mydirectory

first call to mv,

1

Failed in errorHandler first call to mv, Exit code is 1

second call to mv,

1

Failed in errorHandler second call to mv, Exit code is 1

Notice also, that by following the metrics the script in Listing 2 is nicely divided (or modularized) into three parts:

1. Definition of constants

2. Definition of error handler and other functions

3. The main code

Also noteworthy in this example was the fact that we iterated twice through the metrics. Again, this is a good practice - making small, focused changes, reviewing the changes, and adding more minor changes. The combination of the small changes adds up to a far better end result and the code can be tested carefully as you go.

One noteworthy caveat is in relation to spacing. There might be a temptation on the part of a Java (or other high level language) programmer to introduce spaces into Listing 2. This might be done to try to improve readability. One of the things about scripting languages, such as, Bash and Python is that they are often very fussy about spaces, indentation, and so on. Adding spaces to Bash code can introduce hard to find errors. So, be careful with readability requirements!

Up to this point, we've seen the metrics in action in C code and now in Bash scripting. How can the metrics approach be applied to Python code? Let's find out.

A Python example

Given the following Python code.

```
f=open('myfile','r+')
f.write('abcdef012345')
```

As usual, let's apply the metrics to the Python code. Again, here is the list of metrics.

1. Too short variable names and has no usage context

2. Code that provides no context or obvious purpose

3. Uneven spacing

4. Uneven parameter type definition

5. Incomprehensible code

6. Code that is too long

7. No exemption handling

8. No automatic resource management

9. External calls that are not contained in separate methods

10. Inadequate abstraction - need for higher level code

11. Code that is difficult or impossible to change

I would say that the following metrics are violated by the Python code:

- Variable names that are too short and provide no usage context

- Inconsistent spacing

- No exception handling

- No automatic resource management

- External calls that are not contained in separate methods

Also, we have some assumptions lying at the heart of the Python code example.

What are the assumptions? Well, the first line assumes that the file already exists and the second line in turn assumes that the first line was successful.

A simpler and sturdier version is illustrated in Listing 4 where we use the standard exception management of the Python language. Also, I've tried to improve the file handle name by giving it some context in the wider program.

Listing 4 - Incorporating better naming and exception management

```python
try:
  logfile = open('myfile', 'r+')
  logfile.write('abcdef012345')
except IOError:
  print('Encountered an error')
```

Now if the file is deleted before the script runs, then you get a meaningful message rather than a runtime failure. It's essential always to remember that when your code interacts with system resources (such as files), you're handling somebody else's property! System resources are owned by the system, so you have to handle them with care.

The moral of the story is to keep it simple and try to avoid assumptions. Mother nature enjoys assumptions; they give her an opportunity to show us who's boss!

The addition of exception code has still not produced particularly reliable operation. We are still relying on the file existing in order for the code to work. To fix this, before opening the file, we can first check that it exists as illustrated in Listing 5:

Listing 5 - Incorporating an existence check

```
try:
  if(os.path.isfile('myfile')):
    logfile = open('myfile', 'r+')
    logfile.write('abcdef012345')
  else:
    print('File does not exist')
except IOError:
  print('Encountered an error')
```

So, the code now uses isfile() to check if the file exists before attempting to open and update it. This means that we have now removed the assumption about the file existence. If the file does not exist, then we'll know upfront, rather than relying on an exception.

Chapter 13: **_Regular Expressions_**

The Simple Patterns

T he simple patterns are direct literal representations of the anticipated inputs. First we present the necessary characters for the formation of simple regular expression patterns.

Simple Pattern Characters

Characters	Functions
/.../	Patterns are enclosed in between two forward slashes like this /a/. This matches a single alphabetic letter 'a' in an input string "ant".
[...]	The braces represent a character set. The character set matches any of the characters within the braces with no exceptions for special characters and escape sequences, for example [abc] would match the first three letters of the input string "abcdef". A range can be represented with a hyphen like this [1-9], which matches any character from 1 to 9, same as [123456789].
\	When the backslash character precedes a character, it makes the character unique and gives it a special meaning different from its literal meaning.

\d	The lower case letter 'd' preceded by a backslash represents a numerical input and matches a single digit, for example /\d/ matches digit 3 in the input string "32 Highway".
\D	The upper case letter 'D' preceded by a backslash represents any non numerical input and matches a single non digit input, for example /\D/ matches 'H' in "32 Highway".
\w	The lower case letter 'w' proceeded by the backslash character represents a single alphanumeric character in the range 0 - 9, a – z, A – Z including the underscore.
\W	The upper case letter 'W' preceded by the backslash character represents a non alphanumeric character like the followings; @, %, * and so on for example /\W/ matches the '@' in the email address feyi_dos1@yahoo.com.

The Simple Pattern Quantifier

Pattern quantifiers are used for specifying the frequency of occurrence of the affected character under representation by the regular expression. The quantifiers are presented in the table below.

Quantifiers	Function
?	This when applied to regular expression character implies 0 or 1 occurrence of that character. This can also be replaced with {0, 1}. For example the proper expression /Shoes?/ or /Shoes{0,1}/ matches the string "Shoe" in "Shoe lace".
*	The quantifier '*' implies zero or more occurrence of the regular expression character under representation. It can be replaced with {0,}. For example the

	regular expression /lo*/ or /lo{0,}/ would match the character 'l' in string "lives" and the sub-string "loo" in the string "looses"
+	The quantifier '+' implies one or more occurrence of the regular expression character under representation. The quantifier can also be replaced with {1,}. For example the regular expression /lo+/ or /lo{1,}/ would find no match in the string "life" but would find the match "loo" in the string "looses".

The Simple Patterns Formulation

We proceed to the implementation phase of the simple regular expression patterns, starting with the development of an HTML5 input form. It will validate the user inputs with JavaScript using our designed regular expression patterns. We begin with the noun class pattern.

The Noun Class Patterns

The noun class represents the name of a person, a place or a concept on an input form. This can be one of the following input fields; place of birth, religion, nationality, occupation and name.

A name is made up of alphabetic characters with the characters in upper or lower cases. To represent this, we use the following simple regular expression; a combination of simple characters and quantifiers as shown below.

Step 1:

We create the regular expression pattern for the first letters which normally should be a single capital letter and in some exceptional cases can be more than one. We use the character set A to Z to represent the pattern as shown below:

[A-Z]+

Remember the quantifier '+' implies one or more occurrence of the upper case character set A to Z. We need this representation to be followed by lower case character set a to z. The lower case character set is represented as follows:

[a–z]+

Now we want a combination of the two sets, to achieve this we combine the two sets as shown below.

[A-Z]+[a-zA-Z]+

Meaning you can have a noun class written in upper cases all through and a noun class starting with an uppercase character, followed with a combination of high and lowercases. In summary a noun class must begin with a capital letter. The quantifiers ensure there is at least an alphabetical input for both the upper and lower cases.

The Complex Patterns

The complex patterns are the combinations of simple characters, complex characters, the alphanumeric, the non-alphabetic characters and the quantifiers. We start off with the complex characters.

Complex characters	Functions
$	Matches a character occupying the last position in the input string, for example /r$/ matches the last alphabetic character 'r' in the input string "reader", but finds no match in the input string "read" or "READER" for the match is case sensitive.
^	Matches a character occupying the first position in the input string. For example /^e/ matches 'e' in the string "eat".
.	Represents a single character input and matches the character input. For example the regular expression /.n/ matches the letters 'In' in the string "Into" and /.o/ matches the letters "to" in the string "to".
A|B	The '|' special character also called the 'OR' operator matches A or B, whichever it finds in the input string. For example the regular expression /boy|girl/ matches 'boy' in the input string "boy scout", girl in the input string "girl scout" and girl in the input string "girl or boy" whichever it finds first.
\s	Represents and matches a white space character, a tab or a form feed.
\S	Represents and matches a non-space character.
(…)	The capturing parentheses match their contents as single entities and also remember the match for future usage. \1 to \n denotes the sequence number of the parenthesized matched items to be remembered. For example, the regular expression /\w+(\s)\d+\1\w+/ matches the string "No 42

	Highway" in the input string "No 42 Highway road". The only capturing parenthesis is remembered with '\1' in the expression and applied as a white space between "42" and "Highway".
(?:a)	The expression (?:a) represents a set of non capturing parentheses that match but do not remember the match as done by the capturing parentheses. The main purpose of the non capturing parentheses is for creating sub expressions to be matched in a regular expression. For example in the expression /(\w)+\s(?:\d+)\s\1/ the numeric part (?:\d) is matched but never remembered.
A(?=B)	This acts like a look ahead. It matches the expression A provided that it is immediately followed by an expression B. For example the regular expression /Coca(?=Cola)/ matches "Coca" if and only if it is followed by "Cola" and it is case sensitive. The regular expression /No(?=\d+)/ matches "No" if and only if it is followed by one or more numbers.
A(?!B)	The regular expression matches an expression A provided it is not followed by an expression B. For example the regular expression /No(?!\W)/ would match nothing in the strings "No%" and "No@" but would match the "No" in the string "No1 Gateway".
[^abc]	This expression represents a complimented character set that matches any character set not in the complimented set. A range can be represented with a dash. For example the regular expression [^abc] performs the same function as the regular expression [^a-c] and matches the character 'r' in the string "car".

A Username Expression Implementation

The username is a combination of alphanumeric characters beginning with at least an alphabetic character. There are two steps to this.

Step 1:

The alphabetic character is represented with the regular expression /[a-zA-Z]/ which matches any single upper or lower case alphabetic input. We expect that our username should start with a minimum of a single alphabetical input, for this reason we make use of the quantifier "+" to arrive at the following expression:

/[a-zA-Z]+/

Step 2:

We also expect that the above may be followed by a combination of alphanumeric characters. The regular expression /\w/ gives a good fit. The quantifier "*" (zero or more times) is used with the expression for a complete representation as shown below:

/\w*/

Step 3:

The final step is to combine the alphabetic regular expression with the alphanumeric regular expression such that the alphabetic is matched if followed by an alphanumeric expression or not. This is as presented below:

/[a-zA-Z]+\w*/

Complex Regular Expression Implementation

Examples of complex patterns are the email address and dates. We shall be formulating the email address as a follow up practise to our username implementation. An email address is has two parts; the username part and the server address part separated by the '@' sign. Therefore the formulation process is divided into two stages.

Stage 1: Username Formulation

This is as done in 2.2 above..

Stage 2: Server Address Formulation

The sever address will always start with the '@' symbol. This can be represented literally by the '@ symbol itself followed by the organization's name, which can be represented by a username expression as shown below:

/@[a-zA-Z]+\w*/

This is followed by the organization's categorization (.com, .mil, .net, .org, .edu) preceded by a full stop .e.g. yahoo.com as implemented below:

/(\.)[A–Za-z]{2,3}/

Note that the categorization is written in a minimum of two alphabetic characters and a maximum of three, the reason for the use of the quantifier {2,3} and that the expression for the full stop '\.' Is enclosed in a capturing parenthesis in order for it to be matched and remembered for a later re-use. This may be followed by the country name as in .us, .uk, or .ng. As observed this uses a maximum of two letters so that it can be represented with the following regular expression:

/(\.)[A–Za-z]{2}/

The quantifier {2} accepts two character length input only. Now bringing the components together we have the regular expression:

/@[a-zA-Z]+\w*(\.)[A–Za-z]{2,3}(?:\1[A–Za-z]{2})*/

The above regular expression would match the server name "@yahoo.com" in the input string "123@yahoo.common". Please note that the country code component which is enclosed in a non-capturing parenthesis '(?:\1[A–Za-z]{2})*' has been made optional with the use of the quantifier '*'.

Step 3: Combining the Username and the Domain name

The final step is to combine the username and the domain name regular expression to arrive at the complete pattern for matching an email address as shown below:

/[a-zA-Z]+\w*(?:@)[a-zA-Z]+\w*(\.)[A–Za-z]{2,3}(?:\1[A–Za-z]{2})*/

From here on, you can design and implement any desired pattern for any particular validation purpose, all you need is a little more practise though. Remember, practise makes perfection. I wish you success in your practise.

Chapter 14:   *__Data Structures__*

List

E xplanation: A list represents a set of ordered elements, which means that each component can have another element before or after it. A linked list consist of **nodes** that contain **data**. Each node, or position **gets** a certain ordering number, depending on its ordering in the list: we talk about the first element, the second etc. Each node **contains** a value; it can be an integer, a string etc. When we refer to a specific position (for example when we talk about the first element), there is maximum one entry that may satisfy our request. This means that we cannot have two or more elements in a position.

The first node is called **head**. Internally, each node points to the **next** one, and the last one points to **null**. In Python we do not have to worry about pointers.

Implementation: We can name our list with a name of our liking, usually something that represents its functionality (be careful not to use a built-in python name!).

Lets name our list **a**.

In the brackets that follow the name of our list, we place the index, the position which we refer to:

a[0] refers to the element at the **first** position (**position 0**). We need to assign a value in this cell.

a[0] = 5, assigns 5 in the **first** node of our list.

So, we have:

list[index] = value

We can easily create a list in Python. In order to define a list (initially empty) we just do:

a = []

Else, we could initialize our list with some data:

b = [2,5,4]

Note that we do not have to specify the positions of our elements each time, as the first element will always be in position 0 (b[0] is 2), the second in position 1 (b[1] is 5) etc.

We can add add an element x in the end of the list:

list.append(x)

For example, b.append(7) will give us:

b = [2,5,4,7]

We can also add an element x in a certain position I of the list.

list.insert(i,x)

For example in our previous list, we can do b.insert(0,3), which will give us:

b = [3,2,5,4,7]

We can remove an element that contains a certain value:

list.remove(x)

Note that this will delete the first element that contains this certain value.

For example in our previous list, if we do b.remove(2), we will get:

b = [3,5,4,7]

Tuple

Explanation: Tuples serve a similar functionality with lists, with the main difference being that tuples are immutable: as soon as you add your data in a tuple, they cannot be changed or deleted and it is not possible to insert new data. The only way to perform such operations is to create a new tuple containing the new or edited data etc.

In terms of syntax, tuples use parentheses to store the data in place of the lists' square brackets. There is also the possibility not to include parentheses at all, and just separate data with a comma.

When we need to refer to a certain position in the tuple, for example position 0 (first element), position 1 (second element) etc, square brackets are used.

Implementation: We can create an empty tuple named t:

t = ()

We can also create a tuple that contains some numbers:

t_2 = (9,4,6,8,2)

or:

t_2 = 9,4,6,8,2

Now, we can refer to a certain element of the tuple, like for example the first element:

t_2[0] = 9

Dictionary

Explanation: A dictionary is used to store data by using a unique key for each entry. Key is somehow serving the same functionality as indices in lists and tuples, when we want to refer to a certain element. The values where each key refers to are not necessarily unique. Dictionaries are mutable, so we can add, delete or modify the elements in it.

The entries of a dictionary are contained between curly braces {}. Each entry is in the form key: value.

Implementation: We have a dictionary d:

d = {}

and we can populate it with key-value pairs:

d = { key1:value1,

key2:value2,

key3:value3,

...

}

Set

Explanation: A set is a collection of items that in contrast to lists/tuples, it is unordered. There can be no duplicate elements. Sets are efficient when we want to search if an item is contained in them or not. Later on, we are going to talk about hash functions, which implement efficient searching. We can add, delete or modify the items in a set. The set items are contained in {}.

Implementation: We can define an empty set s_empty:

s_empty = {}

or we can construct a set of certain items, like a set of fruits:

s_fruits = {'orange', 'banana', 'apple', 'peach'}

We can add an item using the add() function:

s_fruits.add('cherry')

'cherry' will be added in a random position in the initial set (remember, sets are unordered!). For example:

s_fruits = {'orange', 'banana', 'cherry','apple', 'peach'}

or we can add multiple items in the s_fruits set using the update() function:

s_fruits.update(['grapes', 'mango'])

s_fruits = {'orange', 'grapes', 'banana', 'cherry','apple', 'peach', 'mango'}

Array

Explanation: An array consists of an ordered collection of elements. We can refer to each item by its index in the array. An array can have dimensions: the widely used 2-dimensional table that we encounter very often in our everyday life, but we can also have more dimensions. In computer science theory, the difference between an array and a list is the way data are stored in memory, which affects how we access an element. A list allocates non sequential cells in memory, therefore they need a reference for the next cell; this is what the index does. Lists support sequential access, where you need to search an element by examining the first element, then the next one, afterwards the third one etc until you find the element you are looking for. An array allocates only sequential cells in memory. Arrays support sequential access, as well as direct access.

Implementation: You may have noticed that Python lists have some array-like features, according to the list analysis above. Python in fact uses array functionalities in lists, like for example direct access to a certain position. However, there is an array structure in Python, but it should be imported:

import array

We need to specify the data type that this array contains and also the list of elements that the array is going to contain when we are creating it. For example:

a = array.array('i', [1,2,3])

Yes, array keyword is written twice, because we are calling the array module from the array library. It is easier to rename the imported library array though:

import array as arr

a = arr.array('i', [1,2,3])

'i' refers to int Python type. Below is the list of all supported Python data types and the letter they use to indicate this data type when we construct an array:

Code	C Type	Python Type	Min bytes
'b'	signed char	int	1
'B'	unsigned char	int	1
'u'	Py_UNICODE	Unicode	2
'h'	signed short	int	2
'H'	unsigned short	int	2
'i'	signed int	int	2
'I'	unsigned int	int	2
'l'	signed long	int	4
'L'	unsigned long	int	4
'f'	float	float	4
'd'	double	float	8

Stack

Explanation: Stack is used to store items in the Last in – First out (LIFO) manner. Operations like insert element (push) and remove element (pop) can occur only from the 'upper' end of the stack. An overflow can occur if we exceed the maximum size of the stack, while an underflow can occur if we try to delete an element from an empty stack.

Implementation: In Python a stack can be implemented by using a list structure. We can create a simple stack:

stack = []

Pop elements from the stack

stack.pop()# '3'

stack.pop()# '2'

stack.pop()# '1'

Queue

Explanation: A queue handles item in the first in – first out (FIFO) manner. We can add (enqueue) items from the 'end' of the queue and delete (dequeue) items from the 'beginning' of the queue. Overflow and underflow can occur as in the case of the stack.

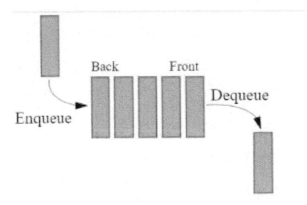

Implementation: In Python we can import the queue module:

import queue

Then we can create a queue by calling the method Queue in that module. We can add (put) elements and we can delete (get) them in the FIFO way:

q = queue.Queue(maxsize = 100)

q.put('a')

q.put('b')

q.put('c')

q = ['a','b','c']

q.get()# 'a'

q.get()# 'b'

q.get()# 'c'

Graph

A graph is a representation of a set of objects (nodes or vertices V) where some of them are connected with links (edges **E**). Formally, a graph G is defined as pairs (V, E) .

We can dynamically add and remove vertices and edges.

Note that the above is an undirected graph: this means that the connections between the vertices have no direction, for example ab = ba etc.

In case of directed graphs there are directed arrows → as edges, and we can move only towards the direction of the arrow.

A sequence of edges that connect a vertex with another, either directly or indirectly, forms a path. \

Tree

Trees are a subtype of graphs, which needs to satisfy the following requirements:

- It needs to be acyclic: to contain no cycles

- It needs to be connected: Any node should be reachable through some path, so there are not 'stray' nodes

Typically, the tree has a structure of a root node and children nodes. Root node can be only one and it can have any number of children nodes (directly connected to the root nodes). Any child can have any number of children etc. Nodes that do not have children are called leaves.

Chapter 15: *Algorithms*

Algorithm

I n the coding phase, all the modules defined by the modular design will become a program; that is, the final application will consist of the sum of all the programs that are designed. But first, we must determine what the instructions or actions of each of these programs are. To do this, algorithms must be used.

An algorithm establishes, in a generic and informal way, the sequence of steps or actions that solves a certain problem. The algorithms constitute the main documentation that is needed to be able to start the coding phase, and, to represent them, two types of notation are essentially used: pseudocode and flowcharts. The design of an algorithm is independent of the language that will later be used to encode it.

Pseudocode

The pseudocode is an algorithmic programming language; It is an intermediate language between natural language and any specific programming language, such as C, FORTRAN, Pascal, etc. There is no formal or standard pseudocode notation, but each programmer can use their own.

An algorithm written in pseudocode is usually organized in three sections: header, declarations, and body. In the header section, the name of the algorithm is written, in this case, add. In the declarations section, some of the objects that the program will use are declared. In the tutorial of the language of Abrirllave, the different types of objects that can be used in a program are studied in detail, such as variables, constants, subprograms, etc. For now, note that, in this example, the variables a, b, and c, they indicate that the program needs three spaces in the main memory of the computer to store three integers. Each of the variables refers to a different memory space.

Flowcharts (Ordinograms)

Algorithms can also be represented, graphically, by means of flowcharts. Flowcharts can be used for other purposes; however, in this tutorial, we will only use them to represent algorithms. Such flow charts are also known as audiograms. In other words, an ordinogram graphically represents the order of the steps or actions of an algorithm.

Pseudocode and flowcharts are the two most used tools to design algorithms in structured programming. Although, between both types of representation, there are the following important differences:

Flowcharts Began To Be Used Before the Pseudocode

In pseudocode, three sections of the algorithm are usually defined (header, declarations, and body). However, in one ordinogram only the body is represented.

In an ordinogram it is usually easier to see, at first glance, what the order of the algorithm's actions is.

The graphic symbols used in a flowchart have been standardized by the American National Standards Institute (ANSI). However, there is no "standard pseudocode."

Qualities of an algorithm

For any given problem there is no single algorithmic solution; It is the task of the person who designs an algorithm to find the most optimal solution, this is none other than one that more faithfully meets the desirable qualities of any well-designed algorithm:

- Finitude. An algorithm always has to end after a finite number of actions. When the Add algorithm is already a program, its execution will always be the same, since, the actions described in the body of the algorithm will always be followed, one by one, from the first to the last and in the established order.

- Accuracy. All the actions of an algorithm must be well defined, that is, no action can be ambiguous, but each one of them must only be interpreted in a unique way. In other words, if the program resulting from an algorithm is executed several times with the same input data, in all cases, the same output data will be obtained.

- Clarity. Normally, a problem can be solved in different ways. Therefore, one of the most important tasks of the designer of an algorithm is to find the most readable solution, that is, the most understandable for the human being.

- Generality. An algorithm must solve general problems. For example, the Add program should be used to make sums of any two whole numbers, and not only to add two specific numbers, such as 3 and 5.

- Efficiency. The execution of the program resulting from coding an algorithm should consume as little as possible the available resources of the computer (memory, CPU time, etc.).

- Simplicity. Sometimes, finding the most efficient algorithmic solution to a problem can lead to writing a very complex algorithm, affecting its clarity. Therefore, we must try to make the solution simple, even at the cost of losing a bit of efficiency, that is, we must find a balance between clarity and efficiency. Writing simple, clear, and efficient algorithms is achieved based on practice.

- Modularity. Never forget the fact that an algorithm can be part of the solution to a bigger problem. But, in turn, this algorithm must be broken down into others, as long as this favors its clarity.

The person who designs an algorithm must be aware that all the properties of an algorithm will be transmitted to the resulting program.

Chapter 16: *Logical Switches*

L ogical Switches are very similar to a series of if statements, in that they allow for many different conditions to be checked and have varied output depending on the value we are checking against. They look cleaner than a series of 'if' statements, and there is some additional functionality that can be done with switches that sometimes makes the desirable. Let's look at a basic switch now.

switch (variable) {

case condition1:

// some code based on what you're doing

break;// exits the switch loop

case condition2:

// more code for what happens for this condition

break;

case condition3:

// you can have as many cases as you like

break;

default;

// code to do if none of the other cases are true

In this example, we can see the format that switches take. The term 'variable' is a component you will use to measure some varying quantity in your sketch. The conditions, one, two, three, as many as you like, are values you are comparing a variable against. They can be anything, numbers, letters, words, even other variables, or the results of functions it is kind of crazy what you can put as a condition. This is why they can be extremely powerful in coding. You can make complex conditions or simple ones, and both will have a clean, readable layout that has a very easy to understand flow when you read it. This readability in your code is so important for us humans to understand what is going on with it.

The code within each case will continue until it reaches the word 'break' which is an Arduino keyword and this tells the compiler that it should exit the current function it is doing. In the case of a switch, it will exit the switch when a break is encountered. If a break is missing from the code, it will instead continue on and run the next line of code below in the next case, which may leave unexpected results. It's best to make sure you add break to your code at the same time as a case to make sure the code you're writing will flow properly.

Let's look at an example sketch:

File → Examples → 05.Control → switchCase

Okay, we start off with initializing our sensor minimum and maximums in the form of constants that the coder determined from experiment. In setup() we turn on serial communication so we can use our serial display. In the loop function, we declare and initialize the variable we will use to read our sensor, sensorReading. Zero to Six Hundred is a lot of cases to cover if we just want to display relative brightness of the display. The user wanted four data points to generalize the brightness, ranging from zero to four. They, therefore, used the map() function, along with sensorReading, sensorMin, sensorMax, 0, and 3 as the arguments, to scale the reading should be within a 0-3 range instead. Notably, the map function will scale to the nearest integer so we can safely know it will only contain four data points.

We now set up a switch to check the reading. We send 'range' to our mapped sensor reading and have the switch as our variable. Our cases are 0, 1, 2, 3, which corresponds to the expected data range of our variable, good so far. Now, if range got mapped to 0, we will print, dark. If range gets mapped to 1, we will print dim. For range 2, medium, and for range 3, bright. The user added a 1-millisecond delay for stability, forcing it to read once per millisecond instead of much faster. Essentially the chip clock speed, which by default, is 16Mhz or sixteen million instructions per second.

Let's take a look at another switch example. Open up:

> File → Examples → 05.Control → switchCase2

In this next example, again we see and initialize 'Serial' communications like we've done before. Then we initialize our pins to OUTPUT using a 'for' loop, cycling from pins two through seven by one each pass. Next, we have to check if we have received a character input from the serial port (greater than zero means not FALSE), we will then create an integer which will read the input from our keyboard. Alphanumeric keys come in the form of ASCII characters, so for example 'a' = 97, 'b' = 98, 'c' = 99, etc. This is why we record the input as an integer from Serial.read().

Next, we reach our switch, which varies based on the value we recorded from our keyboard input inByte. We have set five possible cases and a default in case we get a character other than our case values. For any character a, b, c, d, e, we will toggle an LED to high. For any other value, we will sequentially turn the LEDs off going from lowest to highest, using a 'for' loop.

This example shows that you can base your cases off of almost any kind of variable. It doesn't have to be an integer. They can be anything you feel you need to check what is happening in your sketch and react to that condition.

Switches are a fantastic way to keep your code elegant and organized.

Chapter 17: <u>*Coding Practices*</u>

C ontained in this will be some of the best practices you can adapt to take your coding to a higher standard. We have touched on this first topic already, but we will expand and reiterate here. First up is naming conventions.

Here are some best practices for your comments that will help other readers understand you easier:

- Start with a summary of the sketch and what it will accomplish. Provide any links if it helps the understanding of your design. Try to approach your block comments from a user-friendly stance as much as possible to give a clear idea of what you will be doing.

- Write in the active voice. Use a clear, conversational tone for your writing, as if you were speaking to another person standing next to you.

- For instructions to the user, use the second person, to invoke in the user that they should be the ones to carry out your instructions.

- Use short descriptive phrases rather than complex phrases. It is easier to understand one simple idea at a time.

- Be explicit about what you are doing with your actions. For example: "Next, you'll read the value of the sensor on pin thisPin."

- Avoid phrases or words that are 'fluff' or do not contribute to the explanation, e.g. you see, you'd want to, etc. Instead, skip those words and give a statement that's direct to the point, e.g. set the pins.

- Check your assumptions, make sure you have explained all of your ideas and haven't left something that can only be explained 'in your head.'

- Give a description for every variable or constant with a comment of its purpose either before, or in line with the variable or constant.

- Similarly, give an explanation of a block of code that you're about to perform before the instructions are executed, so it's clear what's about to happen.

- Every loop should have comments explaining why this loop exists (e.g. what it is doing), and a verbal explanation of its condition if it's still not clear.

Coding Best Practices

- Follow naming conventions

Do not create one letter variable names! Your naming conventions exist so that you can, at a glance, read your code without having to refer to other places to understand what is going on.

- Write code that is reusable or modular

User-defined functions are a great way to accomplish this. By doing this, you can write a segment of code in just one place and refer to it each time it is necessary. This makes better sense and is much cleaner and simpler to read.

- Write a flow-chart of your sketch before you start coding

Seriously, this cannot be overstated how valuable this step is to write clean code. By knowing all the pieces you will need to accomplish your sketch's task ahead of time conceptually, you can successfully plan ahead and use things like functions in a smart way.

- Keep things organize and together

If you make a function to smooth an analog sensor, make sure that's all it does. Don't start doing other parts of your code within that function. If your function needs to, you can have it call yet another function to help it accomplish its task. Again think modular (small pieces make a big part).

- Make yourself a toolbox

Make functions that do specific things. Then use your tools as needed in your code.

- Keep your sketches

Even if you think you won't need a sketch you made anymore, keep them. If you need a piece of code that you've already written for another project and you have followed these practices, you can simply snag that piece of code and drop it into the new project you're working on. Brilliant!

- Write your functions in a generalized way whenever possible for these exact reasons

To put this simply, it means that if you were making a function to draw a square, make a function to draw a rectangle instead since a square is a special case of a rectangle, where the edges are equal.

- Make sure your functions do what they say they will do

E.g., if it is a function named 'flickerLeds' (pinValue), it better be flickering some LEDs!

- Avoid pointers

We didn't even touch on them in this document, and we are only going to tell you they exist to tell you not to use them unless you're an advanced user. They are the most likely 'tool' to cause the crazy, bad kinds of problems from happening in your coding, and are notoriously tough for a beginner to use properly. So avoid them until you are sure you know what you are doing.

- Embrace self-improvement

Understand from day 1 that as a fledgling coder that you will grow and improve over time. Use each challenge you come across to try writing new sketches as an opportunity to grow and hone your skills.

- Reach out to the community for help and advice!

There are some really fantastic people in our big community of hobbyists that are willing to help you learn and grow as an enthusiast.

- Try to make things foolproof when you code

Try to make sure your for loops terminate, try to account for unexpected inputs when checking values, try to constrain your data within expected values. These 'tedious' steps are what keeps your program running smooth and bug-free!

- Know how to use debugging tools and techniques

It's a more advanced topic but learning about debugging tools and techniques for large-scale projects such as robotics, or as a controller for something like a pump mechanism will help expand your knowledge further.

- Write both brackets or both braces at the start then fill in the date in-between

When writing functions, loops or anything with brackets and braces, this trick helps to ensure that you will be closing all of your brackets and braces, preventing unexpected results.

- Try new ways to use your Arduino!

This is how you can really develop new skills. When you have more skills, you can think of even more things you can do with the chip! The possibilities with this micro-controller are nearly limitless and are bound only by the limits of your imagination.

More Naming Best Practices

- Functions follow the same rules as variables

The name should start with a lower-case letter, all one word, and additional words are distinguished with capital letters.

- Functions should use verb names to describe their function

E.g. stepMotor(), getValue(), smoothReadings(), etc. All these names explain with an action word what this function should be doing.

- Make the name describe the purpose of the function

- Make sure the for loop variables are clear on what they represent

Having a variable of x can work, but it really offers nothing to the person reading your code for them to understand exactly what that variable is for.

Chapter 18: *How to Be an Expert Coder in the Shortest Time Possible*

C oding is not the easiest thing to do; at least this is something almost everyone new to coding will agree with. However, as you actually go on, you'd discover that coding is actually not so hard, challenging, yes, and it will actually always remain challenging, but difficult and almost impossible, that is just at the beginning. You'll also discover that what you might find infinitely difficult might just be learning your first language. This is quite understandable as you're just getting into a new field. As you learn more languages, you'll discover that it actually becomes easier. The previous languages just seem to prepare you to learn a newer one, irrespective of the language that you've learned. This, I guess, is the reason lots of coders advise that you learn HTML first. Although it's not a programming language, it is very easy to learn and put into practice, and it has a way of preparing yours for more difficult language in no time.

So how does one become an expert coder in the shortest possible time? In fact, who's an expert coder, and how long will it take before someone can be regarded as that?

The fact is that if you ask 5 different people in tech, they'll give you five different answers about who an expert coder is. Here's the way I'd define an expert coder. I consider an expert coder as one who can write good code. Anyone can actually learn how to write code; writing good code, though, is a different thing entirely. And this is where the tough part is, I think it should be the aspiration of every coder to be able to write, neat, good, free-flowing code.

Refuse To Be Intimidated

This is usually the first problem that beguiles most people learning code for the first time. Especially those who think it is for the mathematical geniuses. It all starts in your mind; you have to rid yourself of any form of intimidation. "Anything can be learned," never forget this phrase. I'm not trying to excite you up like a motivational speaker, though I'm not saying this is bad in any way, I'm just trying to present the facts before you. And with the array of resources available on coding, you'd be able to find a class or two that totally resonates with your learning pattern.

Learn How To Learn

This, for me, is the most important skill every developer needs. Irrespective of how far you've gone into coding, or how little about coding that you know. Learn how to effectively learn, because you'd continue learning as long as you're a coder. There's no point in the life of a programmer when he can really say I have arrived, I have learned all that needs to be learned. This character is something I have found amongst musicians, both professional and those who do it as a hobby. When we meet at events and someone does an introduction, which goes thus, "meet my badass keyboardist friend," and then the badass keyboardist will say something along these lines "please pay him no mind, I'm just a learner." And as the introductions go round, and someone introduces someone who he thinks is an excellent musician, the instrumentalist friend says, "I'm still learning." At the event, a lot of times, it would turn out that a lot of the guys are actually excellent instrument players. At first, I thought it was fake humility until I started learning to play the keyboard. And the better I got, the more I realized that there was so much more to learn about playing the instrument.

This is something most programmers understand; there's always something to be learned. There are new code bases, new challenges you encounter as you tackle novel projects, both personal and at work.

The rate at which the tech world is changing is astronomical. There are new updates to languages, new tools and frameworks, and many other new features coming out every day. A developer needs to be able to keep up; otherwise, he/she will be left behind.

Learning is not easy. If it were, well, we'd have knowledgeable people around us every day. If you really want to learn how to learn, then I'd suggest that you take coursera's course. The course title is "Learning How to Learn: Powerful mental tools to help you master tough subjects." At this point, you'd agree that learning to code is a tough subject. The course is free, and you'd be able to apply the skills and techniques you learn there to any form of learning in your life, both technical and non-technical. This is like the best free course I have taken all year, and I recommend it to everyone who needs to or wants to keep on learning. It's going to make your learning more efficient. I'll also suggest that you read Cal Newport's book "Deep Work."

The book contains strategies on how to learn faster and also be more productive. It also has a very inspiring story about some guy learning how to code and becoming very good at it and getting well paid. I don't remember the fellow's name, but the thing is that this guy was an entry-level accountant, but he wanted more, so he taught himself how to code. And all these happened in less than a year.

As far as learning code is concerned, there'll be no point where you might be able to say; I have learned it all; therefore, I know it all. Learning for a coder is a continuous process; it never ends, the challenges, the pressure to be the best you can be, it will not end. Perhaps until you decide to stop coding, but one thing though that it that learning coding will get easier as you go along. The better you get, the easier and faster it becomes for you to learn more coding related things.

Learn To Write Code; Try the Hands-on Approach

There is the temptation by certain persons wanting to learn code to read all the materials they can get on the language, read blog posts, and watch videos before even writing a line for code. For effective learning, I'll say you should begin writing code as soon as possible. That's another reason I suggest you start learning from HTML; you can see the results of your code immediately. You might think that you've gotten the concept of how to code a certain feature because you saw the documentation, or you read it in a book only to want to try it out, and you're stumped. This, I think, is one reason I love freecodecamp, each concept you learn is paired with a relevant exercise so that you can try out your hand on a concept. Until then, no matter how much you think that you understood the concept from the lesson until you do something with it, you can't be so sure. Something else with coding is that things don't usually work right the first time; you'd be stumped many times. So it's better you get used to getting stumped and learning also to get yourself out of the quagmire.

Another way to reinforce learning faster is to use coding games, challenges, and other interactive tutorials to reinforce learning. Hour of Code is one coding game you might want to give a try, CodinGame is another coding game you might want to try, it is more complex, but also you might be able to put it on your resume.

Learn Computational Skills

Computational thinking is very important for a programmer. This is where you learn to solve problems in the way a computer can interpret. These skills are what people acquire when they study computer science. So you see, a computer science degree is not a waste after all. Some of the topics you'll encounter include loops, algorithms, recognizing patterns, amongst others. These concepts will equip you with the skills to understand programming languages easier and faster. With this knowledge, too, you can take on more difficult projects and even design better products. Ideally, the place you'll get this knowledge is from a degree program in computer science from a university. However, there are online resources where you can learn computer science for free or a token price. EdX, Coursera and MIT OpenCourseware are some of the places you can learn about computer science. You can also get videos on this YouTube channel.

Projects

You really can't say that you've understood a language well until you've used it in a project. In fact, if you don't have projects in a certain language, you might not be able to prove in a job interview that you really understood a certain language. A project tasks you on most or all of the knowledge you have acquired in a certain language. It reinforces what you've learned, and also it pushes you to learn more. See, you don't have to wait until you've gotten to the end of the course before you start attempting projects. Some platforms like freecode camp have projects, real-life projects for real-life organizations which you can tackle as a way to challenge yourself.

If you're looking to get into coding things very fast, you should start coding with a project in mind, even without knowing jack about the language. It is one easy way to learn about the features and tools. So you might decide that you want to learn Android development, and then with your skills, you want to be able to build an alarm clock app for your phone. So you go online to search for resources on how to make that happen. In the process of learning to build an alarm clock, you'll definitely learn a lot. It's a more difficult route to use in learning, but it is a very effective one.

Tinker with Other Peoples' Code

This is after you've grasped the basics of whatever language you're learning. At this point, it is time to find someone else's code, play around with it, and see what happens. There are places where you can find code files; one of them is GitHub. Open the file in your code editor and get to work. Try to read the lines of code and try to see if you can understand what each line does. If you can improve it, so if you have questions about the code, ask, if you have comments, make them. And if, for any reason, you improved on the code, upload it to GitHub or any developer forum you're on and see people's feedback.

Join Developer Forums

This goes without saying. Development is not done in isolation. It's a group of people building on what others have built and improving what others have created. Most developers are open-hearted as far as sharing coding knowledge is concerned. On these platforms, you can get people to answer your questions, give you advice, share knowledge, and even get mentored. Slack Overflow is a good place to be as someone learning to code. You'd be inspired; you'd be challenged and encouraged by what you see in these forums.

Chapter 19: <u>*Other Factors*</u>

B ecoming the best programmers depends on many factors besides learning programming techniques in classes or over the internet. In simple terms, it is not about programming as most beginners think. From my experience, your level of impacts plays a lot in determining the level of your success or how best you are as a programmer. Truly, people will not measure your experience from how happy you look when doing programing projects but how your programming projects are impacting the lives of many people in society. For example, there are some people who always feel happy after spending the whole day without doing any programming tasks while others feel unhappy if they do not handle any projects. Also, drinking alcohol everyday can make a person feel happy. Therefore, you level of experience and knowledge does not on how happy you are but how you use the learned skills.

Several studies have proved that slacking off in computer programming not only makes person's programming logic weaker but also destroys his/her tempo. Normally, we miss many things when we don't attend the classes just like drinking coke every day ruins both our teeth and internal organs. Just like alcohol has impacts in our bodies, your success in programming is measured through its impacts. We will see you as a weaker programmer if you do not use the learned programming skills to create positive impact to you or to the society.

Levels of Impacts Resulting From Programming

Ideally, there are different levels of impacts we can use to determine how perfect you are with programming. Yes, most programmers do not know that their programming knowledge is judged on how it impacts them or the society. The following are levels of the impacts:

First Level of Impact: You/ A Person

One of the step to determine how you can measure the impact is by looking at the effects of programming has made on an individual. It is not only the simplest way but also very important since all programmers have goals in their mind before starting programming. Usually, you engage in various activities or jobs because you want a result not nothing. For example, we take our children to schools with two reasons; (1) get job in their future lives to live better life, and (2) obtain knowledge that will help them associate with other people in the society. It is important to know that doing something without a purpose makes you to experience an unexpected result on your way. Therefore, the impacts of programming on you show how best and successful you are as a programmer.

Relationships in Life

Do you know that programming can cause certain impacts on your relationship? In order to determine the effects of programming on your relationship, we always look at how close you are to your love, friends, and other people in the society. Some people chose to be software programmers because it is their passion while others chose it because their friends are doing it or their parents forced them.

Another main reason why people chose programming is getting jobs. In most cases, we work in projects, deliver them, and earn income once users use them. As programmers, we are only required to maintain the projects if there are crashes or bugs. This gives us more time to spend on our relationships. Truly, human life is all about relationship but not how much we earn per day. You may be earning five or six digits but you are not happy at all because you lack freedom to associate with people, particularly your love ones and relatives. Let me tell you, people get more fulfillments out of life when there are some people whom they love and care for. You should spend your earnings with the people you love. As such, work is supposed to improve your relationship with love and relatives.

Impacts on Your Health and Life

In this modern life, your mind and body are the two main assets you must value most. Both body and mind are irreplaceable in our life. Therefore, you must take care of our mind and bodies to avoid them deteriorating over the time. Surely, every person wants to have a longer life, and as such, it is important to consider health when measuring how best you are as a programmer. You career as a programmer would not be either good if you are not healthy.

Money is worthless when compared to our mind and health. I tell you, money will always come on your way when you develop a good mind, which include practicing daily to solve problems, looking for answers, and thinking deep and creatively. You should not only get enough sleep but also build a habit that will train your mind just like writing and reading books. Make coding to be a favorite way to train you. The best programmers always spend at least thirty to forty minutes per day on programming. This is very important to their health. We can say health is your life and you should take care of it in order to live longer.

Having Full Enjoyment

We have seen previously that happy is not the measurement of the success of a person; it is only a part of it, though we need it. You can increase your productivity in programming by engaging in things that you enjoy. What do I mean? I mean that a person can be more productivity in his/her programming work if he/she gives himself/herself a chance to enjoy life. Being more productivity in programming has more impact too. In addition, you should know that there is a great difference between passion and hobbies. While hobby refers to doing something you enjoy, passion refers to thing you like doing throughout the life. For example, my passion is coding and my hobby is learning Japanese language. I always study Japanese when I am a little bit frustrated with some complex coding. This gives enough time to refresh my mind before diving back into the world of coding.

It is always better to give yourself enough time to relax or take a break to make your brain work on the problem subconsciously. But what do you do if you find it hard to solve the problem even after relaxing? It is easy. Just give your brain enough time to solve the problem in the background. In fact, this is one of the main reasons why most ideas come in our minds when we are eating, showering, or drinking tea.

The Second Level of Impact:

This is to know how your programming knowledge and skills impact other people and the society at large.

Impact on Others

Before you consider yourself as the best programmers, it is important to ask yourself about the impact you cause to other people when you are coding. Okay, you may be like that you know how to code because it is the most useful tool available for impacting the lives of many people positively. You can impact people by either enabling them to get data easily, improve their websites, or increase sales. Every person must have a goal in mind why you are doing a particular job. One of the goals in programming is helping other people achieve their objectives. You will be recognized as the best programmers when you help others and organizations to succeed and at the same time meeting your goals. I know it is sometimes difficult for most programmers, but you can become the best programmers if you do this.

Giving Purpose to Other People

Every person has a purpose in life, and this is seen when an individual dedicate his/her life to doing certain thing. For programmers, their purpose is revealed when they engage in building projects and software. Now, let us ask ourselves where this sense of purpose comes from. In normal cases, our purpose comes from the surrounding, society, friends, and internet. For example, we develop an interest in programming after we encounter those who do programming and have achieved a lot in their lives. To be precise, they are the main people who can inspire you to engage in programming. But what will you do in case those people fail to give us ideas? There is a higher chance that you will not have a right purpose. We all have different purpose in our lives and that is the main reason why we all do different work. We were not born to do the same job. While some people are born to be developers, others are born to be doctors, teachers, or politicians.

According to Mark Zuckerberg during his Harvard Commencement Speech, people must have a generational challenge for our society to continue moving forward. We should not only create new jobs for the youth or our people but promote a sense of purpose. However, it is not easy to have a purpose for yourself. You should also create a sense of purpose to other people in the society. Let us take the following example. You need to hire workers if you build a company. These workers play a significant role to the growth of your company. It is, however, your responsibility, as an employer, not only to give them a sense of purpose but also help them to grow in society.

Chapter 20: *Landing a Job*

Getting A Job Without Experience

Getting started with finding your first job can be difficult. There is quite a bit of competition. Many recent college graduates compete for the same position as you.

How to be chosen from all the other candidates?

The answer is to differentiate yourself, stand out from the rest.

What is the type of job you want?

The first thing you should do to stand out from the rest and get your first job even if you don't have experience is to know what you want.

Do you want to be a front end developer, a back end developer or a mobile developer? Neither is better than the other, it is about what you like, you will spend the following years of your life coding, what better it is in those technologies that you love.

Study the market offers

You have already decided the type of developer you will be, now you must know what you need to know or know to get the desired job.

Depending on the country where you live, there are Internet portals where employers publish the available job offers. Perform a search, you can try for example with "Developer backend jr". Do not be in a hurry to apply for whatever job that appears in your search. What you should do is analyze the market.

Most of the job offers will ask you for technologies that you must know and divide them into two sections,

Required which you must know to get the job and the desired ones that are a plus or extra if you know them.

Analyze various job offers and analyze the technologies that are repeated and make a list of them. It will serve you later.

Some job offers publish the salary range and the benefits they offer in others wait to make a call if they are interested in your profile. I'm going to tell you this to give you an idea of what you can earn in your first job, since getting out of that rank can affect your chances of being hired.

Acquire the skills you need for your dream job

Here is a news that will be a bit harsh. Everything you learned in college during your 4 or 5 years spent in it is not enough for the world of work.

Most of what you learned just lays the groundwork for what's next (in addition to giving you that valuable piece of paper called a title that companies still ask to employ you).

Do you remember the list you made with the desired and required technologies that are most repeated to you according to your choice of type of development you want to dedicate yourself to? It is time to use it.

You will have to study and master these technologies. Most companies will give you an oral or written exam to verify that you can perform the job for which they are hiring you. So study and strive.

You can choose to review free tutorials on the Internet or videos on YouTube. But my recommendation is that you buy courses on Udemy or Platzi since their teachers and community will answer your questions and guide you step by step. This will save you a lot of time, unlike searching for information scattered throughout the Internet.

Show your knowledge

Now how do you show the employer that you have the necessary knowledge?

Having no experience, you must demonstrate in another way that you have the ability you claim to have.

In programming there is nothing better than github to demonstrate your skills.

If you do not know Git and Github you are one step behind your competition, but do not worry it is not something that with a little study you cannot remedy.

Show off your skills by writing a blog or YouTube. Do not expect to fill the blog with advertising or become a youtuber. The objective is not that. The objective is to demonstrate that you have the necessary knowledge.

You want to go one step further, buy a domain with your name and a hosting. It will make you look more professional.

The last option to demonstrate your knowledge is certifications. Certifications are documents issued by authorized companies that when you pass an exam (quite difficult at times) certify that you have extensive knowledge of this technology.

Create a linkedIn account, fill out your profile to be visible and have an online presence make sure to link your github or website.

Creating a Perfect Resume

Forget about putting the information of your preschool and high school, just put relevant information, and put the information of your university only. You can also put information about your middle school if it has technical training in computer science or similar if it is not, also omit it.

The information you fill out will be related to your acquired skills.

Write all the technologies in which you have knowledge and link to the blog, YouTube channel, Github or website where you demonstrate it.

Never you to put technologies that you do not know in your CV, it will automatically untie you from the selection process and if it is very easy to notice it in a technical interview, believe me.

Postulant

It's time to go back to the Job Search Portals and fill them with your information, your new knowledge and your online github profiles and personal sites.

Do a search with the characteristics you want from the job.

In the course you will find dubious offers, it is better to avoid them since they will slow down your development.

I don't know if you noticed it during your search, but it is in the big cities that most of the offers are concentrated in addition to being the best paid. If you live in one of them you will have no problems, but if not, sooner or later you will have to move.

In your search you have already found several companies where you would like to work, contact them and send that resume that you made with so much effort and patiently waiting for an answer. You can do this once a day with new offers.

Conclusion

T he best way to learn programming is really just to challenge yourself. Start putting yourself out there and seeking programming challenges. Think of something that you want to do and then start looking into whether other people have done it. If they have, look into the way that they did it and try to find a way that you could do it yourself. If they haven't, then this gives you a perfect opportunity to be the first to do something. Get your hands dirty and start looking into and learning as much about things having to do with programming as you possibly can.

I'm going to say this right now: Programming is not easy. You have a long and arduous journey ahead of you, and the truth about programming is that to be a programmer means to submit yourself to constantly learning. At no point in programming do you ever consider yourself "done with learning'.

One of the big problems they face when starting in this programming world is that when you start you want to make complex programs, pages, and professional applications, but at the critical moment there can be some difficulties, even when you have the experience, for this reason, we decided to share some tips to shorten the learning curve:

1-Know the origins first.

This does not mean that you completely learn the history of the computer, but you must know it, that will give you the notion of how everything came about, so you will know how everything works, from data to an operating system.

2-Master basic concepts.

Know computer concepts such as what is a data, record, field, information among others. As theoretical and boring as this may seem, it will help a future to understand how multiple functions work and why they are made that way.

3- Make an algorithm before starting to throw codes.

If you do not know what it is sincerely I tell you that you will less understand what you do, this is a serious mistake that many programmers make that we do not give importance to the analysis before starting, I advise you that if you are starting as a programmer, you first practice informal algorithms, then it happens to the computations.

This will open up your logic as a programmer and will make a kind of connection between your mind and the computer so that both friends can easily understand.

4-Study fundamental functions of programming

When we start as a programmer, it is necessary that we know perfectly the functions like for "for," while "while," if "if" but "else," among others, where our code starts, because it must have an end and a set of fundamental operations that are in general use.

And you will ask yourself: What is all this for me to learn any programming language? Simple and straightforward programming in general, and in any programming language be it Python, PHP, C ++, C, C #, Java, etc. a "for" will remain a "for" an "if" will continue to be "if" and a "function" will continue to be "function" the only thing that varies are the details of the language's own syntax.

5-Anyone can program

You must trust yourself and be persevering, what makes good programmers is not that they have exceptional talent better than everyone or anything like that, rather they know and master the concepts that I have mentioned before, This means that they are made to learn both a new language and to understand well what they do as programmers.

Be patient read, study, use the documentation that is offered, one of my teachers says that when he started as a programmer he made many mistakes, and it was very difficult to adapt to programming, today he is one of the best and most recognized programmers from my country.

If you take these tips to the letter, success as a programmer awaits you, and many doors will open in this wonderful world of technology.

CODING WITH PYTHON:

A SIMPLE AND STRAIGHTFORWARD GUIDE FOR BEGINNERS TO LEARN FAST PROGRAMMING WITH PYTHON.

Ashton Miller

Introduction

T here are various operating systems that you are able to work without there. Each of them is set up to handle different situations and help you to get different things done with your work. But you will find that one of the best coding languages out there, the one that will help you to get the most done while still being easy to maintain and work with, is the Python language.

There are a lot of coders and programmers out there who love to work with the Python language. And as we go through this guidebook and learn a bit more about this language and what it is able to help us do, you will not take long before you realize why it is such a popular option to work with, and why so many people love it. Some of the different benefits that you will be able to see when it is time to work with the Python language includes:

Python is an easy coding language to learn how to use. If you have never had a chance to work with any coding language at all, then you are going to really enjoy working with the Python language overall. This is going to make it easier for us to handle some of the coding that we are not used to, and you will be able to catch on to some of the basics that come with coding in Python and more in no time at all.

Python has a lot of power and resources behind it. Sometimes there is worry that working with this language is going to be too easy that you will not be able to handle some of the more complicated codes that you would like to work with. The Python language is often going to be advertised as a beginner's language, and this can keep a few programmers away from it.

The good news here is that the Python language is not just a good coding language for beginners to get started with. It is also a good language that is going to help you to get a lot of the different codes that you want. We will take a look at some of the different options that you can do when it is time to code, and we are going to spend some time on them in this guidebook as well. And you will be able to handle them with plenty of strength that comes in the Python language.

And if there are a few things that you may struggle within this language, or that are not strong enough to handle, then you will be able to combine in another language, while still relying on the Python syntax. You will find that Python works well with a lot of other coding languages, and several of the libraries that work with Python can help you to get this done. This will ensure that the few tasks you need help with will work well, while still choosing the Python language.

Python has a great standard library to work with. For the beginner coder, and someone who is just getting started with some of the work that comes with the Python language, or any coding for that matter, you will find that the regular library of Python is going to have all of the parts that you need. You will be able to use the standard library of Python in order to handle all of the coding that we are going to explore in this guidebook.

Python has a lot of extensions and other libraries that can help to add to the capabilities that come with this language. Even though there is a lot that we are able to do when it comes to working on the Python language, you will find that there are also some good extensions that you can take a look at as well. These are going to be good options to go with because they will extend out what the Python language is able to handle, and will make it easier to handle things like science, math, machine learning, data science, and so much more.

The kinds of extensions that you are going to use will really depend on what your goals are overall with the language. If you want to work with machine learning and this language, then there are a lot of great libraries and extensions that you are able to choose to help with that as well. But there are also some that work with other features and capabilities as well, so you need to make sure that you are choosing the right one for your needs.

Python has a large community that can provide beginners with the support and helps they need. At some point, there will be some part of coding that you are not sure how to do, or you are going to run into something that may not make sense when it is time to work on your coding. This is going to happen with many beginners, so it is nothing to be worried about But since there is a nice community out there of other programmers and coders who like to use Python, you will be able to find the assistance that you need in no time.

This community will be there to help you to get going overall, and they can answer all of your questions, make sure that you understand what is going on, and just provide you with all of the resources that you need to make sure you are doing well. You can visit this community as often as you need to make sure that you are able to handle all of the different coding options that you want to work with too.

Python is considered an OOP language that relies on classes and objects to keep things nice and organized Right now, that may not seem to mean all that much for you. But in the long run, it is going to help us to make sure that we can keep all of the parts of our code organized and easy to work with. The code is set up so that you can create the classes that you need while still ensuring that you can add in the objects of the code and find everything later on.

This was not something that we were able to find with some of the traditional coding languages out there. These could sometimes be harder to work with than Python and other options because they are not going to be that organized and things can move around on you. But in Python, the code is going to rely on those classes and more to ensure that it works the way that you want, and that you are able to find the objects that you need.

Python is a great general-purpose language that is easy to learn, has all of the features that you would want in a coding language, and so much more. If you don't want to get into a language that is too technical, but you do want to make sure that you pick out a language that is able to handle a lot of different programming tasks at the same time, then Python is the right language for your needs.

You would want to go through and work with the Python language for many reasons, especially when you are new to the world of coding. For those who have never been able to do any coding in the past, you will find that the Python coding adds in all of the ease of use that you need to see success while still ensuring that you are going to be able to get all of the power that you need actually to complete some of the coding that you would like.

Chapter 1   <u>*What is Python?*</u>

T he introduction of technologies, especially computers, has influenced our behavior differently. Some people spend most of their time on computers that create programs and websites to make a living, while others mess around with computers to try to understand many different things about how machines work. Programming is one of the areas in networks that most people in the world focus on as a source of income. They can work in a company or computer repair to protect computers from attacks such as hackers or viruses. One of the most advanced programming tools is Python because anyone, including beginners or experts, can easily use and read it. The secret to using Python is that you can read it because it contains syntax, which allows you as a programmer to express your concepts without necessarily creating a coding page. This is what makes Python easier to use and read than the other codes, including C ++ and Java. Overall, Python is the best language for you because of its usability and readability. We are therefore confident that it will be easy for you to read and understand all the codes you enter while creating your first program during and after this course.

Features of the Python

Python has the following characteristics:

- **Large library:** it works with other programming projects such as searching for texts, connecting to the web servers and exchanging files.

- **Interactive:** Using the Python is very simple because you can easily test codes to determine if they work.

- **It is free software:** so you can always download it from the internet with your computer.

- **Python programming language can be extended to other modules such as C ++ and C.**

- **Has an elegant syntax** that makes it easy for beginners to read and use.

- **Has several basic data types to choose from.**

History of the Python

Python programming was discovered by Guido Van Rossum in 1989 while he was carrying out a project at the Dutch research institute CWI, but it was later discontinued. Guido has successfully used a number of basic languages, the so-called ABC language, to work on the Python. According to Van Rossum, the strength of the python language is that you can either keep it simple or extend it to more platforms to support many platforms at once. The design allowed the system to communicate with the libraries and various file formats easily.

Since its introduction, many programmers now use Python in the world, and in fact, many tools are included to improve operation and efficiency. Many programmers have taken various initiatives to educate everyone about using python programming language and how it can help ease the fear of complex computer codes.

However, the Python was made open source by Van Rossum a few years ago to allow all programmers access and even make changes to it. This has changed a lot in the field of programming. For example, there was a release of the Python 2.0. Python 2.0 was community-oriented, making it transparent in the development process. While many people don't use Python, there are still some programmers and organizations that use part of the version.

The Python 3, a unique version, was released in 2008. Although the version has many different functions, it is completely different from the first two versions and it is not easy to update the program. While this version is not backwards compatible, it has a small creator to show what needs to be changed when uploading the files.

Why You Should Use Python

There are many types of computer coding programs in the world, each with its advantages and disadvantages. However, Python has proven to be the best option for a variety of reasons, such as readability, and can be used on many platforms without changing things. Using Python has the following advantages;

Readability

Since it is designed in the English language, a beginner will find it easy to read and us. There are also a number of rules that help the programmer understand how to format everything, and this makes it easy for a programmer to create a simple code that other people can follow when using their projects with it.

Community

Today, there are many workshops for Python worldwide. A beginner can visit online, offline or both to learn more or even seek clarification on Python. Also, online and offline workshops can improve your understanding of Python, as well as your socialization skills. It is best for the personal computer as it works successfully on many different platforms. In fact, all beginners find it easy to code or learn from the expert.

Libraries

For over 25 years, programmers have been using Python to teach the beginners how to use different codes written with it. The system is very open to programmers and they can use the available codes indefinitely. In fact, a student can download and install the system and use it for their personal use, such as writing your codes and completing the product.

General Terms in the Python

Understanding the standard terms used in Python is essential to you. It makes everything easy to know when you get started. Following are the most common terms in the Python programming language;

- **Function:** refers to a code block that is called when a programmer uses a calling program. The goal is also to provide free services and accurate calculation.

- **Class:** a template used for developing user-defined objects. It is friendly and easy to use by everyone including the beginners.

- **Ver Immutable:** refers to an object with a fixed value and is contained within the code. These can be numbers, strings, or tuples. Such an object cannot be changed.

- **St Docstring:** Refers to a string that is displayed in the function, class definition, and module. This object is always available in the documentation tools.

- **List:** refers to the data type built into the Python and contains values sorted. Such values include strings and numbers.

- **LE IDLE:** Stands for an integrated development environment that allows the users to type the code while interpreting and editing it in the same window. Best suited for beginners because it is an excellent example of code.

- **Interactive:** Python has become the most suitable programming language for beginners due to its interactive nature. As a beginner, you can try out many things in the IDLE (interpreter to see their response and effects).

- **Qu Triple Quoted String:** The string helps an individual to have single and double quotes in the string, making it easy to go through different lines of code.

- **Object:** it refers to all data in a state such as attitudes, methods, defined behaviors or values.

- **Type:** refers to a group of data categories in the programming language and differences in properties, functions and methods.

- **Tuple:** Refers to the datatype built into the Python and is an unchanging set of values, although it contains some changeable values.

Advantages of Python Language

Using the Python program has many advantages over other programming languages such as C ++ and Java. You will be happy to see the availability and how easy it is to learn and use the Python program. Ideally, these are the best programming languages you can use right now, especially if you are a beginner. Following are some of the advantages of using Python language;

It is easy to use, write and read

Many programmers face some challenges when using programming languages such as Java and C ++. They are difficult to view due to their design. One has to spend a lot of his / her time learning about the use of parentheses and it is not easy to recognize some of the words used in these programming languages. Such words can scare you, especially if you are just getting acquainted with the programming languages. Unlike Java and C ++ languages, Python does not use crazy brackets. It only uses indents, making it easy to read the page. It uses English which makes it easy to understand characters.

In addition to using indents, Python uses a lot of white spaces, making it easy to learn and read what's needed. It consists of many places with comments to allow you to understand or get clarification in case the program confuses you. So check it out and you will see how easy it is to use the Python programming language.

It uses English as the primary language

Using Python is easy because the main language is English. As a beginner, you will spend less time reading and understanding the basic words used when programming in Python. So, whether you speak native or non-native English, Python is best for you because most words are simple and easy to understand.

Python is already available on some computers

Some computers such as macOS systems and Ubuntu come with Python pre-installed. In this case, you just need to download the text interpreter to get started with Python programming. However, you must download the program on your computer if you are using a Windows computer. In fact, Python works fine even if you didn't install it from the beginning.

Python works perfectly with other programming languages

For the first time, you will be using Python alone. However, you will realize that Python can work with other languages as you continue programming. Some of the programming languages that you can work with Python include C ++ and JavaScript. Try to learn more about Python and what it can do practically. You will be able to discover many things over time.

Th Python can be used to test many things

You need to download the test interpreter once you have downloaded the Python. Test interpreter plays an important role in enabling Python to read the information. It's good to use a simple product like Notepad that is available in your Windows or other interpreters.

Disadvantages of using Python programming

While there are many advantages to using Python, it is essential to recognize some of the adverse effects of using it. Some individuals prefer to use other programming languages such as C ++ and JavaScript for Python because of the following negative effects of Python.

Python has a slow speed

While Python works well with other programming languages and is suitable for beginners, it is unfortunate that Python is not ideal for programmers looking for a high speed program as it is a slower translated language than the other options. The level of speed depends on the content you are translating because some benchmarks with Python code work faster compared to other codes. Currently, many programmers around the world are trying to solve this problem by making the interpreting speed faster. It is hopeful that Python will run at the same rate or even faster than C and C ++ soon.

Python is not available in most mobile browsers

While Python works well for those who have regular computers and is accessible on many server platforms and desktops to help individuals create the codes they are looking for, it is not yet ready for mobile computing. Programmers are trying to transition the program to mobile computing to cater to today's large numbers of people who use cell phones.

Limited design

Python program is not a better option for programmers looking for a program with many design options. For example, the design language is not available in some other options; so you will need more time to test and sometimes a lot of errors can occur when you run the program.

Chapter 2   *Why Python?*

I have experience coding in several programming languages. Last week, I was discussing a project with a friend who is a developer, and out of nowhere, he asked me the question "Why Python? Of all the languages that are available, why did you settle with Python?" My friend definitely caught me off guard because I had never thought about it. The day I started programming with Python was the day I almost stopped coding in any other language. I still occasionally use other languages depending upon the project, but, if given the choice, I pick Python every time.

But, why? Yes, this is a small question but it carries a lot of weight. I spent a few days figuring out the advantages of using Python over other languages. Of course, I can list a few problems, too. I am going to share my point of view with you now.

The Alternatives

Before we look into Python, let's talk about the alternatives we can use for programming.

The C Family

UNIX is arguably the first operating system that was widely used across different computer systems. AT&T Bell Laboratories developed the operating system for minicomputers in the late 1960s based upon a language that we now call the C language. AT&T forced companies using Bell systems to use UNIX which meant UNIX was ported to various different computer systems along with the C language. Because the C language became so common, many languages that were developed later provided a similar coding environment to make it easier for C language programmers to use them.

The list of C-family programming languages is a long one, but some became more famous than others. C, C++ and C# are the three most popular, closely followed by Objective C.

Advantages

- As of October 2019, C is the most widely used language family after Java and Python. Embedded systems and operating systems still depend heavily on C language

- Every programmer should learn at least one of the C, C++ or C# languages to understand what happens in the background during program execution

Disadvantages

- It is difficult to learn as it forces programmer to focus on things that modern programming languages take care of automatically

- The syntax, although it inspired a lot of other languages, is very ugly.

- A lot of extraneous lines of codes are required even to perform the most basic tasks.

Java Platform

Thanks to the millions of web applications developed using the language, ***Java is possibly the most widely used programming language in the world.*** Released as a core component of the Java platform in 1995 by Sun Microsystems, it enabled applications built using Java to run on any computer system that has Java Virtual Machine (JVM). Although it has a syntax similar to C and C++ languages, it doesn't demand low-level considerations from the programmers. Oracle has acquired Sun Microsystems and now manages Java platform.

For years, Microsoft's C# and Sun's Java remained in a cold war, each trying to outdo the other programming language. Both languages were heavily criticized for adding new features just to win a competition instead of following a standard direction. It was not until 2004 that both languages took to separate ways and developed into the unique languages as we know them today.

Even then, Java remains the top programming language in the world and Java platform runs on almost every laptop, game console, data center, and even supercomputers.

Advantages

- Java frees the programmer from computer dependencies and offers a vast degree of freedom

- Java is compatible with almost all computer systems. It means almost every program created using Java language will run on all those systems without any issues.

Disadvantages

- There have been serious security issues with Java over the years. Severe security vulnerabilities were found in the last Java version and Oracle advised every Java user to update to the latest version.

- Java programs are known to be slower than the competition even though there have been huge performance improvements in recent versions.

- For a long time Java remained a proprietary platform. Even after Sun declared it open-source, a long copyright battle ensued between Oracle and Google over the use of Java in Google's Android.

Python is Different

We have briefly tackled the best options we have if we don't want to use Python. They are great options but before you jump ship, let me tell you why I chose Python over others.

- **Python is one of the easiest high-level programming languages to learn.** It means the time it takes from setup to coding programs is very short.

- **Code written in Python is easier to understand.** It enables programmers to consult codes written by other programmers to adapt for their project.

- Python is an interpreter language. Code is executed one line at a time which makes debugging easier for beginners.

- Python code can run on any computer no matter if it's Windows, Linux, UNIS, or a macOS based system.

- Python has a vast standard library that provides methods for unique project requirements.

- Python supports various coding paradigms including Object Oriented Programming (OOP) and functional programming.

- Python programming language is free and open source. This has helped create an active programmer community and detailed tutorials are available for free on the Internet.

- The open source nature of the language has also enabled many programmers to extend Python capabilities by writing special libraries. These libraries are available on the Internet free of charge for everyone's use.

- It's very easy to create Graphical User Interface (GUI) through Python.

- One of the biggest advantages of Python is its ability to integrate with different programming languages. You can import a specific library and start coding in a completely different language and Python will understand the codes. Python supports extended integration with C++ and Java. Not only that, Python code can be placed inside a code written with another programming language.

These are the general advantages of Python over other programming languages. Depending upon your project, Python might be able to provide even more benefits. We are going to see how Python makes data analysis easy.

Advantages of Using Python in Data Analysis

Strong with Strings

Python has a special place for strings. There are multiple string related operations supported by Python. These operations are a big help in data analysis stages of parsing and processing if you are dealing with string data.

Dedicated Libraries

There are dedicated libraries in Python that help make data analysis projects easier to handle. The libraries are regularly updated which means they are compatible with the latest analysis algorithms.

Some of the popular data analysis libraries available on Python are:

1. NumPy: Collection of mathematical functions for fast calculations

2. SciPy: Offers advanced scientific tools

3. Pandas: Offers robust handling of mathematical components using data structures

4. Matplotlib: Offers data visualization methods including line plots, bar charts, and scatter plots.

Highly Scalable

Python is very efficient in handling large and complex datasets. This quality has made this programming language invaluable to companies like YouTube, Facebook, and Amazon that deal with huge data on a consistent basis.

Fast Deployment

With a simple coding syntax and straightforward development process, it's definitely faster to create and deploy applications using Python as compared to other languages.

If you look at the larger picture, Python provides the easiest yet most robust coding environment. It's faster to learn and deploy applications. It integrates well with other programming languages and technologies. There are tons of free tutorials and documentations available online for help if you are not able to resolve an issue.

All of the above qualities make Python the best package when it comes to programming languages. Yes, you might find that another programming language suits your needs better for a specific application, for example, for web applications JavaScript is more popular, and for database, SQL is used more. But, as a whole, Python offers you everything you need for 90% of the programming tasks.

Knowing all this, do you still think I made a mistake sticking with Python? Personally, I think it was a great decision. I told my friend all these points and he was amazed by how versatile Python is. Whenever I meet someone who asks me where they should start with programming, I recommend they start with Python.

Chapter 3   *Installing Python*

Ｔo code in Python, you must have the Python Interpreter installed in your computer. You must also have a text editor in which you will be writing and saving your Python codes. The good thing with Python is that it can run on various platforms like Windows, Linux, and Mac OS. Most of the current versions of these operating systems come installed with Python. You can check whether Python has been installed on your operating system by running this command on the terminal or operating system console:

Python

Type the above command on the terminal of your operating system then hit the Enter/Return key.

The command should return the version of Python installed on your system. If Python is not installed, you will be informed that the command is not recognized; hence you have to install Python.

Choosing a Python Version

The main two versions of Python are 2.x and 3.x. Python 3.x is obviously the latest one but Python 2.x as of today is most likely still the most used one. Python 3.x is however growing much faster in terms of adoption. Python 2.x is still in use in many software companies. More and more enterprises however are moving to Python 3.x. There are several technical differences between the 2 versions. We can summarize in very a simple way as Python 2.x is legacy and Python 3.x is the future. The advice for you is to go for the latest version Python 3.x. From 2020 Python 2.x is not be supported anymore.

General Installations Instruction

Installing Python is very easy. All you need to do is follow the steps described below:

1. Go to Python downloads page https://www.python.org/downloads/

2. Click the link related to your operating system

> Looking for Python with a different OS? Python for Windows, Linux/UNIX, Mac OS X, Other

3. Click on the latest release and download according to your operating system

4. Launch the package and follow the installation instructions (we recommend to leave the default settings)

> Make sure you click on Add Python 3.x to PATH. Once the installation is finished you are set to go!

5. Access your terminal IDLE

Test that all works by writing your first Python code:

☐   print ("I'm running my first Python code")

Press enter or return, this is what you should get

```
>>> print ("I'm running my first Python code")
I'm running my first Python code
```

You can do the same also by launching this command using a file. We will address this after we address the Python IDLE or another code editor.

Installation on Windows

To install Python on Windows, download Python from its official website then double click the downloaded setup package to launch the installation. You can download the package by clicking this link:

https://www.python.org/downloads/windows/

It will be good for you to download and install the latest package of Python as you will be able to enjoy using the latest Python packages. After downloading the package, double click on it and you will be guided through on-screen instructions on how to install Python on your Windows OS.

Installation on Linux (Ubuntu)

In Linux, there are a number of package managers that can be used for installation of Python in various Linux distributions. For example, if you are using Ubuntu Linux, run this command to install Python:

$ sudo apt-get install python3-minimal

Python will be installed on your system. However, most of the latest versions of various Linux distributions come installed with Python. Just run the "python" command. If you get a Python version as the return, then Python has been installed on your system. If not, go ahead and install Python.

Installation on Mac OS

To install Python in Mac OS, you must first download the package. You can find it by opening the following link on your web browser:

https://www.python.org/downloads/mac-osx/

After the setup has been downloaded, double click it to launch the installation. You will be presented with on screen instructions that will guide through the installation process. Lastly, you will have Python running on your Mac OS system.

Running Programs

One can run Python programs in two main ways:

- Interactive interpreter

- Script from command line

Interactive Interpreter or Interactive Mode via Shell

Python comes with a command line which is commonly referred to as the interactive interpreter. You can write your Python code directly on this interpreter and press the enter key. You will get instant results. If you are on Linux, you only have to open the Linux terminal then type "python". Hit the enter key and you will be presented with the Python interpreter with the >>> symbol. To access the interactive Python interpreter on Windows, click Start -> All programs, then identify "Python …" from the list of programs. In my case, I find "Python 3.5" as I have installed Python 3.5. Expand this option and click "Python …". In my case, I click "Python 3.5(64-bit)" and I get the interactive Python interpreter.

Here, you can write and run your Python scripts directly. To write the "Hello" example, type the following on the interpreter terminal:

print("Hello")

Hit the enter/return key and the text "Hello" will be printed on the interpreter:

Script from Command Line

This method involves writing Python programs in a file, then invoking the Python interpreter to work on the file. Files with Python should be saved with a .py extension. This is a designation to signify that it is a Python file. For example, script.py, myscript.py, etc. After writing your code in the file and saving with the name "mycode.py", you can open the operating system command line and invoke the Python interpreter to work on the file. For example, you can run this command on the command line to execute the code on the file mycode.py:

- python mycode.py

The Python interpreter will work on the file and print the results on the terminal.

Python IDE (Integrated Development Environment)

If you have a GUI (Graphical User Interface) application capable of supporting Python, you can run the Python on a GUI environment. The following are the Python IDEs for the various operating systems:

- UNIX- IDLE

- Windows- PythonWin

Macintosh comes along with IDLE IDE, downloadable from the official website as MacBinary or BinHex'd files.

Chapter 4   <u>**What are Data Types?**</u>

E very program has certain data that allows it to function and operate in the way we want. The data can be a text, a number, or any other thing in between. Whether complex in nature or as simple as you like, these data types are the cogs in a machine that allow the rest of the mechanism to connect and work.

Python is a host to a few data types and, unlike its competitors, it does not deal with an extensive range of things. That is good because we have less to worry about and yet achieve accurate results despite the lapse. Python was created to make our lives, as programmers, a lot easier.

Strings

In Python, and other programming languages, any text value that we may use, such as names, places, sentences, they are all referred to as strings. A string is a collection of characters, not words or letters, which is marked by the use of single or double quotation marks.

To display a string, use the print command, open up a parenthesis, put in a quotation mark, and write anything. Once done, we generally end the quotation marks and close the bracket.

Numeric Data Type

Just as the number suggests, Python is able to recognize numbers rather well. The numbers are divided into two pairs:

- Integer – A positive and negative whole numbers that are represented without any decimal points.
- Float – A real number that has a decimal point representation.

This means, if you were to use 100 and 100.00, one would be identified as an integer while the other will be deemed as a float. So why do we need to use two various number representations?

If you are designing a program, suppose a small game that has a character's life of 10, you might wish to keep the program in a way that whenever a said character takes a hit, his life reduces by one or two points. However, to make things a little more precise, you may need to use float numbers. Now, each hit might vary and may take 1.5, 2.1, or 1.8 points away from the life total.

Using floats allows us to use greater precision, especially when calculations are on the cards. If you aren't too troubled about the accuracy, or your programming involves whole numbers only, stick to integers.

Booleans

Boolean (or bool) is a data type that can only operate on and return two values: True or False. Booleans are a vital part of any program, except the ones where you may never need them, such as our first program. These are what allow programs to take various paths if the result is true or false.

Here's an example. Suppose you are traveling to a country you have never been to. There are two choices you are most likely to face.

If it is cold, you will be packing your winter clothes. If it is warm, you will be packing clothes which are appropriate for warm weather. Simple, right? That is exactly how the Booleans work. We will look into the coding aspect of it as well. For now, just remember, when it comes to true and false, you are dealing with a bool value.

List

While this is slightly more advanced for someone at this stage of learning, the list is a data type that does exactly what it sounds like. It lists objects, values, or stores data within square brackets ([]). Here's what a list would look like:

month = ['Jan', 'Feb', 'March', 'And so on!']

Variables

You have the passengers, but you do not have a mode of commuting; they will have nowhere to go. These passengers would just be folks standing around, waiting for some kind of transportation to pick them up. Similarly, data types cannot function alone. They need to be 'stored' in these vehicles, which can take them places. These special vehicles, or as we programmers refer to as containers, are called 'variables,' and they are exactly what perform the magic for us.

Variables are specialized containers that store a specific value in them and can then be accessed, called, modified, or even removed when the need arises. Every variable that you may create will hold a specific type of data in them. You cannot add more than one type of data within a variable.

In other programming languages, you will find that in order to create a variable, you need to use the keyword 'var' followed by an equals mark '=' and then the value. In Python, it is a lot easier, as shown below:

name = "John"

age = 33

weight = 131.50

is_married = True

In the above, we have created a variable named 'name' and given it a value of characters. If you recall strings, we have used double quotation marks to let the program know that this is a string.

We then created a variable called age. Here, we simply wrote 33, which is an integer as there are no decimal figures following that. You do not need to use quotation marks here at all.

Next, we created a variable 'weight' and assigned it a float value.

Finally, we created a variable called 'is_married' and assigned it a 'True' bool value. If you were to change the 'T' to 't' the system will not recognize it as a bool and will end up giving an error.

Focus on how we used the naming convention for the last variable. We will be ensuring that our variables follow the same naming convention.

You can even create blank variables in case you feel like you may need these at a later point in time or wish to initiate them at no value at the start of the application. For variables with numeric values, you can create a variable with a name of your choosing and assign it a value of zero. Alternatively, you can create an empty string as well by using opening and closing quotation marks only.

empty_variable1 = 0

empty_variable2 = ""

You do not have to name them like this necessarily; you can come up with more meaningful names so that you and any other programmer who may read your code would understand. I have given them these names to ensure anyone can immediately understand their purpose.

Now we have learned how to create variables, let's learn how to call them. What's the point of having these variables if we are never going to use them, right?

Let's create a new set of variables. Have a look here:

name = "Jonah"

age = 47

height_in_cm = 170

occupation = "Programmer"

I do encourage you to use your own values and play around with variables if you like.

In order for us to call the name variable, we simply need to type the name of the variable. In order to print that to the console, we will do this:

print(name)

Output

Jonah

The same goes for the age, the height variable, and occupation. But what if we wanted to print them together and not separately?

Try running the code below and see what happens:

print(name age height_in_cm occupation)

Surprised? Did you end up with this?

print(name age height_in_cm occupation)

^

SyntaxError: invalid syntax

Process finished with exit code 1

Here is the reason why that happened. When you were using a single variable, the program knew what variable that was. The minute you added a second, a third, and a fourth variable, it tried to look for something that was written in that manner. Since there wasn't any, it returned with an error that otherwise says:

"Umm… Are you sure, Sir? I tried looking everywhere, but I couldn't find this 'name age height_in_cm occupation' element anywhere."

All you need to do is add a comma to act as a separator like so:

print(name, age, height_in_cm, occupation)

Output:

Jonah 47 170 Programmer

"Your variables, Sir!"

And now, it knew what we were talking about. The system recalled these variables and was successfully able to show us what their values were. But what happens if you try to add two strings together? What if you wish to merge two separate strings and create a third-string as a result?

first_name = "John"

last_name = "Wick"

To join these two strings into one, we can use the '+' sign. The resulting string will now be called a String Object, and since this is Python we are dealing with, everything within this language is considered as an object.

first_name = "John"

last_name = "Wick"

first_name + last_name

Here, we did not ask the program to print the two strings. If you wish to print these two instead, simply add the print function and type in the string variables with a + sign in the middle within parentheses. Sounds good, but the result will not be quite what you expect:

first_name = "John"

last_name = "Wick"

print(first_name + last_name)

Output:

JohnWick

Why do you think that happened? Certainly, we did use a space between the two variables. The problem is that the two strings have combined together, quite literally here, and we did not provide a white space (blank space) after John or before Wick; it will not include that. Even the white space can be a part of a string. To test it out, add one character of space within the first line of code by tapping on the friendly spacebar after John. Now try running the same command again, and you should see "John Wick" as your result.

The process of merging two strings is called concatenation. While you can concatenate as many strings as you like, you cannot concatenate a string and an integer together. If you really need to do that, you will need to use another technique first to convert the integer into a string and then concatenate the same. To convert an integer, we use the str() function.

text1 = "Zero is equal to "

text2 = 0

print(text1 + str(text2))

Output:

Zero is equal to 0

Python reads the codes in a line-by-line method. First, it will read the first line, then the second, then third, and so on. This means we can do a few things beforehand as well, to save some time for ourselves.

text1 = "Zero is still equal to "

text2 = str(0)

print(text1 + text2)

Output:

Zero is still equal to 0

You may wish to remember this as we will be visiting the conversion of values into strings a lot sooner than you might expect.

There is one more way through which you can print out both string variables and numeric variables, all at the same time, without the need for '+' signs or conversion. This way is called String Formatting. To create a formatted string, we follow a simple process, as shown here:

print(f" This is where {var 1} will be. Then {var 2}, then {var 3} and so on")

Var 1, 2, and 3 are variables. You can have as many as you like here. Notice the importance of whitespace. Try not to use the spacebar as much. You might struggle at the start but will eventually get the hang of it.

When we start the string, we place the character 'f' to let Python know that this is a formatted string. Here, the curly brackets are performing a part of placeholders. Within these curly brackets, you can recall your variables. One set of curly brackets will be a placeholder for each variable that you would like to call upon. To put this in practical terms, let's look at an example:

show = "GOT"

name1 = "Daenerys"

name2 = "Jon"

name3 = "Tyrion"

seasons = 8

print(f"The show called {show} had characters like {name1}, {name2} and {name3} in all {seasons} seasons. ")

Output:

The show called GOT had characters like Daenerys, Jon, and Tyrion in all 8 seasons.

Chapter 5   How to Read Errors and Troubleshooting Your Code

These codes are great because they will save you a lot of time and will make your code look nicer because you can reuse parts of your code without tiring yourself out by having to rewrite it so many times. This is something that you can do with object-oriented programming, or OOP, languages, a category which Python is a part of. You can work with inheritances so you can use a parent code and then make some adjustments to the parts of the code that you want and make the code unique. As a beginner, you will find that these inheritances can be quite easy to work with because you can get the code to work the way you want it to work without having to write it out a million times over.

To help you keep things simple and to understand how inheritances work a little better, an inheritance is when you will take a 'parent' code and copy it down into a 'child' code. You will then be able to work on the child code and make some adjustments without having to make any changes in the parent part of the code. You can do this one time and stop there, or you can keep on going down the line and change the child code at each level without making any changes to the parent code.

Working with inheritances can be a fun part of making your own code, and you can make it look so much nicer without all that mess.

How to override the base class

The next thing that we can work on when it comes to inheritance codes is how to override a base class. There will be a lot of times that while you are working on a derived class, you have to go in and override what you have placed inside a base class. What this means is that you will take a look at what was placed inside the base class and then make changes to alter some of the behavior that was programmed inside of it. This helps to bring in new behavior which will then be available inside the child class that you plan to create from that base class.

This does sound a little bit complicated to work with, but it can really be useful because you can choose and pick the parental features that you would like to place inside the derived class, which ones you would like to keep around, and which ones you no longer want to use. This whole process will make it easier for you to make some changes to the new class and keep the original parts from your base class that might help you out later. It is a simple process that you can use to make some changes in the code and get rid of parts of the base class that is no longer working and replaces them with something that will work better.

Overloading

Another process that you may want to consider when you're working with inheritances is learning how to 'overload.' When you work on the process known as overloading, you can take one of the identifiers that you are working with and then use that to define at least two methods, if not more. For the most part, there will only be two methods that are inside of each class, but sometimes this number will be higher. The two methods should be inside the exact same class, but they need to have different parameters so that they can be kept separate in this process. You will find that it is a good idea to use this method when you want the two matched methods to do the same tasks, but you would like them to do that task while having different parameters.

This is not something that is common to work with, and as a beginner, you will have very little need to use this since many experts don't actually use it either. But it is still something that you may want to spend your time learning about just in case you do need to use it inside of your code. There are some extra modules available for you that you can download so you can make sure that overloading will work for you.

Final Notes about Inheritances

As you are working on your codes, you will find that it is possible that you could work on more than one inheritance code. If you are doing this, it means that you can make a line of inheritances that are similar to each other, but you can also make some changes to them as well if needed. You will notice that multiple inheritances are not all that different from what you did with a normal inheritance. Instead, you are just adding more steps and continuously repeating yourself so you can make the changes that you want.

When you want to work with multiple inheritances, you have to take one class and then give it two or more parent classes to get it started. This is important once you are ready to write your own code, but you can also use the inheritances to make sure the code looks nice as you write it out.

Now, as a beginner, you may be worried that working with these multiple inheritances might be difficult because it sounds too complicated. When you are working with these types of inheritances, you will create a new class, which we will call Class3, and you will find that this class was created from the features that were inside of Class2. Then you can go back a bit further and will find that Class2 was created with the features that come from Class1 and so on and so forth. Each layer will contain features from the class that was ahead of it, and you can really go down as far as you would like. You can have ten of these classes if you would like, with features from the past parent class in each one, as long as it works inside of your code.

One of the things that you should remember when you're creating new code and if you are considering to add in some multiple inheritances is that the Python language will not allow you to create a circular inheritance. You can add in as many parent classes as you want, but you are not allowed to go into the code and make the parent class go in a circle, or the program will get mad at you if you do so. Expanding out the example that we did above to make another class or more is fine, but you must make sure that you are copying the codes out properly before you even make changes so you can get this program to work.

As you start to write out some more codes using the Python programming language, you will find that working with different types of inheritances is actually pretty popular. There are many times when you can just stick with the same block of code in the program and then make some changes without having to waste your time and tire yourself out by rewriting the code over and over again.

Chapter 6 <u>*Variables*</u>

Creating a Variable

I t is very easy to create a variable in Python. The assignment operator "=" is used for this purpose. The value to the left of the assignment operator is the variable identifier or name of the variable. The value to the right of the operator is the value assigned to the variable. Take a look at the following code snippet.

Name = 'Mike' # A string variable

Age = 15 # An integer variable

Score = 102.5 # A floating type variable

Pass = True # A Boolean variable

In the script above we created four different types of variables. You can see that we did not specify the type of variable with the variable name. For instance we did not write "string Name" or "int Age". We only wrote the variable name. This is because Python is a loosely typed language. Depending upon the value being stored in a variable, Python assigns type to the variable at runtime. For instance when Python interpreter interprets the line "Age = 15", it checks the type of the value which is integer in this case. Hence, Python understands that Age is an integer type variable.

To check type of a variable, pass the variable name to "type" function as shown below: type(Age)

You will see that the above script, when run, prints "int" in the output which is basically the type of Age variables

Python allows multiple assignment which means that you can assign one value to multiple variables at the same time. Take a look at the following script:

Age = Number = Point = 20 #Multiple Assignment

print (Age)

print (Number)

print (Point)

In the script above, integer 20 is assigned to three variables: Age, Number and Point. If you print the value of these three variables, you will see 20 thrice in the output.

For any programming language, the basic part is to store the data in memory and process it. No matter what kind of operation we are going to perform, we must have the object of operation. It is difficult for a skillful woman to cook without rice. In Python language, constants and variables are the main ones. In fact, both of them are identification codes used by program designers to access data contents in memory.

The biggest difference between the two is that the contents of variables will change with the execution of the program, while the contents of constants are fixed forever. In the process of program execution, it is often necessary to store or use some data. For example, if you want to write a program to calculate the mid-term exam results, you must first input the students' results, and then output the total score, average score and ranking after calculation. This part describes how to store and access this data.

Variable Naming and Assignment

In a program, program statements or instructions tell the computer which Data to access and execute step by step according to the instructions in the program statements. These data may be words or numbers. What we call variable is the most basic role in a programming language, that is, a named memory unit allocated by the compiler in programming to store changeable data contents. The computer will store it in "memory" and take it out for use when necessary. In order to facilitate identification, it must be given a name. We call such an object "variable." For example:

> > firstsample = 3

> > > second sample = 5

> > > result = firstsample + secondsample

In the above program statement, firstsample, secondsample, result are variables, and number 3 is the variable value of firstsample. Since the capacity of memory is limited, in order to avoid wasting memory space, each variable will allocate memory space of different sizes according to requirements, so "Data Type" is used to regulate it.

Variable Declaration and Assignment

Python is an object-oriented language, all data are regarded as objects, and the method of an Object reference is also used in variable processing. The type of variable is determined when the initial value is given, so there is no need to declare the data type in advance. The value of a variable is assigned with "=" and beginners easily confuse the function of the assignment operator (=) with the function of "equal" in mathematics. In programming languages, the "=" sign is mainly used for assignment.

The syntax for declaring a variable is as follows:

variable name = variable value

e.g. number = 10.

The above expression indicates that the value 10 is assigned to the variable number. In short, in Python language, the data type does not need to be declared in advance when using a variable, which is different from that in C language, which must be declared in advance before using a variable. Python interpretation and operation system will automatically determine the data type of the variable according to the value of the variable given or set. For example, the data type of the above variable number is an integer. If the content of the variable is a string, the data type of the variable is a string.

Variable Naming Rules

For an excellent programmer, readability of program code is very important. Although variable names can be defined by themselves as long as they conform to Python's regulations, when there are more and more variables, simply taking variables with letter names such as abc will confuse people and greatly reduce readability. Considering the readability of the program, it is best to name it according to the functions and meanings given by variables. For example, the variable that stores height is named "Height" and the variable that stores weight is named "Weight." Especially when the program scale is larger, meaningful variable names will become more important. For example, when declaring variables, in order to make the program readable, it is generally used to start with lowercase letters, such as score, salary, etc. In Python, variable names also need to conform to certain rules. If inappropriate names are used, errors may occur during program execution. Python is a case-sensitive language. In other words, number and Number are two different variables. Variable names are not limited in length. Variable names have the following limitations: the first character of a variable name must be an English letter, underlined "_" and cannot be a number. Subsequent characters can match other upper- and lower-case English letters, numbers, underlined "_," and no space character is allowed. You cannot use Python's built-in reserved words (or keywords). Although Python version 3. X supports foreign language variable names; it is recommended that you try not to use words to name variables. On the one hand, it is more troublesome to switch input methods when inputting program code. On the other hand, the reading of program code will not be smooth. The so-called reserved word usually has special meaning and function, so it will be reserved in advance and cannot be used as a variable name or any other identifier name.

The following is an example of a valid variable name: pageresponse

fileName4563

level

Number_

dstance

The following is an example of an invalid variable name:

2_sample

for

$ levelone

The user name learning classroom uses the help () function to query Python reserved word. The help () function is Python's built-in function. If you are not sure about the method and property usage of a specific object, you can use the help () function to query.

The Python reserved words mentioned above can be viewed by using the help () function. As long as "help ()" is executed, the help interactive mode will be entered. In this mode, the instructions to be queried will be input, and the relevant instructions will be displayed.

We can continue to input the instructions we want to query in help mode. When we want to exit help interactive mode, we can input Q or quit. You can also take parameters when entering the help () command, such as help (" keywords "), Python will directly display help or description the information without entering help interactive mode.

Although Python uses dynamic data types, it is very strict in data processing, and its data type is "strong type." For example:

> > > firstsample = 5

> > > secondsample = "45"

> > > print (firstsample + secondsample) #

shows that TypeError variable firstsample is of numeric type and variable secondsample is of string type.

Some programming languages will convert the type unconsciously and automatically convert the value A to the string type, so firstsample + secondsample will get 545. Python language prohibits different data types from operating, so executing the above statement obviously Indicates information about the wrong type.

There is a difference between "strongly typed" and "weakly typed" in the data types of strong and weak type programming languages in small classrooms. One of the trade-offs is the safety of data type conversion. The strong type has a strict inspection for data type conversion.

Different types of operations must be explicitly converted, and programs will not automatically convert. For example, Python and Ruby prefer strong types.

However, most weak type programming languages adopt Implicit Conversion. If you don't pay attention to it, unexpected type conversion will occur, which will lead to wrong execution results.

JavaScript is a weak type of programming language.

Static Type and Dynamic Type

When Python is executed, the way to determine the data type belongs to "dynamic type."

What is the dynamic type?

The data types of programming languages can be divided into "Statically-Typed" and "Dynamically-Typed" according to the type checking method.

1.   Static types are compiled with the type checked first, so the variables must be explicitly declared before they are used. The types of variables cannot be arbitrarily changed during execution. Java and C are such programming languages. For example, the following C language program statement declares that the variable number is of int integer type, and the initial value of the variable is set to 10. When we assign "apple" to number again, an error will occur, because "apple" is a string, and compilation will fail due to type discrepancy during compilation.

int firstsample = 10

firstsample = "apple"

#Error:

Types do not match

2.   Dynamic types are compiled without prior type checking, and data types are determined according to variable values during execution. Therefore, there is no need to declare types before variables are used. The same variable can also be given different types of values, and Python is a dynamic type. For example, the following program statement declares the variable number and sets the initial value to the integer 10. When we assign the string apple to number, the type will be automatically converted.

firstsample = 10

firstsample = "love"

Print (firstsample)

output string love

Python has a Garbage Collection mechanism. When the object is no longer in use, the interpreter will automatically recycle and free up memory space. In the above example, when the integer object number is reassigned to another string object, the original integer object will be deleted by the interpreter. If the object is determined not to be used, we can also delete it by using the "del" command with the following syntax: del object name

For example:

 > > number = "apple"

> > > print(number) # output apple

> > > del number # deletes string object number

> > > print(number) #Error: number does not define the execution result.

Since the variable number has been deleted, if the number variable is used again, an undefined error message for the variable will appear.

Chapter 7   Lists

I n Python it is possible to define a list, to which a name can be attributed, inserting elements in square brackets ("[..]"). Those who already work with other languages for programming or development will certainly know arrays, or "vectors", which are variables intended to contain further variables; syntactically and conceptually the lists can remember arrays, but their functioning has some peculiarities that make them different.

Basically a list can exist but be empty, that is, not present any element inside it:

Example of empty list

list_name = []

If a list is not empty, it will be necessary to separate the elements that compose it by a comma. It is therefore possible to define lists that contain elements associated with a single type of data:

Example of a list containing only numeric values

list_name = [15, 25, 35, 45, 55]

Example of a list containing only strings

list_name = ['Homer', 'Bart', 'Lisa']

Just as you can create lists that present elements of different nature:

Example of list containing elements of different types

numbers and strings

list_name = [65, 'Homer', 7.3]

Finally, the creation of nested lists is also allowed, i.e. lists that have other lists among their elements.

Example of nested list

list_name = ['Homer', 3.7, 10, [29, 39, 49]].

Automatic generation of lists of integers

range () is a native Python function (or more properly an "immutable sequence type") designed to automatically generate a list based on a range of values or a numeric value passed as an argument; it is particularly useful when you need to define lists made up of a large number of numerical elements.

In the case of a parameter expressed as an interval, we will have an instruction like the following:

Using range () to generate

a list based on an interval

>>> range (1.8)

will lead to the generation of a list consisting of 7 elements:

[1, 2, 3, 4, 5, 6, 7]

These elements will be the result of the call to the range () function which will evaluate the two arguments of the range by returning a list containing all the integer values starting from the first, included in the list, up to the second, excluded from the list instead.

The two arguments of the interval may be followed by a third argument called step; it specifies the interval between successive values, which is why if, for example, you want to obtain a list made up of only the odd numbers covered between "1" and "8" you could operate in this way:

Using range () to generate

a list based on an interval

with steps equal to 2

>>> range (1,8,2)

list generated

\# [1, 3, 5, 7]

When, on the other hand, we pass the function an integer as in the example below:

\# Using range () to generate

\# a list based on an integer

>>> range (5)

you will get a list populated like this:

[0, 1, 2, 3, 4]

The elements present will therefore be 8, placing the "0" as an element and (not) initial value.

Indexing of the elements of a list

By default and lists in Python, internal elements are indexed numerically; indexing will start from "0", so a list consisting of three elements will have "0", "1" and "2" as indexes. It follows that a specific element of a list can be called up via its index, as in the following example:

\# Access to an element of a list

\# through its index

\# definition of the elements in the list

>>> list_name = ['a', 'b', 'c', 'd', 'e']

\# access to element with index "3"

>>> list_name [3]

In this case, the element called will be "d", ie the fourth inserted in the list, this is because "a" is associated with the index "0", "b" to "1", "c" to "2" and di consequence "d" has as index "3".

Access to the elements in the list could also take place through negative indexing, where the last element will have the index "-1", the penultimate "-2" and so on. A call like the following will therefore have the result of allowing access to the "a" element.

Access to an element of a list

through the negative index

definition of the elements in the list

 >>> list_name = ['a', 'b', 'c', 'd', 'e']

access to element with index "-5"

>>> list_name [-5]

It is also possible to access the elements of a list on the basis of a range of values; be careful that the two components of the range will correspond to the index numbers, which is why an expression like this:

Access to multiple elements of a list

through an interval

definition of the elements in the list

>>> list_name = ['a', 'b', 'c', 'd', 'e']

access to elements with interval "0: 2"

>>> list_name [0: 2]

will allow access to the elements "a", "b", ie those whose index goes from "0" to "2" (excluded). The colon symbol (":"), used for the definition of the interval, is called slicing operator. It can also be used for other purposes, such as defining the index from which to start for data access:

Access to multiple elements of a list

starting from a specific index

definition of the elements in the list

```
>>> list_name = ['a', 'b', 'c', 'd', 'e']
```

access to the first element in the list ('a') via negative index

the last 4 elements will be excluded

```
>>> list_name [: - 4]
```

access from the third element to the last

'c', 'd' and 'e'

```
>>> list_name [2:]
```

access to all items in the list

```
>>> list_name [:]
```

Python has constructs that allow you to perform more advanced operations than simply accessing values, such as those dedicated to manipulating lists.

Chapter 8   Dictionaries

W e will cover a new data type which facilitates a flexible way to organize data. Using the knowledge about lists, soon you will be able to create data structures that will be useful in almost any application you may think of.

A dictionary can store many values just like a list. However, they can index different data types. Keys of a dictionary are associated with values. When combined, that is called the key-value pair. Let's start by creating a new dictionary variable.

1.   flat = {'rooms': '2', 'bathrooms': '1', 'floor': '3rd', 'apartment': '306'} # Note the curly braces

2.   print(f"My Apartment has {flat['rooms']} rooms, {flat['bathrooms']} bathroom")

Program output:

C:\Users\...\PycharmProjects\GettingStarted\venv\Scripts\Python.exe
C:/Users/.../PycharmProjects/GettingStarted/Start.py

My Apartment has 2 rooms, 1 bathroom

Process finished with exit code 0

Dictionaries, unlike lists, can be identified by other data types that are not necessarily integers, although it can use integers as keys as well.

Dictionaries vs. lists

The order of list items does matter when trying to compare them to other lists. Meanwhile, dictionaries can find if a list that already exists, even if the keys are out of order. This does not mean that the order is not important. If a coder maintains a uniform order in their lists, then this is not an issue. However, the main problem appears once you start getting unordered data, especially from users.

Try this following sequence in the editor.

1.   flat = ['rooms', 'bathrooms', 'floor', 'apartment']

2.   apartment = ['apartment', 'bathrooms', 'rooms', 'floor']

3.   print(flat == apartment) # When you use == you are asking if they are equal to each other

4.   flat = {'rooms': '2', 'bathrooms': '1', 'floor': '3rd', 'apartment': '306'} # Note the curly braces

5.   apartment = {'apartment': '306', 'bathrooms': '1', 'rooms': '2', 'floor': '3rd'}

6.   print(flat == apartment)

Program output:

C:\Users\...\PycharmProjects\GettingStarted\venv\Scripts\Python.exe C:/..

False

True

Process finished with exit code 0

Useful methods

There are a few useful methods that you can use with dictionaries. These methods are particularly useful when combined with loops. All of the following methods need to be used by adding a dot notation after the name of the variable followed by a parenthesis.

The first method is the keys(), which will output the keys to a dictionary. The next method is the value(), which will output the values of keys. The last method is the items() which will output both the keys and values between parenthesis and separated by a comma.

Try out the example below.

1.   flat = {'rooms': '2', 'bathrooms': '1', 'floor': '3rd', 'apartment': '306'}

2.   print(flat.keys())

3.   print(flat.values())

4.   print(flat.items())

Program output:

C:\Users\...\PycharmProjects\GettingStarted\venv\Scripts\Python.exe
C:/Users/.../PycharmProjects/GettingStarted/MyFirstProgram.py

dict_keys(['rooms', 'bathrooms', 'floor', 'apartment'])

dict_values(['2', '1', '3rd', '306'])

dict_items([('rooms', '2'), ('bathrooms', '1'), ('floor', '3rd'), ('apartment', '306')])

Process finished with exit code 0

Value or key check

While using a dictionary, one of the functions that will most likely be needed regularly is to check for a certain value in your dictionary. For this exercise, we will be using two operators; the 'in' and the 'not' operators. These two operators can tell you if a certain key or value in a dictionary exists. Note that these operators can also be used in lists as well as logic. These operators will come out with a Boolean output either 'True' or 'False'.

Here are some lines of codes to try out.

1.   flat = {'rooms': 2, 'bathrooms': 1, 'floor': '3rd', 'apartment': 306}

2.   print('rooms' in flat.keys()) # Determining if there is a key called rooms

3.   print('1st' in flat.values()) # Determining if there is a value called 1st

4.   print(3 not in flat.items()) #Determining if there is neither a value nor key of 3

Program output:

C:\Users\...\PycharmProjects\GettingStarted\venv\Scripts\Python.exe
C:/Users/.../PycharmProjects/GettingStarted/MyFirstProgram.py

True

False

True

Process finished with exit code 0

There is another method that can be used with dictionaries, and it makes it easy to fetch a specific piece of data. This is called the get() method.

Check out the example below, to see how it is used inside the editor.

1.   flat = {'rooms': 2, 'bathrooms': 1, 'floor': '3rd', 'apartment': 306}

2.   print(f"I live in the apartment {flat.get('apartment')}") #getting the apartment number

Program Output:

C:\Users\...\PycharmProjects\GettingStarted\venv\Scripts\Python.exe
C:/Users/.../PycharmProjects/GettingStarted/MyFirstProgram.py

I live in the apartment 306

Process finished with exit code 0

Chapter 9   *Functions*

A nother cornerstone of programming are the functions. Unlike the built-in ones that are ready to go once you've started, user-defined functions open up unlimited possibilities. Using functions helps programmers abstract their code and simplify modifications in the future. Think of it as a container which is labeled and will only run once you call it, making it perfect for event-driven programming. In this part, we are going to take a closer look at how to create, alter, and place functions to get the most out of your programs.

Definition Statement and Function Calls

There is a distinct method to define a function. The syntax of that is in the code that follows. In this hypothetical example, we will be creating a function that will square a given number.

1.   def greetUser(): # Definition statement starts with def which is reserved, followed by the function name.

2.   purpose = input('State your purpose: ') # First line of the code block.

3.   print(purpose) # Second line of the code block.

4.   #For good code writing practices, you should add two empty lines (breaks) after your function bloc.

5.   print('You have reached the umbrella corporation website') # This is the first thing that will run in the program.

6.   greetUser() # The function will only run after you call it like that (name of the function followed by parenthesis).

Program output:

C:\Users\...\PycharmProjects\GettingStarted\venv\Scripts\Python.exe
C:/Users/.../PycharmProjects/GettingStarted/MyFirstProgram.py

You have reached the umbrella corporation website

State your purpose: I'm looking for Alice...

I'm looking for Alice...

Process finished with exit code 0

As explained, programs will run in a sequence of lines so that line one will be followed by line two, and so on. For that same reason, a function needs to be defined before calling it. If you try and call a function ahead of time, your IDE will prompt you with an error.

Parameters

Now let's explore how to add parameters to our functions. In many cases, we need to take information from the user or elsewhere and use it inside of a function. This technique is used by all programmers, regardless of what kind of program they are creating. Follow the instructions below to see how it works.

1.   def greetUser(userName): # This is the parameter that we pass when the function is called on lines 7 and 8.

2.   purpose = input('State your purpose: ')

3.   print(f'Hello {userName.title()}, are these your intentions: "{purpose}" ?')

Here we are using the parameter.

We are also using the title method, to avoid any user error.

4.

5.

6.   print('You have reached the umbrella corporation website') # This is the first thing that will run in the program.

7.   greetUser("rEbEcEa") # Once you have added a parameter you need to supply a value while calling the function.

8.   greetUser("dr. Green") # Each time you call a function, the new parameter is passed.

Program output:

C:\Users\...\PycharmProjects\GettingStarted\venv\Scripts\Python.exe
C:/Users/.../PycharmProjects/GettingStarted/MyFirstProgram.py

You have reached the umbrella corporation website

State your purpose: I'm looking for Alice

Hello Rebecea, are these your intentions: "I'm looking for Alice"?

State your purpose: Create a virus!

Hello Dr. Green, are these your intentions: "Create a virus!"?

Process finished with exit code 0

Keyword Arguments

In most cases, you may be passing more than one parameter into your program. In cases like these you need to pass the value of these parameters with respect to how they were defined in the function. Let's see an example.

1.   def greetUser(firstName, lastName):

2.   purpose = input('State your purpose: ')

3.   print(f'Hello   {firstName.title()}   {lastName.title()},   are   these   your   intentions: "{purpose}" ?')

4.

5.

6.   print('You have reached the umbrella corporation website')

7.   greetUser("rebecca", "chambers") # In this function call we have the first name as the first parameter.

8.   greetUser('chambers', 'rebecca') # In this function call we have the last name as the first parameter

Program output:

C:\Users\...\PycharmProjects\GettingStarted\venv\Scripts\Python.exe
C:/Users/.../PycharmProjects/GettingStarted/MyFirstProgram.py

You have reached the umbrella corporation website

State your purpose: Rescue Alice

Hello Rebecca Chambers, are these your intentions: "Rescue Alice"?

State your purpose: Rescue Alice

Hello Chambers Rebecca, are these your intentions: "Rescue Alice"?

Process finished with exit code 0

In rare cases, a programmer will need to pass parameters out of order. Although this is not always recommended, there are cases where it is necessary. To do that, all you have to do is add the parameter name while calling the function. Let's take a look at the next example.

1.   def greetUser(firstName, lastName):

2.   purpose = input('State your purpose: ')

3.   print(f'Hello {firstName.title()} {lastName.title()}, are these your intentions: "{purpose}" ?')

4.

5.

6.   print('You have reached the umbrella corporation website')

7.   greetUser("rebecca", "chambers") # In this function call, we have the first name as the first parameter.

8.   greetUser('chambers', 'rebecca') # In this function call, we have the last name as the first parameter

9.   greetUser(lastName = 'chambers', firstName='Rebecca') # We swapped the order and still were able to pass the

parameters as desired.

Program output:

C:\Users\...\PycharmProjects\GettingStarted\venv\Scripts\Python.exe
C:/Users/.../PycharmProjects/GettingStarted/MyFirstProgram.py

You have reached the umbrella corporation website

State your purpose: Saving Alice

Hello Rebecca Chambers, are these your intentions: "Saving Alice" ?

State your purpose: Saving Alice

Hello Chambers Rebecca, are these your intentions: "Saving Alice" ?

State your purpose: Saving Alice

Hello Rebecca Chambers, are these your intentions: "Saving Alice" ?

Process finished with exit code 0

Return Values

There are many cases where you will take a piece of information from the user, run a function and need to return that value to the user again. It is very simply done by writing 'return' in front of the variables you wish to return. In this next example, we are going to create a very simple function that will calculate the square of any number and return the value to the user.

1.   def squareNum(numA): # Parameter

2.   return numA *numA # Add the return at the beginning or else, by default, it will return none.

3.

4.   print(squareNum(3)) # Note that the function was called as an argument and it can also be saved into a variable if necessary.

Program output:

C:\Users\...\PycharmProjects\GettingStarted\venv\Scripts\Python.exe
C:/Users/.../PycharmProjects/GettingStarted/MyFirstProgram.py

9

Process finished with exit code 0

Chapter 10 *User's Input and Loop*

P ython programming, like all other types of coding, is intended to solve the problems that end users face. To do that, you need to get additional information from the end user. For example, if someone needs to check if he is eligible to play on the basketball team or if he is qualified to vote in the elections, you can create a program that can give him the correct answer he needs.

In this type of program, we need to know the age of the user before we give an answer, which means that we have to build an interface that asks for an answer from the user regarding his or his age. The user will enter his or her age into the program using the input () method. Once he or she reaches age, they can know the answer.

The input () method

The input () method is actually a stop for Python programs because it waits for the user to fill in the program with some text. Once the Python program has received the user's input, it can store the same in some kind mostof variable that you create yourself. This makes programming and operation easy. I have created a program that repeats the information you enter in the shell prompt. It is interesting. Let's check it out.

message = input ("This program repeats everything you write. Just like a parrot:")

print (message)

= RESTART: C: / Users / saifia-computers / Desktop / Python.py

This program repeats everything you write. Like a parrot: Terminator has been destroyed.

Terminator has been destroyed.

>>> Sam

Retrace (most recent call last)

File "<pyshell # 136>", line 1, in <module>

Sam

NameError: name 'Sam' is not defined

>>>

= RESTART: C: / Users / saifia-computers / Desktop / Python.py

>>>

This program repeats everything you write. Just like a parrot: I have been selected for the basketball team.

I have been selected on the basketball team.

>>>

You can see that the program returns whatever you say to it. The second attempt gave an error because I did not run the program again. This means that you have to run the program from the beginning every time you want to run it.

The program took an argument from the user. It was a kind of instruction that the adhering program used exactly the same wording as the user entered. The prompt asks users to enter the information they want to display in the shell. When the user presses enter, he executes the instructions.

You should write a clean code to make it easier for users to understand and act on the instructions. The prompt should be clear and easy to follow so that the user knows what to do. Let's write another program with the input () method.

qualification = input ("Enter your name and educational qualification:")

print ("Your information:" + qualification + "!")

= RESTART: C: / Users / saifia-computers / Desktop / Python.py

Enter your name and teaching qualification: John, MA (English literature)

Your data: John, MA (English literature)!

>>>

If you want to write a longer code that spans multiple lines, you can do that with the input () function in Python. For example, if you want to let the user know why you need a certain type of information, you can add an extra line in the code. This code is longer than one line. This is useful because users cannot easily enter the program with their personal information if you do not tell them why you need a piece of information in the first place. To achieve this goal, you can add the prompt within a variable and then pass the variable to the input () function.

prompt = "We need your information to provide you with a custom job search."

prompt + = "\ nEnter your name and educational qualification:"

qualification = input (prompt)

print ("Your information:" + qualification + "!")

= RESTART: C: / Users / saifia-computers / Desktop / Python.py

We need your data to let you search for a tailor-made job.

Enter your name and teaching qualification: Mazhar, MSc (Computer Science)

Your data: Mazhar, MSc (Computer Science)!

>>>

Let's dig deeper into how the input () function works. When entering information in the input () function, Python interprets it as a string. Let's see how to enter numeric numbers. For example, you require the age of the user to put in the record so you can do that with the following method.

user_age = input ("what is your legal age?")

= RESTART: C: / Users / saifia-computers / Desktop / Python.py

>>>

what is your legal age? 23

>>> user_age

'23'

>>>

= RESTART: C: / Users / saifia-computers / Desktop / Python.py

what is your legal age? 54

>>> user_age

'54'

>>>

The user's age information has been successfully stored in the variable called user_age. When we ask Python to return the number, it returns in quotes, meaning it is interpreted as a string. If you want to use the same as a number, an error is displayed.

= RESTART: C: / Users / saifia-computers / Desktop / Python.py

what is your legal age? 25

>>> user_age> = 25

Retrace (most recent call last)

File "<pyshell # 143>", line 1, in <module>

user_age> = 25

TypeError: '> =' not supported between instances of 'str' and 'int'

>>>

Python displays an error because it cannot compare a string to an integer. This problem can be solved if you use the int () function in your code. It teaches Python how to treat an input as a numeric value. It converts a string representation of a given number into a numeric representation. You can tell Python to interpret a number as it is and to perform the math function you want. You can run a conditional test by Python to see if your age is greater than or equal to 25 or not.

user_age = input ("what is your legal age?")

user_age = int (user_age)

if user_age> = 25:

print ("\ nYou are legally entitled to vote!")

different:

print ("\ nYou are not eligible to vote. Return to your home.")

= RESTART: C: / Users / saifia-computers / Desktop / Python.py

what is your legal age? 20

You are not eligible to vote. Please go back to your house.

>>>

= RESTART: C: / Users / saifia-computers / Desktop / Python.py

>>>

what is your legal age? 25

You are legally eligible to vote!

>>>

= RESTART: C: / Users / saifia-computers / Desktop / Python.py

what is your legal age? 24

You are not eligible to vote. Please go back to your house.

>>>

= RESTART: C: / Users / saifia-computers / Desktop / Python.py

what is your legal age? 30

You are legally eligible to vote!

>>>

You can see in the examples above that Python is fully competent in recognizing the numbers. It calculated perfectly and answered my questions when I entered different numbers in the program.

The While Loop

A while loop can be used to count numbers and perform various other tasks efficiently.

my_num = 1

while my_num <= 10:

print (my_num)

my_num + = 1

= RESTART: C: / Users / saifia-computers / Desktop / Python.py

1

2

3

4

5

6

7

8

9

10

>>>

The while loop requires that all variables in the code remain ready. The Python while loop has a break statement that helps us stop the statement at whatever point we want the loop to stop. We need to add the true element which means that the loop will continue as long as the condition is true.

```
a = 1
while a <10:
print (a)
if a == 5:
break
a + = 1
= RESTART: C: / Users / saifia-computers / Desktop / Python.py
1
2
3
```

4

5

>>>

While loop is very interesting. I'll write the program that repeated what I said to it and then put it in the while loop. The while loop will keep the program running unless you press the keyword that I will put in the program. Let's see.

prompt = "\ nMy creator made me repeat what you say:"

prompt + = "\ nI will continue unless you enter 'stop' to terminate the program."

a = ""

while a! = 'stop':

a = input (prompt)

print (a)

= RESTART: C: / Users / saifia-computers / Desktop / Python.py

My creator made sure to repeat everything you say:

I will continue unless you enter 'stop' to terminate the program. I feel dizzy.

I feel dizzy.

My creator made sure to repeat everything you say:

I will continue unless you enter 'stop' to terminate the program. Are you dizzy

Are you dizzy

My creator made sure to repeat everything you say:

I will continue unless you enter 'stop' to terminate the program. How did you learn Python?

How did you learn Python?

My creator made sure to repeat everything you say:

I will continue unless you enter 'stop' to terminate the program. You repeat so well.

You repeat so well.

My creator made sure to repeat everything you say:

I will continue unless you enter 'stop' to terminate the program. You are like a parrot.

You are like a parrot.

My creator made sure to repeat everything you say:

I will continue unless you enter 'stop' to terminate the program. stop

stop

>>> Can you repeat it now?

SyntaxError: invalid syntax

>>>

You can see that after I quit, the program no longer accepts and repeats my text. This way you can get rid of the while loop. If the thought goes around in your mind that or you can use a different value instead of quitting, I'll make it easier for you to understand the following example. I will use the same program, but a different value to end the program.

prompt = "\ nMy creator made me repeat what you say:"

prompt + = "\ nI will continue unless you enter 'stop it' to terminate the program:"

a = ""

while a! = 'stop it':

a = input (prompt)

print (a)

= RESTART: C: / Users / saifia-computers / Desktop / Python.py

My creator made sure to repeat everything you say:

I will continue unless you enter 'quit' to end the program: I want to reach the top of Mount Everest.

I want to reach the top of Mount Everest.

My creator made sure to repeat everything you say:

I will continue unless you enter 'quit' to end the program: quit it

stop

>>>

The prompt in a while loop defines what action a user should take. It tells him that there are generally two options: write what he or she wants to repeat or exit the program. Python ran the while loop and repeated multiple statements that I entered into the program. When I wanted to end the program, I managed to do it by entering the keyword I set to separate from the while loop.

There is still a problem. Python takes the keyword, stop it, as a message. It ends the loop, but also displays the same text. The rest of the code is retained, but there will be a small change to note.

prompt = "\ nMy creator made me repeat what you say:"

prompt + = "\ nI will continue unless you enter 'stop it' to terminate the program:"

a = ""

while a! = 'stop it':

a = input (prompt)

if a! = 'stop it':

print (a)

= RESTART: C: / Users / saifia-computers / Desktop / Python.py

My creator made sure to repeat everything you say:

I will continue unless you enter 'quit' to end the program: I want to reach the top of Mount Everest.

I want to reach the top of Mount Everest.

My creator made sure to repeat everything you say:

I will continue unless you enter 'quit' to end the program: quit it

>>>

(Matthes, 2016)

Chapter 11   Tuples

A tuple is a sequence type that contains an ordered collection of objects. A tuple, unlike a list, is immutable; you won't be able to change its elements once it is created. A tuple can hold items of different types and can have as many elements as you want subject to availability of memory.

Besides being immutable, you can tell a tuple apart from a list by the use of parentheses instead of square brackets. The use of parentheses, however, is optional. You can create a tuple without them. A tuple can store items of different types as well as contain any number of objects.

How to Create a Tuple

To create a tuple, you can place the items within parentheses and separate them with a comma.

Example of a numeric tuple

mytuple_x = (10, 9, 8, 7, 6, 5, 4, 3, 2, 1)

Example of a mixed-type tuple

mytuple_y = ("soprano", 10, 4.3)

Example of a string tuple

mytuple_z = ("b", "Jon", "library")

It's likewise possible to create a nested tuple:

my_tuple4 = ("Python", (5, 15, 20), [2, 1, 4])

You can create a tuple with only one item but since this will look like a string, you'll have to place a comma after the item to tell Python that it is a tuple.

my_tuple5 = ("program",)

You may also create an empty tuple:

my_tuple = ()

You can create a tuple without the parentheses:

numbers = 5, 3, 4, 0, 9

Accessing Tuple Elements

There are different ways to access items in a tuple.

Indexing

If you know how to access elements in a list through indexing, you can use the same procedure to access items in a tuple. The index operator indicates the index of the element you want to access. The first element is on index zero. Accessing an item outside the scope of the indexed elements will generate an IndexError. In addition, accessing an index with a non-integer numeric type will raise a NameError.

To illustrate how tuples work, create my_tuple with strings as elements.

>>> my_tuple = ('p', 'r', 'o', 'g', 'r', 'a', 'm', 'm', 'e', 'r')

>>>

To access the first element on the tuple:

>>> my_tuple[0]

'p'

>>>

To access the 8th element:

>>> my_tuple[7]

'm'

>>>

To access the 6th element:

>>> my_tuple[5]

'a'

>>>

Negative Indexing

As it is a sequence type, Python allows negative indexing on tuples. The last element has -1 index, the penultimate element has -2 index, and so on.

>>> my_tuple = ('p', 'r', 'o', 'g', 'r', 'a', 'm', 'm', 'e', 'r')

>>> my_tuple[-1]

'r'

>>>my_tuple[-7]

'g'

>>>

Slicing a Tuple

If you want to access several items at the same time, you will have to use the slicing operator, the colon (:). By now, you must be very familiar with how slicing works.

To see how you can slice a range of items from a tuple, create new_tuple:

>>>new_tuple = ('i', 'm', 'm', 'u', 't', 'a', 'b', 'l', 'e')

>>>

To access the elements on the 4th to the 6th index:

>>> new_tuple[4:7]

('t', 'a', 'b')

>>>

4 is the index of the first item and 7 is the index of the first item to be excluded.

To access tuple elements from index 2 to the end:

>>> new_tuple[2:]

('m', 'u', 't', 'a', 'b', 'l', 'e')

>>>

To access tuple items from the beginning to the 3rd index:

>>> new_tuple[:4]

('i', 'm', 'm', 'u')

>>>

Changing, Reassigning, and Deleting Tuples

A tuple is immutable so you cannot alter its elements. However, if it contains an element which is a mutable data type, you can actually modify this particular element. This is true in situations where one of the elements is a list. In such cases, you can modify the nested items within the list element.

>>> my_tuple = ('a', 5, 3.5, ['P', 'y', 't', 'h', 'o', 'n'])

>>>

Replacing a Tuple

To replace the item on index 2 of the list which is on index 3 of my_tuple:

>>>my_tuple[3][2] = 'x'

>>>

3 is the index of the list, 2 is the index.

>>> my_tuple

('a', 5, 3.5, ['P', 'y', 'x', 'h', 'o', 'n'])

>>>

While you may not replace or modify other data types, you can reassign a tuple to an entirely different set of values or elements.

Reassigning a Tuple

To reassign a tuple, you can just list a different set of elements and assign it to the tuple. To reassign new_tuple:

>>> my_tuple = ('c', 'o', 'd', 'e', 'r')

>>>

Deleting a Tuple

To delete a tuple and all the items stored in it, you will use the keyword del.

The syntax is:

del tuple_name

Hence, to delete new_tuple:

>>>del my_tuple

Tuple Membership Test

To test if a tuple contains a specific item, you can use the membership operators 'in' and 'not in'

>>> our_tuple = ('p', 'r', 'o', 'g', 'r', 'a', 'm', 'm', 'e', 'r')

>>>'g'in our_tuple

True

>>>'l'in our_tuple

False

>>>'e'not in our_tuple

False

>>>'x'not in'our_tuple'

True

>>>

Python Tuple Methods

Only two Python methods work with tuples:

Count(x)

Returns the number of elements which is equal to the given element.

The syntax is:

mytuple.count(a)

Example:

>>> new_tuple = ("p", "r", "o", "g", "r", "a", "m", "m", "e", "r")

```
>>> new_tuple.count('m')
```

2

```
>>> new_tuple.count('r')
```

3

```
>>> new_tuple.count('x')
```

0

```
>>>
```

Index(x)

Returns the index of the first element which is equal to the given element.

The syntax is:

mytuple.index(a)

Example:

```
>>> new_tuple = ("p", "r", "o", "g", "r", "a", "m", "m", "e", "r")
```

```
>>> new_tuple.index('m')
```

6

```
>>> new_tuple.index('r')
```

1

```
>>> new_tuple.index('g')
```

3

```
>>>
```

Built-in Functions with Tuples

Several built-in functions are often used with tuple to carry out specific tasks. Here are the functions that you can use with a tuple:

Len()

Returns the number of elements on a tuple.

>>> tuple_one = ('cat', 'dog', 'lion', 'elephant', 'zebra')

>>>len(tuple_one)

5

>>>

Max()

Returns the largest element 0n a tuple.

>>> numbers_tuple = (1, 5, 7, 9, 10, 12)

>>>max(numbers_tuple)

12

>>>

When a tuple holds items of purely string data type, max() evaluates the items alphabetically and returns the last item.

>>> my_tuple = ('car', 'zebra', 'book', 'hat', 'shop', 'art')

>>>max(my_tuple)

'zebra'

>>>

Using max() on tuples with mixed data types (string and numbers) will raise a TypeError due to the use of unorderable types.

Min()

Returns the smallest element on a tuple.

>>> numbers_tuple = (1, 5, 7, 9, 10, 12)

>>>min(numbers_tuple)

1

>>>

When used on a tuple that contains purely string data type min() evaluates the items alphabetically and returns the first item.

>>> my_tuple = ('car', 'zebra', 'book', 'hat', 'shop', 'art')

>>> min(my_tuple)

'art'

>>>

Sorted()

Returns a sorted list but does not sort the tuple itself.

>>> my_tuple = ('dog', 'bird', 'ant', 'cat', 'elephant')

>>> sorted(my_tuple)

['ant', 'bird', 'cat', 'dog', 'elephant']

>>>

The order of elements inside the my_tuple, however, remains the same:

>>> my_tuple

('dog', 'bird', 'ant', 'cat', 'elephant')

>>>

Sum()

Returns the total of all items on a tuple.

>>> my_tuple = (5, 10, 15, 20, 25, 30)

>>>sum(my_tuple)

105

>>>

Tuple()

Converts iterables like string, list, dictionary, or set to a tuple.

How to convert a string to a tuple

Example #1:

>>>tuple("Programmer")

('P', 'r', 'o', 'g', 'r', 'a', 'm', 'm', 'e', 'r')

>>>

Example #2:

>>> my_string = ("Hello World")

>>>tuple(my_string)

('H', 'e', 'l', 'l', 'o', ' ', 'W', 'o', 'r', 'l', 'd')

>>>

How to Convert a Dictionary to a Tuple

Example #1:

>>>tuple({'Name':'Joshua', 'Animal':'elephant', 'Color': 'blue', 'Age':22})

('Age', 'Color', 'Name', 'Animal')

>>>

Example #2:

>>> my_dict = {'Name':'Jack', 'Area':'Florida', 'subscription':'premium'}

>>> tuple(my_dict)

('Name', 'Area', 'subscription')

>>>

How to Convert a List to a Tuple

Example #1:

>>>tuple(['red', 'blue', 'yellow', 'green', 'orange', 'violet'])

('red', 'blue', 'yellow', 'green', 'orange', 'violet')

>>>

Example #2:

>>> my_list = ['interest', 'rate', 'principal', 'discount', 'rollover']

>>>tuple(my_list)

('interest', 'rate', 'principal', 'discount', 'rollover')

>>>

Enumerate()

Returns an enumerate object containing the value and index of all tuple elements as pairs.

>>> my_tuple = (1, 3, 5, 7, 9, 11, 13, 15)

```
>>>enumerate(my_tuple)

<enumerate object at 0x03237698>

>>>
```

Iterating Through a Tuple

You can iterate through each item in a tuple with the 'for' loop.

```
>>> for fruit in ('apple', 'peach', 'pineapple', 'banana', 'orange'):
print("I love " + fruit)
```

I love apple

I love peach

I love pineapple

I love banana

I love orange

Tuples vs. Lists

Except for the symbols used to enclose their elements and the fact that one is mutable and the other is not, tuples and lists are similar in many respects. You will likely use a tuple to hold elements which are of different data types while you will prefer a list when working on elements of similar data types.

There are good reasons to choose tuple over a list to handle your data.

The immutable nature of tuples results in faster iteration which can help improve a program's performance.

Immutable tuple elements can be used as dictionary keys, something that is not possible with a list.

Implementing unchangeable data as a tuple will ensure that it will stay write-protected.

Chapter 12   Control Statements

S ometimes, you may need to run certain statements based on conditions. The goal in control statements is to evaluate an expression or expressions, then determine the action to perform depending on whether the expression is TRUE or FALSE. There are numerous control statements supported in Python:

If Statement

With this statement, the body of the code is only executed if the condition is true. If false, then the statements after If block will be executed. It is a basic conditional statement in Python.

Example:

```
#!/usr/bin/python3

ax = 7

bx = 13

if ax > bx:

print('ax is greater than bx')
```

The above code prints nothing. We defined variables ax and bx. We then compare their values to check whether ax is greater than bx. This is false, hence nothing happens. The > is "greater than" sign. Let us change it to >, this symbol means: "less than sign".

Let see how we can write:

```
#!/usr/bin/python3

ax = 7

bx = 13
```

if ax < bx:

print('ax is greater than bx')

This prints the following:

```
ax is greater than bx
```

The condition/expression was true, hence the code below the If expression is executed. Sometimes, you may need to have the program do something even if the condition is false. This can be done with an indentation in the code.

Example:

```
#!/usr/bin/python3

ax = 10

if ax < 5:

print ("ax is less than 5")

print (ax)

if ax > 15:

print ("ax is greater than 15")

print (ax)

print ("No condition is True!")
```

In the above code, the last print() statement is at the same level as the two Ifs. This means even any of the two is true, this statement will not be executed. However, the statement will be executed if both Ifs are false. Running the program outputs this:

```
No condition is True!
```

The last print() statement as executed as shown in the result above.

If-Else Statement

This statement helps us specify a statement to execute in case the If expression is false. If the expression is true, the Ifblock is executed. If the expression is false, the Else block will run. The two blocks cannot run at the same time. It's only one of that can run. It is an advanced If statement.

Example:

```
#!/usr/bin/python3

ax = 10

bx = 7

if ax > 30:

print('ax is greater than 30')

else:

print('ax isnt greater than 30')
```

The code will give this result once executed:

```
ax isnt greater than 30
```

The value of variable ax is 30. The expression if ax > 30: evaluates into a false. As a result, the statement below If, that is, the first print() statement isn't executed. The else part, which is always executed when the If expression is false will be executed, that is, the print() statement below the else part.

Suppose we had this:

```
#!/usr/bin/python3

ax = 10
```

```
bx = 7

if ax < 30:

print('ax is less than 30')

else:

print('ax is greater than 30')
```

This will give this once executed:

```
ax is less than 30
```

In the above case, the print() statement within the If block was executed. The reason is that the If expression as true.

Another example:

```
#!/usr/bin/python3

ax = 35

if ax % 2 ==0:

print("It is eve")

else:

print("It is odd")
```

The code outputs:

```
It is odd
```

The If expression was false, so the else part was executed.

If Elif Else Statement

This statement helps us test numerous conditions. The block of statements under the elif statement that evaluates to true is executed immediately. You must begin with If statement, followed by elif statements that you need then lastly the else statement, which must only be one.

Example:

```
#!/usr/bin/python3

ax = 6

bx = 9

bz = 11

if ax > bx:

print('ax is greater than bx')

elif ax < bz:

print('ax is less than bz')

else:

print('The else part ran')
```

The code outputs the following:

```
ax is less than bz
```

We have three variables namely ax, bx, and bz. The first expression of the If statement is to check whether ax is greater than bx, which is false. The elif expression checks whether ax is less than bx, which is true. The print() statement below this was executed.

Suppose we had this:

```
#!/usr/bin/python3
```

```
ax = 6

bx = 9

bz = 11

if ax > bx:

print('ax is greater than bx')

elif ax > bz:

print('ax is less than bz')

else:

print('The else part ran')
```

The code will output:

```
The else part ran
```

In the above cases, both the If and elif expressions are false, hence the else part was executed.

Another example:

```
#!/usr/bin/python3

day = "friday"

if day == "monday":

print("Day is monday")

elif day == "tuesday":

print("Day is tuesday")

elif day == "wednesday":
```

```
print("Day is wednesday")

elif day == "thursday":

print("Day is thursday")

elif day == "friday":

print("Day is friday")

elif day == "saturday":

print("Day is saturday")

elif day == "sunday":

print("Day is sunday")

else:

print("Day is unkown")
```

The value of day if friday. We have used multiple elif expressions to check for its value. The elif expression for friday will evaluate to true, hence its print() statement will be executed.

Nested If

An If statement can be written inside another If statement. That is how we get nested If.

Example:

```
#!/usr/bin/python3

day = "holiday"

balance = 110000

if day == "holiday":

if balance > 70000:
```

```
print("Go for outing")

else:

print("Stay indoors")

else:

print("Go to work")
```

We have two variables day and balance. The code gives the following result:

```
Go for outing
```

The first if expression is true as it's a holiday. The second if expression is also true since balance is greater than 70000. The print() statement below that expression is executed. The execution of the program stops there. Suppose the balance is less than 70000 as shown below:

```
#!/usr/bin/python3

day = "holiday"

balance = 50000

if day == "holiday":

if balance > 70000:

print("Go for outing")

else:

print("Stay indoors")

else:

print("Go to work")
```

The value of balance is 50000. The first if expression is true, but the second one is false. The nested else part is executed. We get this result from the code:

```
Stay indoors
```

Note that the nested part will only be executed if and only if the first if expression is true. If the first if is false, then the un-nested else part will run. Example:

```
#!/usr/bin/python3

day = "workday"

balance = 50000

if day == "holiday":

if balance > 70000:

print("Go for outing")

else:

print("Stay indoors")

else:

print("Go to work")
```

The value for day is workday. The first if expression testing whether it's a holiday is false, hence the Python interpreter will move to execute the un-nested else part and skip the entire nested part. The code gives this result:

```
Go to work
```

Chapter 13   *Underline: File Management*

Why Use Modules?

Modules allow us to organize the elements and components inside our codes in an easier way, providing us with a big package of variables that are auto contained. Names that are defined on a superior level in a module file automatically will become an attribute of the object of the imported module.

Another advantage of using modules is that they let us reuse the code, using data services and linking individual files to broaden our program.

The main reason why we think that the modules are a very useful tool when it comes to programming is that they are really helpful to organize and reuse our code. This is very important when we talk about OOP (Object-Oriented Programming) since on that mode, the modularization and reusage are very popular. Since Python is a programming language oriented for that, it comes very user-friendly.

Imagine that you want to create an application or a program, more complicated than what we have been doing until now. For it, you are going to need one of the former codes to complement. Here is when you see the real benefit of the modules since you will be able to simply add one of the old codes to the complex application you want to do.

In modules, we will also have modularization. It is based on dividing our codes into several tiny pieces of codes, so that, at the moment of making the sophisticated program or application, it won't have hundreds and hundreds of lines of codes that could be annoying and hard to read. Instead, the code will be separated into tiny files.

How Create a Module on Python

Creating a module is something straightforward that anyone can do, all that needs to be done is to create a file with the .py extension, then, that file will be stored on a folder of your preference; this is known as import.

In case we want to create a module of our own, you will have to do the following. We will make a program on which we will create a module that could be used later.

The module syntax is as follows:

As you could see, the syntax is straightforward, since it is pretty much like creating a function. After we created it, we must be able to import it from another program, in order to do that, we will use the import statement.

Import Statement

A module is able to contain definitions of a function and even statements, which can be executable. With this, it is possible to initialize a module since they execute only when our module is on the import statement.

Modules are capable of importing other modules that is why people use to put the import type statements at the beginning of each since with the names of our imported modules, they will locate on a space named global; function that modules have for importing.

With the help of the last example, we can manage to import the module created earlier and use the functions that we defined there.

As you see in this example, we created the op variable, who takes the task of storing a string, which will specify the option that the users choose. Then, two variables would be initialized, a and b; they will store the value of the operators we are going to use to perform the mathematical operations.

Afterward, the result variable will store the value that the function calculator returns, according to the operators and the type of operation that the users want. The function calculator comes from the module that we have imported.

When the Python interpreter finds the import statement, it imports the module, as long as it is located on the full search path. The search path is nothing but a list where all the directories that Python accesses before importing any module are located.

How to Import a Module?

For being able to import a module, we just have to follow some instructions and steps that are performed at the moment of the execution:

We look for the module through the module search path, compile to byte code, and lastly, we execute the byte-code of our module to build then an object that defines it.

How can I search for a module through Search Path?

To search for a module, our search system compounds of the concatenation of paths; these can be seen on the directory "Home" of our program. After this, the environment PYTHONPATH will be located from left to right, and that is how we will find the directory of default libraries.

Namespaces in Modules

As you know, modules are files. Python creates a module object in which all the names that we assigned in that module-file will be contained. What does that mean? This means that namespaces are just places where all the names that later become attributes are created.

What Are the Attributes?

Attributes are the names that have been assigned to a value considered of a higher level on a module file, which does not belong to a function or class.

Errors

When working with files, we will have an optional string. That string will specify the way about how we will handle the errors of coding that may arise in our program.

Those errors can only be handled and managed on files .txt

Ignore_errors()= This control statement will ignore the comments that have a wrong format.

Stric_errors()= This control statement will generate a subclass or an UnicodeError error type in case that there is any kind of fail, mistake or error at the code of the file we are working with.

Encoding

Now we'll talk about string encoding, which we often use when we're working with data storage. But what are data storages? This is just to say that they are the representation in characters of the coding; your system is based on bits and bytes in one familiar character.

The string encoding is expressed in the following way:

Newline

When we talk about the newline mode we refer to the mode that controls the functionalities of creating a new line, these can be: '\r', " ", none,'\n', and '\r\n'.

Newline statements are universal, and newlines are universal and can be seen as a way of interpreting the text sequences of our code.

1. The end-of-line sentence in UNIX: "\n".

2. The end-of-line sentence in Windows: "\r\n"?

3. The end-of-line sentence in Max OS: "\r".

Handling Files

Handling the File Not Found Exception Error

There will be times when you will encounter the FileNotFoundError. Handling such error depends on your intent or purpose with regards to opening the file. Here are common reasons you will encounter this error:

- You did not pass the directory and filename as a string.
- You misspelled the directory and filename.
- You did not specify the directory.

- You did not include the correct file extension.

- The file does not exist.

The first method to handle the FileNotFoundError exception is to make sure that all the typical reasons do not cause it. Once you do, then you will need to choose the best way to handle the error, which is entirely dependent on the reason you are opening a file in the first place.

Xlsx files

These files are those that allow us to work in spreadsheets as if we were working in a windows Excel program; if our operating system is windows, these files will have a much smaller weight to a file of type xlsx in another operating system.

This type of file is beneficial when we work with databases, numerical calculations, graphics and any other type of automation.

To start working with this type of file, we will have to install the necessary library and this is done through the command "pip3 install openpyxl" in the Python terminal.

Once our command has been executed, the openpyxl module will be installed in our Python file.

Now we will create our first xlsx file:

In this example we can see that we have created our file by importing the workbook function, which belongs to the openpyxl module, then we have added our parameters such as: "wb" assigning the workbook function and declaring that it will be our working document, then we add the name and save the file.

Add information to the file with the xlsx module:

To add information to our file, we will rely on the append function

Now, to our document docxlsx.xlsx, we have added a tuple that contains words like Python, document. Once we have created this, the append function will allow us to add the information contained in the tuple in a message.

Here we can see that the main function of append() is to admit iterable data such as tuples.

Read documents in xlsx:

To read an xlsx file, we will only need to import the load_workbook class and know the name of the file we are going to work with. It is also very important that the files are in the same folder in which the program is stored; otherwise, an automatic error will be generated.

Once this is done, we will specify the object to work with, and we will ask for the information we need to read in order to print and compile it finally.

What is Sequence in Python?

The sequence of program execution is not a highway linking the north and the south. It can run from the north to the south to the end. The sequence of program execution may be as complicated as a highway in the busy area, with nine turns and 18 turns, which is easy to make people dizzy.

To write a good program, it is very important to control the process of program execution. Therefore, it is necessary to use the process control structure of the program. Without them, it is impossible to use the program to complete any complicated work.

The programming language has been continuously developed for decades. Structured Programming has gradually become the mainstream of program development. Its main idea is to execute the entire program in sequence from top to bottom. Python language is mainly executed from top to bottom according to the sequence of program source code, but sometimes the execution sequence will be changed according to needs.

At this time, the computer can be told which sequence to execute the program preferentially through flow control instructions. The process control of the program is like designing a traffic direction extending in all directions for the highway system.

It is recognized that most program codes for process control are executed in sequence from top to bottom line after line, but for operations with high repeatability, it is not suitable to execute in sequence. Any Python program, no matter how complex its structure is, can be expressed or described using three basic control processes: sequence structure, selection structure, and loop structure.

The first line statement of the sequence structure program is the entry point and is executed from top to bottom to the last line statement of the program. The selection structure allows the program to select the program block to be executed according to whether the test condition is established or not. If the condition is True, some program statements are executed. If the condition is False, other program statements are executed.

Chapter 14   Getting Started; Python Tips and Tricks

We are going to look at some of the tips and tricks that will help you to get started with Python, along with how we can work with web scraping and debugging some of our programs as well.

Let's get started with this one to help us get started and finalize how good our codes can be.

Web Scraping

Imagine for a moment that we are going to pull up a large amount of data from many websites, and we want to be able to do this at a very fast rate.

How would we be able to go through this without having to manually go through each of the websites that we have and gathering the data in this manner?

This is where the process of web scraping is going to come into play.

Web scraping is going to be used by companies in order to collect a large amount of information form websites.

But why does someone want to go through and collect all of this data, in such large amounts, from these websites in the first place?

There are a lot of reasons for this, and some of them are going to include the following:

- Price comparison: Some of the different services that are out there, such as ParseHub, will work with this process in order to collect data from websites for online shopping and then can use this in order to compare prices of similar products.

- Email address gathering: We can use the process of web scraping in order to help with marketing.

This can help us to collect the email IDs that come with customers and then send out bulk emails to these individuals as well.

- Social media scraping: Web scraping is going to be used to collect data from social media sites and then figure out what is trending.

- Research and development: Web scraping is going to be used to help a company collect a lot of data from websites.

We can then analyze this and use it to finish our surveys and to help out with research and development.

- Job listing: Details regarding openings of jobs, interviews, and more can be collected from a variety of websites and then we can list them in one place in order to make them easier for the user to access

Web scraping is going to be more of an automated method that we can use in order to get a huge amount of data from any website that we choose.

The data that we are able to get out of these websites will be unstructured.

And this web scraping helps a company to collect all of this data and then will ensure that they are able to store it in a structured form.

There are a variety of methods that we are able to use in order to scrape these websites that we want, including online Services, writing out some of your own codes, and APIs.

Talking about whether or not scraping of this kind if seen as legal or not, it can depend on what the website says.

Some websites are fine with this, and some are not.

You can check with each website to figure out whether they are fine with it, and if they are, you are able to continue on with your web scraping tools and gather up the information that you need.

Since we are talking about Python here, we are going to take some time to see how we are able to use Python to help out with web scraping.

But this brings up the reasons why we would want to work with Python to help out with this process rather than working with some of the other coding languages that are out there. Some of the features that come with Python and can make it more suitable for web scraping will include:

- It is easy to use: The code that you are able to use along with Python is going to be simple. This ensures that any of the codes that you want to use for web scraping will not be as messy to work with and can be easy to use.

- A large library collection: There are a lot of libraries that work with data science and web scraping that are also compatible with what the Python language is able to do.

These include options like Pandas, Matplotlib, and NumPy.

This is why you will find that the Python language is going to be suitable for web scraping and even for some of the other manipulations that you want to do with the extracted data.

- Dynamically typed: This is something in Python where you will not need to go through and define all of the types of data that you are using with our variables.

Instead, you are able just to use these variables wherever you would like.

This is going to save a lot of time when it comes to working on the codes and can make your job faster than ever.

- The syntax of Python is going to be easy to understand the syntax that we are able to see with Python is easy to understand, mainly because the statements that come with this are going to be written in English.

It is going to be expressive and easy to read, and the indentations will make it easier for us to figure out between the different parts of the code.

- A small line of code is able to handle some large tasks.

Web scraping is a process that we are going to use in order to save some time.

And with Python, you are able to write out a small amount of code in order to get some of the big tasks that you would like to accomplish done.

This is going to save you time not only when it comes to figuring out the important data that comes in that website, but can also help you to save time when you would like to write out the codes.

- Community: At times, when you are a beginner, you are going to find that there are parts of the code that are hard to work with and are not going to go as smoothly as you had hoped in the process.

This is where you will find the Python language to be healthy.

If you get stuck while writing out some of your code, you will like that the Python community is going to help you to answer your questions and get things done on the code in no time.

Now that we know some of the benefits that come with Python, especially the ones that are going to help us to handle some of the web scrapings that we want to do, it is time for us to take things to the next step and look at how the process of web scraping is going to work.

When you run out the code that you want to work within web scraping, you will find that there is a request that is sent out to the URL.

Then there is going to be a response sent back from that request, and then the server is able to send the data and allows you a chance to read the page, whether it is XML or HTML at the time.

The code is then able to go through and parse the XML or HTML page, find the data, and takes it out.

The location where you are going to find this data when it is extracted will depend on what you told the code to do.

Often it is going to be moved over to a database so that you are able to search through it later and learn more from it as well.

There are going to be a few simple steps that you are able to take to make something to help us go through the process of extracting the data with the help of web scraping in Python.

The steps that will help you to use Python to help with web scraping ill include:

- Find the URL that you would like to scrape in the first place.

- Inspect the page that you are planning on using.

- Find the data that is on the page that you would like to extract.

- Write out the code that you would like to use with the help of Python in order to complete this process.

- Run the code that you just wrote and then extract out the data that you would like to use.

- Store the data in the format that would be the most helpful for you in the process.

There are also a few options that you are able to use when it is time to work on the process of web scraping.

As we know, Python is already able to be used for a lot of different types of applications, and there are going to be a ton of libraries with Python that is going to be used for different purposes.

There are a few libraries that work the best when it comes to working with the process of data web scraping will include:

1. Selenium: This is going to be a web testing library.

It is going to be used to help automate some of the activities that are found on your browser.

2. BeautifulSoup: This is going to be one of those packages that you are able to use with Python to help us to parse HTML and XML documents.

It is also able to create parse trees that can help us to extract the data in an easy manner.

3. Pandas: This is one of the best libraries to rely on when it is time to handle any kind of work that you would like in data analysis and data science.

Pandas are often going to be used to help out with any of the data analysis and the data manipulation that you would like.

When it comes to web scraping, you will find that Pandas is going to be used in order to extract the data and then get it stored in the right format in the way that you would like along the way.

There are many times when a company is going to try and gather up data from other websites and from many other sources.

This is one of the first steps that is going to be found when we are working with data analysis and using that information to improve a business through their customers, the industry, or from the other competition out there.

But going through and gathering all of that data in a manual manner is going to take too long, and can be really hard to work with as well.

And with the large amounts of data that are being used and generated on a daily basis, it is no wonder that so many companies are working with processes like web scraping to handle all of the work in a timely manner as well.

When we work with web scraping and do some of the codings that are necessary with the help of Python, we will find that we are able to get through the information in a fast manner and get it stored in the right place for our needs, without having to do all of the work manually.

This can make the process of data analysis much easier overall and will ensure that we are able to see some of the results that we want with this as well.

And with some of the right Python algorithms and codes, we can get data scraping done in no time.

Chapter 15   <u>Things We Can Do in Python</u>

I n this part, we will discuss many things that you can do in Python. Some of the things we can do in Python include the comments, reading and writing, files and integers, strings, and variables. We are sure that after reading this, you will be able to create the program that will run effectively. Due to the interactive and descriptive nature of the Python, a beginner can handle many things using it. Therefore, we will discuss some aspects and comments in Python to help you get started. You can make amazing codes in a short time using the Python programming language.

Comment

A comment, in the Python programming, starts with the # sign. This continues until the programmer gets to the end of the line. A good example is;

This is a comment

Print (hello, thanks for contacting us)

It instructs your computer to print "hello, thanks for contacting us". In fact, the Python interpreter ignores all the comments. As a programmer, however, you should not leave a comment after every line. You can put in a comment when you need to explain something. Since long comments are not supported by Python, it is important to use short and descriptive comments to avoid them going across the lines.

Reading and Writing

You will realize that some program requests specific information or show the text on the screen. Sometimes we start the program code by informing the readers about our programs. To make things look easy for the other coders, it is important to give it the name or title that is simple and descriptive.

As a programmer, you can use a string literal that comprises the print function to get the right data. String literal is a line of the text surrounded by the quotes. They can be either double or single quotes. Although the type of quotes a programmer use matters less, the programmer must end with the quotes that he/she has used at the beginning of the phrase. You can command your computer to display a phrase or a word on the screen by just doing as mentioned above.

Files

Apart from using the print function to obtain a string when printing on the screen, it can be used to write something onto the file. First, you will have to open up the myfile.txt and write on it before assigning it the myfile which is a variable. Once you have completed the first step, you will have to assign "w" in the new line to tell the program that you will only write or make changes after the file has opened. It is not mandatory to use print function; just use the right methods like read method.

Read method is used to open specific files to help you read the available data. You can use this option to open a specific file. Generally, the read method helps the programmers to read the contents into variable data, making it easy for them to open the program they would like to read.

Integers

Always make sure that the integers are kept as whole numbers if you are using them. They can be negative or positive only if there are no decimals. However, if your number has a decimal point, use it as a floating number. Python will automatically display such integers in the screen.

Moreover, you cannot place one number next to others if you are using the integers because Python is a strongly typed language; thus it will not recognize them when you use them together. However, you put both the number and the string together by making sure you turn the number into a string first before going to the next steps.

Triple Quotes

After reading and understanding both the single and double quotes, it is now a time to look at the triple quotes. The triple quotes are used to define the literal that spans many lines. You can use three singles, double, or single when defining an authentic.

Strings

Although a string is seen as a complicated thing to many beginners, it is a term used by the programmers when referring to a sequence of characters and works just like a list. A string contains more functionality which is specific than a list. You will find it challenging to format the strings when writing out the code because some messages will not be fixed easily due to its functionality. String formatting is the only way to go away within such a situation.

Escape Sequences

They are used to donate special characters which are hard to type on the keyboard or those that can be reserved to avoid confusion that may occur in programming.

Operator Precedence

It will help you to track what you are doing in Python. In fact, it makes things easy when ordering the operation to receive the right information. So, take enough time to understand how the operator precedence works to avoid confusion.

Variables

Variables refer to the labels donated somewhere in the computer memory to store something like holding values and numbers. In the programming typed statistically, the variables have predetermined values. However, Python enables you to use one variable to store many different types. For example, in the calculator, variables are like memory function to hold values which can be retrieved in case you need them later. The variables can only be erased if you store them in the newer value. You will have to name the variable and ensure it has an integer value.

Moreover, the programmer can define a variable in Python by providing the label value. For instance, a programmer can name a variable count and even make it an integer of one, and this can be written as; count=1. It allows you to assign the same name to the variable, and in fact, the Python interpreter cannot read through the information if you are trying to access values in the undefined variable. It will display a message showing syntax error. Also, Python provides you with the opportunity of defining different variables in one line even though this not a good according to our experience.

The Scope of a Variable

It is not easy to access everything in Python, and there will be differences in the length of the variables. However, the way we define the variable plays a vital role in determining the location and the duration of accessing the variables. The part of the program that allows you to access the variable is called the Scope while the time taken for accessing the variable is a lifetime.

Global variables refer to the variables defined in the primary file body. These variables are visible throughout the file and also in the file that imports specific data. As such, these variables cause a long-term impact which you may notice when working on your program. This is the reason why it is not good to use global variables in the Python program. We advise programmers to add stuff into the global namespace only if they plan to use them internationally. A local variable is a variable defined within another variable. You can access local variables from the region they are assigned. Also, the variables are available in the specific parts of the program.

Modifying Values

For many programming languages, it is easy for an individual to define a particular variable whose values have been set. The values which cannot be modified or changed, in the programming language, are called constants. Although this kind of restrictions is not allowed in Python, there are used to ensure some variables are marked indicating that no one should change those values. You must write the name in capital letters, separated with underscores. A good example is shown below.

NUMBER_OF_HOURS_IN_A_DAY=24

It is not mandatory to put the correct number at the end. Since Python programming does not keep tracking and has no rules for inserting the correct value at the end, you are free and allowed to say, for example, that they are 25 hours in a day. However, it is important to put the correct value for other coders to use in case they want.

Modifying values is essential in your string as it allows a programmer to change the maximum number in the future. Therefore, understanding the working of the string in the program contributes a lot to the success of your program. One has to learn and know where to store the values, the rules governing each value, and how to make them perform well in a specific area.

The Assignment Operator

It refers to an equal sign (=). You will be using the assignment operator to assign values to the variable located at the left side on the right of the statement. However, you must evaluate if the value on the right side is an arithmetic expression. Note that the assignment operator is not a mathematical sign in the programming because, in programming, we are allowed to add all types of things and make them look like they are equivalent to a certain number. This sign is used to show that those items can be changed or turned into the part on the other side.

Chapter 16   *Working with Files*

I n this part, we'll discuss working with files. Often during your programming journey, you'll want to pull in data from external files and manipulate that data. For example, maybe you have a large word document, but you only want sentences that contain certain words and phrases. With Python, you can read the document, do a search for the desired strings, join these strings into a list, and write a new document containing just the target strings. Python has many built-in functions and features that make loading, reading, and even writing to external files simple. Let's see the various ways we can interact with a file using Python.

Opening and Reading

To begin our exploration of files, we'll first need a text file to work with. Copy any text you'd like into a text editor and save it to the same directory as your Python scripts, saving it with the ".txt" format. If you need text to work with, you can try writing the following and running the script:

import this

Running this script will activate a Python Easter Egg, printing out the Zen of Python (a list of the principles that guide design in Python). If you would like, you can copy that text into a text file and save it.

To open a file in Python, we can use the open() function, which takes two arguments. The first argument is the file that you want to open, while the second argument specifies the mode that the file will be opened in. For instance, if you have a folder called "Projects" on your C drive, you would have to specify that Python looks for the targeted file by passing in:

C:\\Projects\\test_text.txt.

With this in mind, you can assign the contents of a file to a variable by doing this:

text_file = open("text_test.txt", "r")

The first argument specifies where Python should look for the file that you want to open. If the file is in the same directory as the program you are writing, all you need to do is provide the name and extension of the file. If this isn't the case and the file is located elsewhere, you'll need to provide the full path to the file, as mentioned above.

In the case above, the r specifies that we want to open the document in read-only mode. The other file-handling options include:

w mode - Specifies you want to open the file in write-only mode.

w will create the file that has been passed in as the first argument if the file doesn't already exist. Be careful when using this, because the data in the file will be erased if the file already exists.

a mode – Used for opening the file in appending-mode. Appending is for adding text to the current body of the file. If the file doesn't exist yet, the file will be created. Unlike w, the existing data in the file isn't erased if the file already exists. This is because any new data is added to the end of the file.

r+ - Specifies that you want to both read and write to the file.

After you have created a file object by using the open() function and the assignment operator, it's possible to read out individual lines in the document by using the readline() function, which is done by using dot notation on the file object:

text_file.readline()

Each time the readline() function is called, it moves to the next line in the text document. This means that if you call the function and print the results three times, Python will print out the first three lines in the document.

A more efficient way of printing out multiple lines from a file is by using a for loop. We can easily print out all the lines in a text file by writing a statement like:

for i in text_file:

print(i)

Now that you know how to open files in Python, you should also know how to close them. You can close a file you've opened simply by using the close() function on it, like this:

text_file.close()

You should get in the habit of closing files after you are done working with them, because this frees up resources your system is using to keep the file open.

Writing to Text Files

Let's learn how to write text to a file in Python. For us to accomplish this, we can use either the a or w modes, but if we use w, the current content of our text file will be erased whenever our program runs. For this reason, it's often smarter to write to files in a/append mode. Writing to a file in Python can be accomplished using the intuitively named write() function. The function merely takes in the text you want to write as an argument and is invoked with dot notation on the text file object you've created. We could create and write to a text file by doing this:

target_file = open("write_test.txt", "a")

\n creates a new line

target_file.write("All we have to do is type in a sentence to write to the document. \n")

target_file.write("Using the write function multiple times will write multiples lines to the document. \n")

Much like we can use a for loop to read from a text document, we can also use a for loop to write to a text document. We could make a list full of strings to write and then use a for loop to write to the document, which would write our list items on different lines.

list_to_write = ["This", " is", " our", " word", " list"]

for w in list_to_write:

target_file.write(w)

target_file.close()

Remember that you can format how your string is written into the text document by using the escape character and formatting options.

Buffer Size/Binary Files

When you first start writing your programs, you'll probably only be working with small text files that don't take up a lot of memory. However, when you start to work with larger collections of data and bigger text files, you'll want to know how to specify a buffer size. Buffering our file allows us to read it in small chunks, so that it doesn't take up too much memory. Python will divide the text document up, reading it in by the specified buffer size. We can declare the desired buffer size by using the read() function and passing in the buffer size as an argument.

When we pass in the buffer size, Python expects a numerical value. We are specifying the number of bytes to read at one time. Let's say we wanted to read our test text file 20 bytes at a time.

```
text = open("test_text.txt", "r")

print(text.read(20))
```

Printing the text variable would now display the first 20 bytes of the text document. If you wanted to loop through the entire document, you would need to use a while loop, setting the end condition as the length of the file, and then updating the current value of the text variable by using the function again to get the next 20 bytes. After opening the file, try running the code below and notice it prints out the text file in blocks of 20 bytes.

```
text = target_file.read(20)

while len(text):

print(text)

text = target_file.read(20)
```

Python interprets non-text files in binary, so the term "binary file" describes non-text files (as opposed to ASCII or other human-readable file encodings). We can work with these non-text files by using specific modes that let the open() function know we want to read or write binary: rb and wb. If you were aiming to open an image file and copy it over to another file, this could be done simply by opening an image file with the mode set to rb and then copy the lines of data over by opening a new file with the mode set to wb.

Deleting and Renaming

There are two other functions that you should be aware of when working with files in Python. The remove() function and rename() function help you deal with files in a folder, either by deleting the files or renaming the files. These are part of the os library, so this means that the functions will need to be imported before they can be used.

from os import remove, rename

This remove() function takes the name of the target file as its only parameter, so the syntax looks like this:

remove(target_file)

Meanwhile, the rename() function takes in two arguments, the current name of the target file and the name you wish to rename the file to.

rename("old_filename.txt","new_filename.txt")

Chapter 17   Python in the Real World

Now that you know the basics behind Python programming, you might be wondering where exactly could you apply your knowledge. Keep in mind that you only started your journey, so right now, you should focus on practicing all the concepts and techniques you learned. However, having a specific goal in mind can be extremely helpful and motivating.

As mentioned earlier, Python is a powerful and versatile language with many practical applications. It is used in many fields, from robotics to game development and web-based application design. In this part, you are going to explore some of these fields to give you an idea about what you can do with your newly acquired skills.

What is Python Used For?

You're on your way to work listening to your favorite Spotify playlist and scrolling through your Instagram feed. Once you arrive at the office, you head over to the coffee machine, and while waiting for your daily boost, you check your Facebook notifications. Finally, you head to your desk, take a sip of coffee, and you think, "Hey, I should Google to learn what Python is used for." At this point, you realize that every technology you just used has a little bit of Python in it.

Python is used in nearly everything, whether we are talking about a simple app created by a startup company or a giant corporation like Google. Let's go through a brief list of all the ways you can use Python.

Robotics

Without a doubt, you've probably heard about tiny computers like the Raspberry Pi or Arduino board. They are tiny, inexpensive devices that can be used in a variety of projects. Some people create cool little weather stations or drones that can scan the area, while others build killer robots because why not. Once the hardware problems are solved, they all need to take care of the software component.

Python is the ideal solution, and it is used by hobbyists and professionals alike. These tiny computers don't have much power, so they need the most powerful programming language that uses the least amount of resources. After all, resources also consume power, and tiny robots can only pack so much juice. Everything you have learned so far can be used in robotics because Python is easily combined with any hardware components without compatibility issues. Furthermore, there are many Python extensions and libraries specifically designed for the field of robotics.

In addition, Google uses some Python magic in their AI-based self-driving car. If Python is good for Google and for creating killer robots, what more can you want?

Machine Learning

You've probably heard about machine learning because it is the new popular kid on the block that every tech company relies on for something. Machine learning is all about teaching computer programs to learn from experience based on data you already have. Thanks to this concept, computers can learn how to predict various actions and results.

Some of the most popular machine learning examples can be found in:

1. Google Maps: Machine learning is used here to determine the speed of the traffic and to predict for you the most optimal route to your destination based on several other factors as well.

2. Gmail: SPAM used to be a problem, but thanks to Google's machine learning algorithms, SPAM can now be easily detected and contained.

3. Spotify or Netflix: Noticed how any of these streaming platforms have a habit of knowing what new things to recommend to you? That's all because of machine

learning. Some algorithms can predict what you will like based on what you have watched or listened to so far.

Machine learning involves programming, as well as a great deal of mathematics. Python's simplicity makes it attractive for both programmers and mathematicians. Furthermore, unlike other programming languages, Python has a number of add-ons and libraries created explicitly for machine learning and data science, such as Tensorflow, NumPy, Pandas, and Scikit-learn.

Cybersecurity

Data security is one of the biggest concerns of our century. By integrating our lives and business into the digital world, we make it vulnerable to unauthorized access. You probably read every month about some governmental institution or company getting hacked or taken offline. Most of these situations involve terrible security due to outdated systems and working with antiquated programming languages.

Python's own popularity is something that makes it far more secure than any other. How so? When something is popular, it becomes driven by a large community of experts and testers. For this reason, Python is often patched, and security issues are plugged in less than a day. This makes it a popular language in the field of cybersecurity.

Web Development

As mentioned several times before, Python is simple yet powerful. Many companies throughout the world, no matter the size, rely on Python to build their applications, websites, and other tools. Even giants like Google and Facebook rely on Python for many of their solutions.

The main advantages of working with Python so that we won't explore them yet again. However, it is worth mentioning that Python is often used as a glue language, especially in web development. Creating web tools always involves several different programming languages, database management languages, and so on. Python can act as the integration language by calling C++ data types and combining them with other elements, for example. C++ is mentioned because in many tech areas, the critical performance components are written in

C++, which offers unmatched performance. However, Python is used for high-level customization.

Conclusion

T hank you for making it through to the end of Coding with Python: A Simple and Straightforward Guide for Beginners to Learn in the Fast Way the Programming with Python, let's hope it was informative and able to provide you with all of the tools you need to achieve your goals whatever they may be.

The next step is to spend some time taking a look at some of the different parts that we are able to focus on when it is time to work with coding our own applications and more. Many people are worried about getting into coding because they think that it is going to be too difficult for them to get started, and they worry that they will never be able to handle all of the work that is going to come with their coding needs.

And that is part of the beauty that is going to come with using the Python language, and we hope that you are able to see this when it comes with this kind of language and with the examples that are in this guidebook, you will find that you will be able to work with the Python language. This is going to be an easy language for beginners and advanced coders to work with, but you will find that it has a lot of power behind it and will help you to get some of the work done in coding that you would like.

This guidebook has spent some time looking at the benefits of working with the Python language, and all of the different options that you are able to work with when it comes time to work on your program. We spent some time looking at how to write out some of our own conditional statements, our loops, exceptions, inheritances, and so much more. We even spent some time looking more in-depth about the work we can do with OOP languages and the classes that we would like to work with, and this will ensure that we can keep things as organized as possible within the code that we do.

When we are able to put all of these parts together inside of our work of coding, you will find that it is a lot easier to work with some of the coding that we want, even when we are a beginner. You will find that this is easier to accomplish than you think, and we are able to make codes that work with all sorts of projects. And considering that Python is going to work well with a lot of the major companies out there and some of the platforms that they want to use as well, including the Google search engine and some of the functionality of the YouTube site, you can see why this is a language that you are able to learn, and get a lot of use out of as well.

You no longer have to be worried or scared about working with a coding language. While some of the coding languages in the past may have been a bit difficult to work with and would not provide you with the results that you wanted all of the time, you will find that Python is not going to come with this kind of situation at all. You may have even glanced through some of the different parts of this ahead of time and noticed that it is easy enough to read some of these codes, before even starting. Take that as a confidence boost, and see how easy working with this language can be.

There may be a lot of different coding languages that we are able to work with when it comes to focusing on the coding that you would like to accomplish. But Python keeps proving that it is one of the best options out there for us to work with. When you are ready to learn more about coding in Python and all of the neat things that we are able to do with it, make sure to check out this guidebook and take a look at how great it can be.

SQL PROGRAMMING FOR BEGINNERS:

THE ULTIMATE BEGINNERS GUIDE TO ANALYZE AND MANIPULATE DATA WITH SQL

Ashton Miller

Introduction

N etwork programs have become larger and more flexible.

In many cases, the fundamental scheme of operations is mainly a mix of scripts that handle the command of a database.

When you look at the structure of any business, you will see that it generates, holds, and then uses data.

Because of the different ways that the company will need to handle this data, they will need to find some method of storing the information.

In the traditional methods, known as Database Management System or DBMS, business organizations would have all the data in one place to help them out.

These systems are pretty simple to use, but modern technology has forced about some changes.

Even the most essential or basic data management systems have changed, and now they are more powerful than before.

This can be an advantage to some companies that have a large amount of data to keep track of or who may need to be careful with some sensitive information.

Out of all this, there was a new breed of data management that has been implemented known as the Relational Database Management System or RDBMS.

This was derived from the renown traditional DBMS, but it is going to have some more to do with the web as well as server and client technologies.

This basically means that they are going to help various companies with the management of data.

One of these new relational databases that will help to store the data in an easy and simple to use a method that also keeps it all safe is SQL.

What is SQL?

It is best to start at the beginning. SQL stands for 'Structured Query Language,' and it is a simple language to learn, considering it will allow interaction to occur between various databases found in a particular system.

The original version was established in the 1970s.

This continued to progress in 1979 until IBM released a new prototype, the Relational Software Inc. that published one of the first SQL tools in the world.

This tool was at first called ORACLE, and it gained so much success that the company was able to split off from IBM and create the Oracle Corporation.

Even today, ORACLE is one of the leaders thanks to being able to use the SQL language.

The SQL is a set of instructions that you can use to interact with your relational database.

While there are a lot of languages that you can use to do this, SQL is the only language that most databases can understand.

Whenever you are ready to interact with one of these databases, the software can go in and translate the commands that you are given, whether you are giving them in form entries or mouse clicks.

These will be translated into SQL statements that the database will already be able to interpret.

If you have ever worked with a software program that is database-driven, then it is likely that you have used some form of SQL in the past.

It is likely that you didn't even know that you were doing this, though.

For example, there are a lot of dynamic web pages that are database driven.

These will take some user input from the forms and clicks that you are making and then will use this information to compose a SQL query.

This query will then go through and retrieve the information from the database to perform the action, such as switch over to a new page.

To illustrate how this functions, think about a simple online catalog that allows you to search.

The search page will often contain a form that will just have a text box.

You can enter the name of the item that you would like to search using the form, and then you would simply need to click on the search button.

As soon as you click on the search button, the web server will go through and search through the database to find anything related to that search term.

It will bring those back to create a new web page that will go along with your specific request.

For those who have not spent that much time at all learning a programming language and who would not consider themselves programmers, the commands that you would use in SQL are not too hard to learn.

Take your time in reading this book for this will be very helpful in guiding you as a beginner to SQL Programming.

Chapter 1   SQL Basics

T he SQL (the Structured Query Language, Structured Query Language) is a special language used to define data, provide access to data and their processing. The SQL language refers to nonprocedural languages - it only describes the necessary components (for example, tables) and the desired results, without specifying how these results should be obtained. Each SQL implementation is an add-on on the database engine, which interprets SQL statements and determines the order of accessing the database structures for the correct and effective formation of the desired result.

SQL to Work with Databases?

To process the request, the database server translates SQL commands into internal procedures. Due to the fact that SQL hides the details of data processing, it is easy to use.

You can use SQL to help out in the following ways:

- SQL helps when you want to create tables based on the data you have.

- SQL can store the data that you collect.

- SQL can look at your database and retrieves the information on there.

- SQL allows you to modify data.

- SQL can take some of the structures in your database and change them up.

- SQL allows you to combine data.

- SQL allows you to perform calculations.

- SQL allows data protection.

Traditionally, many companies would choose to work with the 'Database Management System,' or the DBMS to help them to keep organized and to keep track of their customers and their products. This was the first option that was on the market for this kind of organization, and it does work well. But over the years there have been some newer methods that have changed the way that companies can sort and hold their information. Even when it comes to the most basic management system for data that you can choose, you will see that there is a ton more power and security than you would have found in the past.

Big companies will be responsible for holding onto a lot of data, and some of this data will include personal information about their customers like address, names, and credit card information. Because of the more complex sort of information that these businesses need to store, a new 'Relational Database Management System' has been created to help keep this information safe in a way that the DBMS has not been able to.

Now, as a business owner, there are some different options that you can pick from when you want to get a good database management system. Most business owners like to go with SQL because it is one of the best options out there. The SQL language is easy to use, was designed to work well with businesses, and it will give you all the tools that you need to make sure that your information is safe. Let's take some more time to look at this SQL and learn how to make it work for your business.

How This Works with Your Database

If you decide that SQL is the language that you will work on for managing your database, you can take a look at the database. You will notice that when you look at this, you are basically just looking at groups of information. Some people will consider these to be organizational mechanisms that will be used to store information that you, as the user, can look at later on, and it can do this as effectively as possible. There are a ton of things that SQL can help you with when it comes to managing your database, and you will see some great results.

There are times when you are working on a project with your company, and you may be working with some kind of database that is very similar to SQL, and you may not even realize that you are doing this. For example, one database that you commonly use is the phone book. This will contain a ton of information about people in your area including their name, what business they are in, their address, and their phone numbers. And all this information is found in one place so you won't have to search all over to find it.

This is kind of how the SQL database works as well. It will do this by looking through the information that you have available through your company database. It will sort through that information so that you are better able to find what you need the most without making a mess or wasting time.

Relational Databases

First, we need to take a look at the relational databases. This database is the one that you will want to use when you want to work with databases that are aggregated into logical units or other types of tables, and then these tables have the ability to be interconnected inside of your database in a way that will make sense depending on what you are looking for at the time. These databases can also be good to use if you want to take in some complex information, and then get the program to break it down into some smaller pieces so that you can manage it a little bit better.

The relational databases are good ones to work with because they allow you to grab on to all the information that you have stored for your business, and then manipulate it in a way that makes it easier to use. You can take that complex information and then break it up into a way that you and others are more likely to understand. While you might be confused by all the information and how to break it all up, the system would be able to go through this and sort it the way that you need in no time. You are also able to get some more security so that if you place personal information about the customer into that database, you can keep it away from others, in other words, it will be kept completely safe from people who would want to steal it.

Client and Server Technology

In the past, if you were working with a computer for your business, you were most likely using a mainframe computer. What this means is that the machines were able to hold onto a large system, and this system would be good at storing all the information that you need and for processing options.

Now, these systems were able to work, and they got the job done for a very long time. If your company uses these and this is what you are most comfortable with using, it does get the work done. But there are some options on the market that will do a better job. These options can be found in the client-server system.

These systems will use some different processes to help you to get the results that are needed. With this one, the main computer that you are using, which would be called the 'server,' will be accessible to any user who is on the network. Now, these users must have the right credentials to do this, which helps to keep the system safe and secure. But if the user has the right information and is on your network, they can reach the information without a lot of trouble and barely any effort. The user can get the server from other servers or from their desktop computer, and the user will then be known as the 'client' so that the client and server are easily able to interact through this database.

How to Work With Databases That Are Online

There are a lot of business owners who will find that the client and server technology is the one that works for them. This system is great for many companies, but there are some things that you will need to add or take away at times because of how technology has been changing lately. There are some companies that like the idea that their database will do better with the internet so that they can work on this database anywhere they are located, whether they are at home or at the office. There are even times when a customer will have an account with the company, and they will need to be able to access the database online as well. For example, if you have an account with Amazon, you are a part of their database, and you can gain access to certain parts through this.

As the trend continues for companies to move online, it is more common to see that databases are moving online as well and that you must have a website and a good web browser so that the customer can come in and check them out. You can always add in usernames and passwords to make it more secure and to ensure that only the right user can gain access to their information. This is a great idea to help protect personal and payment information of your customers. Most companies will require that their users pick out security credentials to get on the account, but they will offer the account for free.

Of course, this is a system that is pretty easy to work with, but there will be a number of things going on behind the scenes to make sure that the program will work properly. The customer can simply go onto the system and check the information with ease, but there will be a lot of work for the server to do to make sure that the information is showing up on the screen in the right way, and to ensure that the user will have a good experience and actually see their own account information on the screen.

For example, you may be able to see that the web browser that you are using uses SQL or a program that is similar to it, to figure out the user that your data is hoping to see.

Why is SQL So Great?

Now that we have spent some time talking about the various types of database management systems that you can work with; it is time to discuss why you would want to choose SQL over some of the other options that are out there. You not only have the option of working with other databases but also with other coding languages, and there are benefits to choosing each one. So, why would you want to work with SQL in particular? Some of the great benefits that you can get from using SQL as your database management system includes:

Incredibly Fast

If you would like to pick out a management system that can sort through the information quickly and will get the results back in no time, then SQL is one of the best programs to use for this. Just give it a try, and you will be surprised at how much information you can get back, and how quickly it will come back to you. In fact, out of all the options, this is the most efficient one that you can go with.

Well-Defined Standards

The database that comes with SQL is one that has been working well for a long time. In addition, it has been able to develop some good standards that ensure the database is strong and works the way that you want. Some of the other databases that you may want to work with will miss out on these standards, and this can be frustrating when you use them.

Chapter 2 *Relational Database*

A relational database management system is a management system based on the relational database model.

Its most common representation is as a table that contains rows and columns.

First introduced by E.F Codd, A RDBMS has several key components.

They include:

- Table

- Record/Tuple

- Field/ Column

- Instance

- Schema

- Keys

We will cover some of these components as we progress further into the SQL lessons covered in the book. For now, let us look at tables and columns.

SQL Tables

Tables are objects used to store data in a Relational Database Management System. Tables contain a group of related data entries with numeric columns and rows.

Tables are the simplest form of data storage for relational databases. They are also a convenient representation of relations. However, a table can contain duplicate rows while a relation cannot contain any duplicate. The following is an example of a DVD rental database table:

	customer_id [PK] integer	store_id smallint	first_name character varying (45)	last_name character varying (45)
1	524	1	Jared	Ely
2	1	1	Mary	Smith
3	2	1	Patricia	Johnson
4	3	1	Linda	Williams
5	4	2	Barbara	Jones
6	5	1	Elizabeth	Brown
7	6	2	Jennifer	Davis
8	7	1	Maria	Miller

The table shows information about customers in a DVD rental database.

SQL Fields

Tables break down further into smaller entities referred to as fields. Fields are columns in tables designed to hold information about records in the specified table. For example, in the table above, we can see fields that contain Customer_id, store_id, first_name and last_name.

SQL Records

In a database, we use Records or Rows to refer to a single entry in a database table. It represents a collection or related data. We can also regard it as the horizontal entity in a database table. For example, in the above table, we have five records or tuples.

1	524	1	Jared	Ely
2	1	1	Mary	Smith
3	2	1	Patricia	Johnson
4	3	1	Linda	Williams

SQL Columns

In a database table, we use a column to refer to the vertical entity containing data related to specific fields in a table. For example, in the above table, a column could be first_name or last_name.

first_name character varying (45)
Jared
Mary
Patricia
Linda
Barbara
Elizabeth
Jennifer
Maria

NULL Values

A null value is a value assigned to a blank field. This means that a field with a value NULL has no value. In SQL, a zero or a space is not a NULL value. NULL value mainly refers to a field that is blank in a record.

SQL Constraints

Constraints are rules applied to columns in a database table. We mainly use them to govern the type of data stored within the table. This ensures that the database is accurate and reliable thus minimizing errors.

We can set constraints on columnar or tabular level. Columnar level rules apply only to the specified column while tabular level rules apply to the entire database level.

SQL contains various rules applied to the stored data.

They include:

- NOT NULL: This rule ensures that a table or column does not contain null value, which means during record creation, you must enter either a zero, Space, or another value

- UNIQUE: Ensures each value is unique and no duplicates are available

- DEFAULT: We use this constraint rule to set a default value for a column where we have an unspecified value

- PRIMARY KEY: Identifies each record distinctively in a table. We create this rule by combining NOT NULL and UNIQUE constraints

- FOREIGN KEY: We use this constraint to identify (distinctively) a record in another database table

- CHECK constraint: We use this constraint to confirm if the values in a column fulfill defined conditions

- INDEX constraint: We use this to create and retrieve data from a database

Data Integrity

Data integrity refers to the consistency and accuracy of the data. When creating databases, you MUST pay attention to data integrity. A good database must ensure reinforcement of data integrity as much as possible. Data integrity must also remain maintained during manipulation and update of the database.

Various factors can lead to compromised data integrity within a database. These factors include:

- Connection failure during transfer of data between databases

- Data input that is outside the range.

- Deletion of wrong database records

- Hacking and malicious attacks

- Database backup failures

- Updating of primary key value with the presence of foreign key in a related table

- Using test data in the database

These primary factors are often the ones that lead to loss of data integrity. To avoid compromised data integrity, it is good practice to back up the database before any operation.

Let us look at the types of data integrity available: These data integrity types exist to each RDBMS:

- Entity Data Integrity

- Referential Data Integrity

- Domain Data Integrity

- User-Defined Integrity

Entity Data Integrity

Entity data integrity ensures that rows in a database table are unique and thus, no row can be the same within the same database table. The best way to achieve this is by primary key definition. The field in which the primary key is stored contains a unique identifier thus no row can contain the same identifier.

Referential Data Integrity

Referential Data integrity means consistency and accuracy of data between a relationship. A database relationship refers to the data link within 2 or more tables. In a relationship, we use a certain foreign key to reference another primary key of a certain table. Due to this referencing, we always need to observe data integrity between database relationships.

Hence, Referential Data Integrity requires that the use of a foreign key must reference to an existing and valid primary key.

Referential integrity prevents:

- Addition of records to a related table if no record is available in the parent table

- Deletion of records in a parent table if records are matching a related table

- Changing values in a primary table resulting in orphaned records in the child table

Domain Data Integrity

Domain data integrity is the consistency and accuracy of data within a column. We achieve this by selecting the suitable data type for a column. Other steps to preserve this type of data integrity could include setting suitable constraints and defining the data forms and range restrictions.

User-Defined Data Integrity

This type of data integrity is custom defined by the database administrator. It allows the administrator to define rules that are not available using any of the other type of data integrity.

Normalization

Normalization refers to the process of organizing databases to improve data integrity and reduce data redundancy. This process aids the simplification of the database design. Database normalization offers a range of advantages including:

- Removes the null values available in the databases

- It helps in query simplification

- Helps in speed up operations such as searching and sorting the database indexes

- Helps to clean and optimize database structure

- Removes data redundancy

- Helps in achieving compact databases

Database Normalization Levels

Normalization occurs in various levels where each level builds upon the previous levels. Databases must satisfy all the rules of the lower levels to attain a specific level.

Let us discuss the types of database normalization levels. These levels appear arranged in the order of their strength from the strongest to the weakest.

1: Domain-Key Normal Form

In this type of normalization level, the relation is to Domain-Key Normal Form (DKNF) when every constraint in the relation follows a logical sequence of the definition keys and domains. This removes the probability of non-temporal anomalies as the domain restraint and enforcing keys roots all the constraints to be met.

2: Sixth Normal Form

We say a database relation is in the sixth form normalization when every join dependency of the relation is said to be trivial. We classify a join dependency as trivial if only one of the components is equivalent to the related heading in its total.

3: Fifth Normal Form

We say a database relation is in fifth normalization level if non-trivial join dependency in the stated table is indirect by candidate keys.

4: Essential Tuple Normal Form

A database relational schema is in ENTF normalization level if it is in Boyce-Codd form and components of every openly declared join dependency are a super key.

5: Fourth Normal Form

We say that a database table or relation is in Fourth Normal form if all of its non-trivial multivalued dependencies are super-keys.

NOTE: We have many other database normalization levels not covered in this book. They include:

- Unnormalized Form

- First Normal Form

- Second Normal Form

- Third Normal Form

- Elementary-Key Normal Form

- Boyce-Codd Normal Form

DBMS VS RDBMS

We have already covered RDBMS. DBMS is not different either. DBMS is a software package we use to create and manipulate databases.

DBMS and RDBMS give programmers and users an organized way of working with databases. DBMS and RDBMS are not very different since both provide a physical database storage.

With the above noted, some relevant difference between them are worth mentioning.

They include:

	RDBMS	DBMS
	Supports Normalization	Normalization is not available in a DBMS
	Supports Distributed Database System	Does not support Distributed Database System
	Stores data in a table format	Stores data is a normal computer form
	Integrity constraints are defined for the purpose of ACID property	Security for data manipulation is not applied by DBMS
	Can handle large amounts of data such as a Company database	Designed to small scale data and personal use
	It supports multiple users	Supports a single user
	Cases of data redundancy are close to none	Data redundancy is a very common scenario

	Stores data in tabular form and utilizes primary keys	Mainly stores data in hierarchical or navigational format
	Requires complex software and high-performance hardware to implement	Low software and hardware requirements for implementation
	Supports client-server architecture	Client-side architectures is not supported
	They include PostgreSQL, MySQL and Oracle etc.	Include file system files, xml files, and windows registry.

At this point in the guide, you know enough to start working with SQL and databases.

Chapter 3 *Data Types*

The Basic Types of Data

D ata types are attributes of the information itself, whose characteristics are placed inside a table. For instance, you may require that a field should hold numeric values only, stopping any user from entering alphanumeric data. By assigning data types to certain fields in a database, you can minimize the possibility of errors in data entry.

☐ Important Note: Each version of SQL has its own array of data types. Nowadays, you should use version-specific data types if you want to manage your database properly. The basics, however, are the same for all SQL versions.

Here are the basic types of data:

- Numeric strings

- Character strings

- Time and date values

The Fixed-Length Characters

Constant characters, or strings that have constant length, are saved via fixed length data types. Here is the typical data type for a fixed-length character in SQL:

CHARACTER(n)

"n" is the assigned (or maximum) length of the field you are working on.

Some SQL implementations utilize the "CHAR" data type to save fixed-length information. You can use this data type to store alphanumeric information. State abbreviations serve as excellent example for this: each state abbreviation is composed of two characters.

When using fixed data types, database users often add spaces to fill excess fields. That means if the assigned length was 15 and the data you entered filled only 11 places, you should fill the remaining four places with spaces. This method helps you to make sure that each value is fixed-length.

Important Note:

☐ If you're working on fields that may hold values of different lengths (e.g. usernames), make sure that you are not using fixed-length data types. If you used this type incorrectly, you may encounter problems related to data accuracy and storage space.

The Variable Characters

SQL also allows you to use varying-length strings (i.e. strings whose length may change from one data unit to another). Here's the standard notation for varying-length characters:

CHARACTER VARYING (n)

"n" is a number that identifies the maximum or assigned field length.

VARCHAR2 and VARCHAR are two of the well-known variable-length data types. ANSI (American National Standards Institute) considers VARCHAR as the standard data type for variable-length characters. Because of this, popular services such as MySQL and Microsoft SQL Server use it for their regular operations. Oracle, a top-notch database system provider, uses VARCHAR2 and VARCHAR. Character-defined columns may hold alphanumeric data: you can enter letters and numbers into these columns.

Varying-length data types don't need spaces to fill excess fields. For example, if the assigned length for a field is 15, and you enter a string of 11 characters, the overall length of that value is just 11. You don't have to use spaces to populate empty places.

Important Note:

☐ If you are working with variable character strings, you should use a varying-length data type. This allows you to maximize database space.

The Numeric Values

A numeric value is stored in a field defined as a number. Numeric values are commonly referred to as REAL, NUMBER, DECIMAL, and INTEGER.

Here are the SQL standards for numeric values:

INTEGER

FLOAT(p)

BIT(n)

REAL(s)

DECIMAL(p, s)

BIT VARYING(n)

DOUBLE PRECISION(P)

"p" is a number that shows the maximum or assigned field length.

"s" is a number located at the right side of a decimal point (e.g. 15.ss).

The Decimal Values

A decimal value is a numeric value that contains a decimal point. Here is the SQL standard for decimal values. Remember that p represents precision and s represents the scale of the decimal.

DECIMAL(p, s)

Important Notes:

☐   Precision is the overall length of a numeric value. For this value: (5.3), 5 is the precision. It is the length assigned to a numeric value.

☐   Scale refers to the total number of digits found on the decimal point's right side..

The Integers

Integers are numeric values that don't involve a decimal point. That means integers are whole numbers (regardless if they are negative or positive). Here are some examples of valid integers:

2

0

-3

99

-199

200

The Floating-Point Decimals

A floating-point decimal is a decimal value whose scale and precision have varying lengths. Virtually, floating-point decimals have unlimited character lengths. That means any scale and precision is valid. The data type called "REAL" assigns a column that holds single-precision, floating-point decimals. The data type called "DOUBLE PRECISION," on the other hand, assigns a column that holds double-precision, floating-point decimals.

A floating-point number is only considered as single-precision if its precision is 1 to 21. A floating-point number will be considered double-precision if its precision is 22 to 53.

Time and Dates

Obviously, these data types are used to record data regarding time and dates. Typical SQL distributions support data types known as DATETIME. Here are some of the popular members of this category:

TIME

DATE

TIMESTAMP

INTERVAL

When working with these data types, you'll encounter the following elements:

Day

Year

Hour

Second

Minute

Month

The Literal Strings

Literal strings are series of characters (e.g. names, phone numbers, etc.) that are specified by a program or database user. In general, a literal string is composed of data with similar characteristics. The value of the entire string is identified. The column's value, on the other hand, is often unknown since different values exist between data columns and data rows.

When using literal strings, you don't really specify the data types. You are just specifying the strings. The following list shows some literal strings:

'Morning'

50000

"50000"

5.60

'August 1, 1991'

Alphanumeric strings require quotation marks (either single or double). Number strings, on the other hand, can be stored without any quotation mark.

The Null Values

Basically, null values are missing values or columns in a data row that hasn't received a value yet. These values play an important role in almost every aspect of SQL. You will use null values in creating tables, assigning search conditions, and entering literal strings.

If you need to reference null values, you may use the following methods:

' ' (i.e. single quotation marks with a space between them)

Enter "NULL" (i.e. the word NULL itself)

When working with a null value, you should know that data doesn't have to be entered in any field. If the fields you are working on require data, use a data type followed by NOT NULL. If there's a possibility that a field doesn't require data, you should use the null data type.

The Boolean Values

Boolean values are values that can be NULL, TRUE, OR FALSE. You should use BOOLEAN values when comparing data units. For instance, when you specify parameters for a search, every condition results to either a FALSE, TRUE, OR NULL. If all of the parameters return the BOOLEAN value of NULL or FALSE, data might not be retrieved. If the value is TRUE, however, data is retrieved.

Here's a simple example:

```
WHERE NAME = 'SMITH'
```

A database user may have used this line to perform a search. The system will evaluate this line for each data row. If NAME's value is equal to SMITH in one of the data rows, the search gives TRUE as the result. Afterward, the user will get the data linked with that search result.

Chapter 4 *Exploring a Database*

A database is properly organized and collected data that are stored and can be accessed through electronic means from a particular computer. Formal design and modeling methods are essential in developing a database. Before a designer develops a database, his first assignment is to create a conceptual data model that reflects the type of information to be kept in the database.

The database management system provides the access to the stored data. The DBMS interacts with application users, and the database to analyze and capture the stored data. It also allows end users have seamless interaction with more than one database. Although there may be restrictions in accessing some data, however this will be based on the security level made by the programmer or database owner. The functions of a database are diverse; it allows entry of information, storage of data and also retrieving large files of information. Aside from doing all of these, it also provides ways in which the data stored can be managed and organized effectively.

The Functions of a Database Management Systems

A database is known as the collection of data and a common example is a spreadsheet or card index form. The DBMSs manages the data stored in the below four categories.

Data Definition: Data definition consists of defining the structure of your data, creation and modification of your data.

Update: After you have saved your data on your database, the DBMS gives you the permission to insert new information, alter or modify the former information, or even delete any of the information stored.

Retrieval: DBMS helps you provide information in a readable and usable form. The stored data when retrieved may be available in the exact format it was saved, or a new format.

Administration: For every data stored, there is an end-user, data and a future need for the data. Every data stored needs to be secured properly, and DBMS makes it easy for the application administrator to register and monitor the data effectively, enforces data security to prevent unauthorized personnel from accessing the data, to maintain the integrity and value of the data without any corruption.

Benefits of Database

Database is helps to facilitate the development of a new application, improves factors like data security, data access to enabled users, promotes data integrity and also reduces data errors and redundancy.

Classification of Database

Database can be classified using the following criteria; type of the contents stored, application area and technicality of the database, such as the structure of the database. The classification you are about to read is made based on database distribution, and there are four major distribution systems for DBMS.

Centralized Systems: Databases that are stored in a single location so that the data can be accessed and used by other systems are stored with a centralized database system.

Distributed Database System: The actual databases in this system are distributed evenly from different locations, which are connected to a computer network.

Homogenous Distributed Database System: The same DBMS is used in this database system, though they are from different location.

Heterogonous Distributed Database System: In this database system, different DBMS are used by different sites, however there is a presence of additional software to support easy exchange of data.

Types of Databases

The type of database you want is based on the usage requirements. You are about to learn the available database in the market today.

Centralized database

Centralized database is abbreviated as CDB, it is a database that is stored, located and maintained in a single location, and this location can be a database system or in the central computer. Centralized database is often used by organizations like a business company or a university.

The centralized database has a good number of advantages compared to other types of databases. CBD maximizes the quality of a data properly, helping the data to maintain its integrity, accuracy, and reliability. For the fact that there is only one storage location, there is a higher level of security, and better data preservation. Although CBD is easy to maintain and change at any time, given it needs to be updated, yet it is highly dependent on network connectivity.

The disadvantages of CBD are few, but they are however detrimental to the organization. If for any reason the unexpected occurs, all data will be lost and it may be difficult to retrieve the data, because it was saved in one location.

Distributed database

When information is stored on multiple storage devices, or locations, it is called distributed database. This information may be stored on difference computers in the same physical place, but they are not stored on the same processor. Distributed database can be subdivided into two groups namely, homogenous database and heterogeneous database.

Distributed database involves two processes, the replication and duplication.

Replication is the use of specific software that looks for changes in the distributed database. The replication process is complex and time consuming.

While duplication identifies one of the stored databases as the master and duplicates what it does. However, both replication and duplication can keep the integrity of the data in all distributed locations.

The distributed database should not be confused for centralized database. Although the distributed database has a multiple storage location, it still relies on the central DBMS which manages the storage devices remotely. The benefits of having a distributed database will increase the reliability and availability of your data, easy expansion improved performance and it is also a mean of saving cost.

DBAs are very complex, which makes it a disadvantage because it needs extra effort to ensure that all data are evenly distributed to all locations. It also needs experienced hands to be able to manage the data, and provide maximum security on the stored data.

Personal database

A personal database is a stored data on a personal computer, it is created to be used, organized and managed by one person. It can be created by a computer programming language like Practical Extraction and Reporting Language (PERP). A personal database only support one application, makes use of one computer.

End-user database

An end user is not usually concerned about the about the kind of transactions and operations done, but it is only concerned about the software or application. The end user database is specially meant for the end user, who can be a manager who summarizes the collected information in a database.

Commercial database

Commercial databases are information collected and presented electronically, which are managed by commercial entities. These databases are stored, and maintained for customers' services, they are available to customers for commercial purposes. There are 5 reliable sources where you can access a commercial database; a commercial database retailer, internet sources, library or places with site license, a help of a professional, and personal subscription source.

Commercial databases have advantages and disadvantage, like every other database.

The commercial database requires no physical space, since it is online, unlike printed materials that need library or bookshelf. Aside from this part, the database can be easily monitored, and can be accessed by multiple users at the same time.

The disadvantages of commercial database are that it needs constant network connectivity and cost of management can be expensive for both the administrator and user.

NoSQL database

A NoSQL database was originally referred to as a non-relational database or a non-SQL. It is used in managing big data, and real time web applications. It is a database that is built to provide mechanism for retrieval and storage of data that are modeled in other means used in such relational database. There are different classifications, and sub-categories of NoSQL database.

The Basic Classification of NoSQL Based On Data Model

Column

Column is the lowest level NoSQL object in a key space, which consists of a name, value and timestamp. The name is a unique factor that is used to reference the column. On other hand, the content of the column is referred to as the value and the timestamp is used to determine the validity of the content.

- HBase is an open source non-relational database written in Java language and modelled after Google's Bigitable

- Cassandra is a Java based system that is designed to manage large data across commodity servers, and provide availability without any iota of error or failure.

- Scylla is an open source distributed database that was designed to work with the Casandra database.

- Accumulo is a popular NoSQL database that is written in Java language. It is ranked as the third most popular column database.

Document

This is a computer program that was designed for the storage and retrieval of document oriented information. The document NoSQL category is also sub-divided into fourteen.

- Apache

- CouchDB

- ArangoDB

- BaseX

- Clusterpoint

- Couchbase

- Cosmos

- DB

Operational database

An operational database is used to manage stored data in real time. Organizations make use of operational database because things like clients' information, payroll records and employees bio-data

Relational database

A relational database consists of set of tables where data can be accessed in various ways without an enabled user having to reorganize the tables. Relational database allows users to access and categorize stored data that can later be filtered to retrieve data. Relational database shares few similarities with a database; however, the major difference between a database and a relational database is that the later stores data in rows and columns while the former stores data in files or document.

Cloud database

This is a database that is kept and managed on a cloud application. The benefits of cloud database include fast automated recovery for lost files, increased accessibility, maintenance of in-house hardware, and a better performance. Despite all of these advantages, cloud databases have their own drawbacks such as security issues and potential loss of data in case of bankruptcy or disaster.

Object-oriented database

This is a database management system that represents information as objects.

Graph database

Graph database (GDB) is a database that uses graph structures for semantic queries that have nodes and edges to store data. It is a part of NoSQL database, created for the purpose of addressing limitations attached to the existence of relational databases. GDB is designed to allow a fast retrieval of complex data.

There are notable graph database that have used for various purpose and here are their descriptions.

- AllegroGraph was designed as a metadata data model, and its programming language is C, C#, Common Lisp, Java and Python.

- Amazon Neptune is a graph database that is managed Amazon. Notable users of Amazon Neptune databases include Samsung Electronics, Intuit, FINRA, Siemens, AstraZeneca, LifeOmic, Blackfynn and Amazon Alexa.

- AnzoGraph was developed to interact with sets of semantic data. Its programming is C, C++

- ArangoDB is a multi-model database that supports key, documents and graphs which are the three important data models. It uses languages like C++, JavaScript, .NET, Java, Python, Ruby, Node.

- DataStax is a distributed real time database that supports Cassandra. It is a Java only database.

- Microsoft SQL Server is software developed by Microsoft, to store and retrieve data requested by other software applications.

Chapter 5 *Creating a Database*

B   efore you can be able to do anything on your data, create a database. My assumption is
    that you have installed either MySQL or SQL Server in your computer.

To create a database in SQL, we use the CREATE DATABASE statement. This statement
takes the syntax given below:

CREATE DATABASE database_name;

First, login to MySQL by running the following command:

mysql -u root –p

Now you have logged into the MySQL database, it is time for you to create a new database. In
the command given below, we are creating a database named school:

CREATE DATABASE school;

```
mysql> CREATE DATABASE school;
Query OK, 1 row affected (0.00 sec)

mysql>
```

The output shows that the database was created successfully. However, it will be good for you
to confirm whether or not the database was created. To do this, use the SHOW command as
shown below:

SHOW databases;

```
mysql> SHOW databases;
+--------------------+
| Database           |
+--------------------+
| information_schema |
| company1           |
| easydrive          |
| library_system     |
| movies             |
| mysql              |
| performance_schema |
| school             |
| sys                |
| wordpress          |
+--------------------+
10 rows in set (0.00 sec)

mysql>
```

The above output shows that the school database was created successfully. The above command returns the list of databases you have in your system.

An attempt to create a database that already exists generates an error. To confirm this, try to recreate the school database by running the following command:

CREATE DATABASE school;

```
mysql> CREATE DATABASE school;
ERROR 1007 (HY000): Can't create database 'school'; database exists
mysql>
```

The above output shows an error because the database already exists. To avoid this error, we can use the optional clause IF NOT EXISTS. This is showed below:

```
mysql> CREATE DATABASE IF NOT EXISTS school;
Query OK, 1 row affected, 1 warning (0.00 sec)

mysql>
```

The statement executed without returning an error.

Once you have created a database, it doesn't mean that you have select it for use. The target database must be selected using the USE statement. To select the school database, for example, run the following command:

USE school;

After running the above command, the school database will receive all the commands you execute.

RENAME Database

Sometimes, you may need changing the name of a database. This is after you realize that the name you have given to the database is not much relevant to it. You may also need giving the database a database name. This can be done using the SQL RENAME DATABASE command.

The command takes the syntax given below:

RENAME DATABASE old_database_name TO new_database_name;

For example, in my case, I have the following list of databases:

```
mysql> SHOW DATABASES;
+--------------------+
| Database           |
+--------------------+
| information_schema |
| company1           |
| easydrive          |
| library_system     |
| movies             |
| mysql              |
| performance_schema |
| school             |
| sys                |
| wordpress          |
+--------------------+
10 rows in set (0.01 sec)

mysql>
```

Let us rename the database named movies by giving it the name movies_db. This means we run the following command:

RENAME DATABASE movies TO movies_db;

The database should be renamed successfully.

Database Backup

It is always important to back up your database. This is because an unexpected and unforeseen event may happen to the database. Examples of such unforeseen events include Cyber-criminality and natural disasters. In case of such an occurrence, it will be impossible for you to recover your database if you had not backed it up. However, if your database had been backed up, it will be easy to recover the database and resume normal operations. You also need to back up your database to prevent the loss of your data. SQL provides you with an easy way of creating a backup of your database.

To create a database backup, you use the BACKUP DATABASE command. This command takes the syntax given below:

BACKUP DATABASE database_name

TO DISK = 'file_path';

The database_name parameter denotes the name of the database you need to back up. The file_path parameter denotes the file leading to the directory where you need to back up your database. The above command should be done when you need to back up the database from the beginning.

However, the differential command can be used if you need to create a differential backup. When you do this, the backup will only be created from the time you did your last full backup of the database. To do this, you must change the command to:

BACKUP DATABASE database_name

TO DISK = 'file_path'

WITH DIFFERENTIAL;

We have changed the command by adding the WITH DIFFERENTIAL statement. This means that the command will perform a differential backup on the database.

Suppose we need to create a full backup of the database named school. We will store the backup file in the local disk D.

The following command will help us accomplish this:

BACKUP DATABASE school

TO DISK = 'D:\schoolDB.bak';

If you need to create a differential backup of the database, just run the following command:

BACKUP DATABASE school

TO DISK = 'D:\schoolDB.bak'

WITH DIFFERENTIAL;

We have just added the WITH DIFFERENTIAL statement to the command.

Note that with a differential backup, the backup will be created within a short time. This is because you are only backing up changes that have occurred within a short period. However, a full backup will take a longer time to complete.

Creating Tables

To create a table, we have to define the table name, its column names and their corresponding data types.

We create tables by running the CREATE TABLE command. The tables are created within the database, meaning that one database can have many tables. The tables hold the data. The table stores the data in the form of rows and columns. The CREATE TABLE command takes the syntax given below:

CREATE TABLE tableName (

```
    column1_name datatype constraints,

    column2_name datatype constraints,

....

);
```

To make it the above syntax easy to understand, we need to create a table within the school database. Just run the following command from the MySQL command line.

```
-- Syntax for MySQL Database

CREATE TABLE students (

    regno INT NOT NULL PRIMARY KEY AUTO_INCREMENT UNIQUE,

    name VARCHAR(30) NOT NULL,

    birth_date DATE,

    age int NOT NULL

);
```

```
mysql> CREATE TABLE students (
    ->        regno INT NOT NULL PRIMARY KEY AUTO_INCREMENT UNIQUE,
    ->        name VARCHAR(30) NOT NULL,
    ->        birth_date DATE,
    ->        age int NOT NULL
    -> );
Query OK, 0 rows affected (0.85 sec)

mysql>
```

In the above example, we have created a table named students with 4 columns. These columns include regno, name, birth_date, and age. Note that the name of each column has been followed by a data type representation, which dictates the type of data that the column will accept for storage. For the case of some data types, we can define the length of data we will store in it. This means you will not store more characters that exceed what you have defined.

If you attempt to create a table that already exists, you will get an error. Let us show this by trying to recreate the students' table:

```
mysql> CREATE TABLE students (
    ->         regno INT NOT NULL PRIMARY KEY AUTO_INCREMENT UNIQUE,
    ->         name VARCHAR(30) NOT NULL,
    ->         birth_date DATE,
    ->         age int NOT NULL
    -> );
ERROR 1050 (42S01): Table 'students' already exists
mysql>
```

The statement generates an error as shown above.

To avoid this, the IF NOT EXISTS statement can be used. This will create the table if doesn't exist and exit without an error if the table exists. It can be used as follows:

-- Syntax for MySQL Database

CREATE TABLE IF NOT EXISTS students (

   regno INT NOT NULL PRIMARY KEY AUTO_INCREMENT UNIQUE,

   name VARCHAR(30) NOT NULL,

   birth_date DATE,

   age int NOT NULL

)

The statement runs without an error as shown below:

```
mysql> CREATE TABLE IF NOT EXISTS students (
    ->         regno INT NOT NULL PRIMARY KEY AUTO_INCREMENT UNIQUE,
    ->         name VARCHAR(30) NOT NULL,
    ->         birth_date DATE,
    ->         age int NOT NULL
    -> );
Query OK, 0 rows affected, 1 warning (0.00 sec)

mysql>
```

RENAME TABLE

Sometimes, you may need to change the name of your database table. This could be after you realize that the current name of the table is not meaningful. It then becomes necessary for you to change the name of the table. This is possible by the use of the RENAME TABLE command. The command takes the following syntax:

ALTER TABLE old_table_name

RENAME TO new_table_name;

;

For example, to change a table named employees to workers, we run the following command:

ALTER TABLE employees

RENAME TO workers;

The table will be renamed successfully.

ALTER TABLE

This is the statement we use any time we need to change the columns of a table. The modification in this can mean the need to add, change or delete a table column. This command can also help you add or drop the various constraints that may have been imposed on an existing table.

Adding a Column

To add a new column to a table, use the ALTER TABLE command with the following syntax:

ALTER TABLE tableName ADD columnName column-definition;

However, you may sometimes to add multiple columns to the table. In such a case, use the command with the following syntax:

ALTER TABLE tableName

ADD (column1 column-definition,

column2 column-definition,

.....

column_n column-definition);

Let us show this with an example. Suppose we have the workers table with the following columns:

```
mysql> desc workers;
+---------+--------------+------+-----+---------+-------+
| Field   | Type         | Null | Key | Default | Extra |
+---------+--------------+------+-----+---------+-------+
| ID      | int(11)      | NO   | PRI | NULL    |       |
| NAME    | varchar(15)  | NO   |     | NULL    |       |
| ADDRESS | char(20)     | YES  |     | NULL    |       |
| AGE     | int(11)      | NO   |     | NULL    |       |
| SALARY  | decimal(16,2)| YES  |     | NULL    |       |
+---------+--------------+------+-----+---------+-------+
5 rows in set (0.00 sec)
```

We need to add a column named home_town in which we will add the hometown for each worker. We can do this by running the following command:

```
mysql> ALTER TABLE workers ADD home_town varchar(15);
Query OK, 6 rows affected (0.38 sec)
Records: 6  Duplicates: 0  Warnings: 0

mysql>
```

ALTER TABLE workers ADD home_town varchar(15);

We have added a column named home_town of the varchar data type. To confirm whether this happened, we can describe the table again:

```
mysql> desc workers;
+-----------+--------------+------+-----+---------+-------+
| Field     | Type         | Null | Key | Default | Extra |
+-----------+--------------+------+-----+---------+-------+
| ID        | int(11)      | NO   | PRI | NULL    |       |
| NAME      | varchar(15)  | NO   |     | NULL    |       |
| ADDRESS   | char(20)     | YES  |     | NULL    |       |
| AGE       | int(11)      | NO   |     | NULL    |       |
| SALARY    | decimal(16,2)| YES  |     | NULL    |       |
| home_town | varchar(15)  | YES  |     | NULL    |       |
+-----------+--------------+------+-----+---------+-------+
6 rows in set (0.03 sec)

mysql>
```

It is very clear that the table was added successfully.

Modifying a Column

Sometimes, you may need changing a particular column table. This can be done using the ALTER TABLE command with the following syntax:

ALTER TABLE tableName MODIFY column_name column_type;

If you need to change over one table columns, use the command with the following syntax:

ALTER TABLE tableName

MODIFY (column1 column_type,

      column2 column_type,

      .....

      column_n column_type);

Consider the workers table with the following data:

```
mysql> desc workers;
+-----------+--------------+------+-----+---------+-------+
| Field     | Type         | Null | Key | Default | Extra |
+-----------+--------------+------+-----+---------+-------+
| ID        | int(11)      | NO   | PRI | NULL    |       |
| NAME      | varchar(15)  | NO   |     | NULL    |       |
| ADDRESS   | char(20)     | YES  |     | NULL    |       |
| AGE       | int(11)      | NO   |     | NULL    |       |
| SALARY    | decimal(16,2)| YES  |     | NULL    |       |
| home_town | varchar(15)  | YES  |     | NULL    |       |
+-----------+--------------+------+-----+---------+-------+
6 rows in set (0.03 sec)

mysql>
```

We need to change the datatype of the column named home_town from varchar(15) to varchar(20). To do this, we run the command given below:

ALTER TABLE workers MODIFY home_town char(20);

The command should run successfully as follows:

```
mysql> ALTER TABLE workers MODIFY home_town char(20);
Query OK, 6 rows affected (0.95 sec)
Records: 6  Duplicates: 0  Warnings: 0

mysql>
```

To confirm whether the change happened, we can describe the table as follows:

```
mysql> desc workers;
+-----------+--------------+------+-----+---------+-------+
| Field     | Type         | Null | Key | Default | Extra |
+-----------+--------------+------+-----+---------+-------+
| ID        | int(11)      | NO   | PRI | NULL    |       |
| NAME      | varchar(15)  | NO   |     | NULL    |       |
| ADDRESS   | char(20)     | YES  |     | NULL    |       |
| AGE       | int(11)      | NO   |     | NULL    |       |
| SALARY    | decimal(16,2)| YES  |     | NULL    |       |
| home_town | char(20)     | YES  |     | NULL    |       |
+-----------+--------------+------+-----+---------+-------+
6 rows in set (0.08 sec)

mysql>
```

The above output shows that the change was successful.

Renaming a Column

You may need to change the name of a certain table column. This could be when you need to give the table column a more meaningful name. To make this change, use the ALTER TABLE command with the following syntax:

ALTER TABLE "tableName"

Change "column_1" "column_2" ["Data Type"];

The parameter column_1 should be the old column of the table while the parameter column_2 should be the new name you need to assign to the column. If you don't specify the old column name correctly, you will get an error since the column won't be found.

Consider the workers' table with the following columns:

```
mysql> desc workers;
+-------------+---------------+------+-----+---------+-------+
| Field       | Type          | Null | Key | Default | Extra |
+-------------+---------------+------+-----+---------+-------+
| ID          | int(11)       | NO   | PRI | NULL    |       |
| NAME        | varchar(15)   | NO   |     | NULL    |       |
| ADDRESS     | char(20)      | YES  |     | NULL    |       |
| AGE         | int(11)       | NO   |     | NULL    |       |
| SALARY      | decimal(16,2) | YES  |     | NULL    |       |
| home_town   | char(20)      | YES  |     | NULL    |       |
+-------------+---------------+------+-----+---------+-------+
6 rows in set (0.30 sec)

mysql>
```

Suppose we need to change the column named home_town to home_city. We can achieve this by running the following command:

ALTER TABLE workers

Change home_town home_city varchar(20);

The command should run successfully as shown below:

```
mysql> ALTER TABLE workers
    -> Change home_town home_city varchar(20);
Query OK, 6 rows affected (0.23 sec)
Records: 6  Duplicates: 0  Warnings: 0
```

We can describe the table to see whether or not the change was reflected:

```
mysql> desc workers;
+-----------+---------------+------+-----+---------+-------+
| Field     | Type          | Null | Key | Default | Extra |
+-----------+---------------+------+-----+---------+-------+
| ID        | int(11)       | NO   | PRI | NULL    |       |
| NAME      | varchar(15)   | NO   |     | NULL    |       |
| ADDRESS   | char(20)      | YES  |     | NULL    |       |
| AGE       | int(11)       | NO   |     | NULL    |       |
| SALARY    | decimal(16,2) | YES  |     | NULL    |       |
| home_city | varchar(20)   | YES  |     | NULL    |       |
+-----------+---------------+------+-----+---------+-------+
6 rows in set (0.09 sec)

mysql>
```

Dropping Columns

Sometimes, you may need to reduce the number of columns you have in a certain table. In such a case, it will be necessary for you to drop or delete some table columns. It is possible with SQL.

To delete a table column, we combine the ALTER TABLE and the DROP statements. This is done using the syntax given below:

ALTER TABLE tableName DROP COLUMN column_name;

Again, we will use the workers table to show how to use the above command. The table has the following set of columns:

```
mysql> desc workers;
+------------+---------------+------+-----+---------+-------+
| Field      | Type          | Null | Key | Default | Extra |
+------------+---------------+------+-----+---------+-------+
| ID         | int(11)       | NO   | PRI | NULL    |       |
| NAME       | varchar(15)   | NO   |     | NULL    |       |
| ADDRESS    | char(20)      | YES  |     | NULL    |       |
| AGE        | int(11)       | NO   |     | NULL    |       |
| SALARY     | decimal(16,2) | YES  |     | NULL    |       |
| home_city  | varchar(20)   | YES  |     | NULL    |       |
+------------+---------------+------+-----+---------+-------+
6 rows in set (0.04 sec)

mysql>
```

We need to delete the last column of the table, which is home_city. To delete it, we run the command given below:

ALTER TABLE workers DROP COLUMN home_city;

The command should run successfully as shown below:

```
mysql> ALTER TABLE workers DROP COLUMN home_city;
Query OK, 6 rows affected (0.29 sec)
Records: 6  Duplicates: 0  Warnings: 0

mysql>
```

To confirm whether or not the column was deleted, we run the describe command against the table as shown below:

```
mysql> desc workers;
+------------+---------------+------+-----+---------+-------+
| Field      | Type          | Null | Key | Default | Extra |
+------------+---------------+------+-----+---------+-------+
| ID         | int(11)       | NO   | PRI | NULL    |       |
| NAME       | varchar(15)   | NO   |     | NULL    |       |
| ADDRESS    | char(20)      | YES  |     | NULL    |       |
| AGE        | int(11)       | NO   |     | NULL    |       |
| SALARY     | decimal(16,2) | YES  |     | NULL    |       |
+------------+---------------+------+-----+---------+-------+
5 rows in set (0.05 sec)

mysql>
```

The above figure shows that the column deleted from the table successfully.

It is important to know the various data types supported in SQL. SQL data types specify the data for every object. Every variable, column and expression in SQL has an associated data type.

Chapter 6 *Getting Started with Queries*

How Do Queries Work?

Q ueries are a principal working flow for SQL servers. Without querying operations, it is technically impossible to maintain or regulate database operations.

For successful querying database checks the following essentials:

1) Does the authorized user have permissions to execute this statement? If not terminate the statement and show Authorization error.

2) If the user is authorized then the SQL server will check whether the authorized user has permission to retrieve the data he is asking for? If not terminate the procedure and display data retrieval errors for the user.

3) If the author is authorized and has permission to retrieve the data then the SQL server will check the SQL syntax that the user has entered. If SQL syntax is correct then the querying process will start and display results to the end-user. If the SQL syntax is not right then syntax error will be shown.

If the statement entered satisfies these three complexities then your statement will be sent to a query optimizer to analyze the syntax in detail.

What is a Query optimizer?

The query optimizer is a system that helps you to analyze the syntactical structure of the syntax given. The optimizer will first check at all the from clauses that are present and then will look at all of the indexes that are supported. After analyzing all the clauses optimizer will choose the best way to query the operation provided. According to the resources provided it will proceed.

What Happens Next?

After an execution procedure is selected by the Query optimizer it is then sent to the tool that you are using. This tool is the SQL application itself. Then the SQL application will conduct the procedure and display results for the query operation. If the operation succeeds the result will be shown if not then an error will appear. There is also a chance for the query process with no results.

Before knowing about the SELECT function it is necessary to know about the importance of the FROM clause.

FROM

FROM is a simple SQL clause that helps you to point out an instance. When using the SELECT statement it is mandatory to look out at an instance for selecting the columns. This is where the FROM clause helps you to select the columns from the databases.

An SQL statement is here:

FROM {instance name}

Here the instance name belongs to either database or table name. You can also individually enter the column or primary key values to extract information.

As we have sufficient knowledge about the FROM statement now, we will discuss the SELECT cause in detail.

SELECT

The SELECT statement is usually used to select the columns provided using the logical entities that are given. The select clause can often be simple but sometimes it may lead to complex query operations.

Usually, select statements are performed at the end of the query operation by the SQL server software because it is technically not possible to select the things without having an update and changed table. For this reason, SELECT statements are usually performed at the end and often take much longer time than the other query operations.

Here is the SQL statement:

SELECT {Table or column values}

-> FROM {Instance name}

Now, we will discuss the parameters that are present in the syntax.

1) Table/ Column values - In this instance you need to enter all the columns that you are going or willing to select by this query. You can use logical expressions to denote the columns you need to select automatically. If you want to select all the columns present then you can use an asterisk '*'.

2) Instance names - In this, we need to enter the database name we need to retrieve the columns from. Without mentioning FROM statement, it is technically not possible to select the columns.

To say in a single sentence, the Select clause is used to determine all the columns for a query operation.

What else can you do with a SELECT statement?

1) You can use any numerical information such as the primary key id for selecting it.

2) You can enter various logical and conditional expressions to expect automated results.

3) You can sometimes also use inbuilt or scalar functions that SQL offers for its users.

4) If there is no system function satisfying for your requirement then you can build a user-defined function from scratch and use it for selecting.

ALIASES

Aliases are column names that are generated for the queries. Usually, SQL generates custom column names for the query results. However, they are often clumsy and it is essential to generate our columns for both query results and function results. To make your column names usually aliases are used.

Aliases can also be used to return column names that are generated using logical expressions.

Here is the SQL statement:

ALIAS {Column name} {Logical expression}

Creating Indexes

When querying large amounts of data, indexing technology can be applied. An index is a special type of database object that holds the sort structure of one or more columns in a data table. Effective use of indexes can improve the efficiency of the data query. This part focuses on the creation of indexes and related maintenance work.

An index is a separate, physical database structure. In SQL Server, an index is a decentralized storage structure created to speed up the retrieval of data rows in a table. It is built for a table, and the rows in each index page contain logical pointers to physical locations in the data table to speed up retrieval of physical data.

Therefore, whether to create indexes on the columns in the table will have a great impact on the query speed. The storage of a table is composed of two parts, one part is used to store the data pages of the table and the other part is used to store the index pages.

Usually, index pages are much smaller for data pages. In data retrieval, the system first searches the index page to find the pointer of the required data, and then directly reads the data from the data page through the pointer, thus improving the query speed.

The way the database uses indexes is very similar to the catalog of books. Indexes allow a chance of viewing through a complete book. In a database, indexes can be used for introspecting a table without having to scan the entire table.

After understanding the basic concepts of indexes, the following describes the advantages and disadvantages of using indexes and the conditions for using indexes.

1. Advantages of using indexes

(1) Create a unique index to ensure the uniqueness of each row of data in the database table.

(2) The creation of indexes is directly proportional to the increase in the speed of the system.

(3) The accelerator and the table are of special significance in realizing the extra advantages of the data.

(4) When using GROUP BY and ORDER BY you should be aware that the grouping and ordering time in the query can also be reduced.

2. Disadvantages of Using Index

(1) It is a very high turmoil to look at indexes and maintain indexes, which increases with the increase in data volume.

(2) The index needs a lot of storage indication. In addition to the data table occupying data space, each index also occupies a certain amount of physical space. If cluster indexes are to be established, the space required will be larger.

(3) When adding, deleting and modifying the data irrespective of circumstances, the index is used in a separate mechanism such that it reduces the overall capability of the system.

Classification of Indexes

The data in the database page of SQL Server can be divided into two types according to the storage structure: Clustered Index and Non clustered Index.

1. Cluster index

Cluster index (also called "clustered index") means that the physical storage order of data rows in the table is the same as the index order. Cluster index consists of upper and lower layers: the upper layer is an index page, which contains index pages in the table and is used for data retrieval; The lower layer is the data page, which contains the actual data page and stores the data in the table.

When creating a clustered index in a column of a table, the data in the table will be reordered according to the index order of the columns and the table will be modified. Therefore, only one cluster index can be created in each table. Cluster indexes are created on columns that are frequently searched or accessed sequentially.

2. Non-cluster index

The non-clustered index (also called "non-clustered index") does not change the physical storage location of the data rows in the table. Data is stored separately from the index and is linked to the data in the table through the pointer carried by the index. Non-clustered indexes are similar to those in textbooks.

The data is present in one place, the index is present in another place, and the index has a pointer to the storage location of the data. The items in the index are stored in the order of index key values, while the information in the table is stored in another order (non-clustered indexes can specify this).

A table can contain multiple non-clustered indexes, and a non-clustered index can be created for each column commonly used when looking up data in the table.

The method of creating a clustered index is similar to that of the non-cluster index, both uses CREATE INDEX statement, except that the CLUSTERED clause needs to be specified to create a clustered index.

How to Create An Index?

All you need to do is enter the following syntax for creating indexes. As explained above clustered index needs a separate parameter for creation.

Here is the syntax:

CREATE INDEX {Parameters}

In these parameters, we will define whether it is a clustered or non-clustered index.

You can also use SQL server management software to create indexes with a click.

MySQL Functions

Functions are an easy way to repeat a task. Functions consist of a set of code that can be used in logical execution and expressions. SQL provides a lot of scalar and aggregation functions for the database users.

Why are Functions Used?

For example, you can use SQL functions to find maximum or minimum values for your column values. You can also use functions created by yourself from scratch to repeat tasks automatically.

Chapter 7 *Turning Data into Information*

T hrough this part, when we bring up the topic of the operators that are inside of the database, we are going to talk about the characters and the words that we have reserved, and any that can be used along with the WHERE clause of the statements we write. Operators are helpful because we are able to use them to perform operations in the statements, such as comparisons and any of the equations that we need in math, but they can also come in to make it easier to set up some of the parameters that we want to see around our statements. And we need always to remember that they are there to help us connect together two or more parameters that we have in the same statement if this is something that our code needs.

During this process, we are going to need to remember that there are a few options of operators that you are able to use in these statements. The four most common options that we are able to work with include:

Operators that are used to help negate conditions.

- Logical operators

- Comparison operators

- Arithmetic operators.

Logical Operators

The first operator type that we are going to spend some time focusing on in this guidebook will be the logical operators. These are going to be the kinds of operators that we are able to use with the keywords of our statements, and they are going to be easier to form with comparisons inside of the statements. Some of the different logical operators that we are able to add into our statements will include:

- In—this operator will allow you to compare the value of specified literal values that are set. You will get a true if one or more of the specified values is equal to the value that you test.

- Like—the like operator is going to make it so that you can compare a value against others that are similar. You will usually combine it with the "_" or the "%" sign to get more done. The underscore is used to represent a number or a character ad the % is used for several characters, zero, or one.

- Unique—with the unique operator, you will be able to take a look at one or more of your data rows and see if they are unique or not.

- Exists—you will need to use this operator to find the data rows that will meet the criteria that you put down. It basically allows you to put down some criteria and see if there are any rows that exist that meet with this.

- Between—you can use this operator in order to find values that will fall into a specific range. You will need to assign the maximum and the minimum values to make this work.

- Is null—the is null operator will allow you to compare the value of your choosing with a NULL one.

- Any and all—any and all values often go together. Any operator is going to compare a value against all of the values on a list. The list of values is to be set up with predetermined conditions. ALL, on the other hand, will compare the values that you select against the values that are in a different value set.

These are good operators to learn how to use because they will help us to make some good comparisons and to help us look at a few of the points of data that are already inside of our database that we are working with. You are able to work with a few of these logical operators and see how they can work with some of the different statements that you want to work with, and see what will be the best for you.

Comparison Operators

The second operator that we are able to work with inside of the SQL language is going to be the comparison operators. These are going to be the ones that you would choose to use when you want to check on some of the single values that are found in the statement here. This category is going to be composed of a few mathematical signs, some that you are even familiar with so it is not going to be too hard for us to figure out. Some of the best comparison operators that we are able to work within this database will include:

- Non-equality—if you are testing the non-equality operator, you will use the "<>" signs. The operation is going to give you the result of TRUE if the data does not equal and FALSE if the data does equal. You can also use the "!=" to check for this as well.

- Equality—you will be able to use this operator in order to test out some single values in your statement. You will simply need to use the "=" sign to check for this. You are only going to get a response if the data that you chose has identical values. If the values aren't equal, you will get a false and if they are equal, you will get a true.

- Greater-than values and Less-than values—these two are going to rely on the "<" and ">" signs to help you out. They will work as stand-alone operators if you would like but often, they are more effective when you combine them together with some of the other operators.

These are going to help us to see some of the single values that are found in any of the statements of our database, and sometimes they are able to bring out some unique things like the less than and great than options, resulting in a few true and false statements that add in some power to the code we are writing and can make our program stronger than ever before.

Arithmetic Operators

The third type of operator that we need to focus on is going to be the arithmetic operator. These are going to be the most useful when we are trying to add in some of the different mathematical operations that are useful in the SQL language. There are going to be four main arithmetic operators that we are able to use inside of these equations, and we are able to combine a few of them together in the same statement if that is what is needed for our code. The four main types of operators that we are able to focus on here will include:

- Addition—you will just need to use the "+" sign to get started on using addition. For this example, we are going to add up the values for the overhead column and the materials column. The statement that works for this is:

- SELECT MATERIALS + OVERHEAD FROM PRODUCTION_COST_TBL.

- Subtraction—you can also do some basic subtraction when it comes to your SQL statements. You will simply need to use the "-" sign to do this.

- Multiplication—it is possible to do multiplication from your tables as well. You would need to use the "*" sign to do this.

- Division—this one will just need the "/" sign to get started.

With the arithmetic operators, you will be able to gain a lot of freedom in some of the codes that you are writing. You can combine a few of these operators together and even end up with your own equation inside of the statement. For example, you could have one statement with a bit of multiplication along with some division and addition if you would like. You can also have it so that you are just using a few multiplication signs in the same statement as well. Whatever is needed to bring the code together and make it work in the way that you want is available when it comes to these arithmetic operators.

One thing that we need to remember when we decide to add in more than one of these operators to our statement at a time is that we need to work with something known as the principles of precedence to make sure that we get it right. This means that the syntax is going to be able to take care of the arithmetic operators in a certain way to help us get the right answer.

When we are doing this kind of principle in SQL, the syntax is going to take care of everything that we need to multiply first, and then it will pay attention to everything that we need to divide, and then it will do those that should be added together, before finishing up with the things that should be subtracted from one another. And the syntax is going to do this in a manner that goes from left to right, along with going through the symbols in the order that we did above. This makes sure that we are going to get the right answers, and is similar to what we should remember from basic algebra classes in the past.

Working with the Conjunctive Operators

Another type of operator that we need to spend some of our time on here is the conjunctive operators. When you are doing some work with your statements, you may find that there will be some times when new criteria will be needed in order to make sure that the command is going to behave the way that we want.

For example, if you are sending out a database search and your results that might be a bit more confusing, you may find that adding in some different criteria to the mix to get the results you want is a much better idea. You can also use these when you would like to be able to combine together a few different types of criteria within the single statement, and then you would create a brand-new conjunctive operator that works for your needs.

Even though you are able to create one of the conjunctive operators that you want technically, there are going to be a few of these that are already predefined inside of the SQL language, and you are able to use them as you need. Some of these operators are going to include:

- OR—you will use this statement to combine the conditions of the WHERE clause. Before this statement can take action, the criteria need to be separated by the "OR" or it should be TRUE.

- AND—this operator is going to make it easier to include multiple criteria into the WHERE section of your statement. The statement will then only take action when the criteria have been segregated by the "AND" and they are all true.

These operators are all important and each of the categories is going to make a big difference in what we are able to do with some of our own statements. You are able to use the arithmetic operators to help with mathematical equations, work on how to compare different parts of the database, and so much more. You will not have to work longer with the SQL language in order to see all of the cool things that you are able to do with this language in no time at all.

Chapter 8 *Working with Multiple Tables*

D atabases usually consist of different tables with different column values and types. However, some tables in the database consist of the same entities and can be used to query two database columns with precision. To retrieve data using this technique we use JOINS in SQL.

What are Joins?

Usually, we can query columns and rows using the SELECT statement. However, SELECT statements only work for a single table and so is often not useful for complex query operations. At this Joins come into operative where they can query data from two or more tables with the help of common columns present in the tables.

What are Unions?

Unions also are used to retrieve data from two or more tables. The only difference between Joins and Unions is that Joins use only SELECT statement whereas Unions use a different number of SELECT statement to achieve the results.

How to Implement Joins?

Joins are usually implemented using two types of syntaxes. Explicit syntax deals with the cartesian product of two tables. Whereas implicit syntax deals with Where clauses. It is always recommended to use explicit functionality because it is easy for queries to function and operate.

Cartesian product

Before going to learn about the advanced functionalities of Joins it is important to know about the simple cartesian product.

Cartesian product is a simple mathematical operation that multiplies with any entity without restrictions. By using the cartesian product you can combine with any column of the other table.

To understand the cartesian product in layman terms it is just keeping two tables side by side. For example, if Table A has 10 rows and Table B has 5 rows then the cartesian product will have a total of 50 rows.

Cartesian product is often under-discussed even though after being simple is because it gives large output tables.

This cartesian product from SQL is explicitly known as cross join. However, with the time SQL server has restricted cross join operations for its huge data taking.

Here is the SQL statement for your reference:

SELECT * [CROSS JOIN] {Enter parameters here}

SQL Inner Join

If cross join talks about the cartesian product of two tables natural join discusses natural join of tables.

What is a Natural Join?

To explain natural join, we need to be aware of the tables we are trying to target. There will be two tables known as the Source table and Target table. The source table is which we use a SELECT statement to extract columns and the Target table is the table that we use after the JOIN statement.

To understand Natural joins in a better way we will discuss this concept in three scenarios. Follow along!

Scenario 1:

If there is only one same column in both of the tables

Explanation:

To demonstrate this example, we will introduce two tables known as College and Place.

College table has 4 columns namely - BRANCH, BRANCH_NAME, HOD, STREAM

Place table has 6 columns namely - PLACE_ID, STREET, PINCODE, TOWN, COUNTY, STREAM

Now, if we carefully observe you can notice that both tables contain a similar column known as STREAM. This column can be used as a Foreign key to perform a natural join.

Here is the SQL statement to perform Natural join:

SELECT {enter columns here} FROM { Source table} JOIN { target table}

Note:

Always enter all the columns you want to retrieve in the second parameter position. For the table mentioned above, we will enter Stream as a parameter for join to function.

Scenario 2:

If there are more than two identical columns

Explanation:

If you have observed more than two identical columns in the target and source table then it is important to enter only one column for retrieving user desired columns. This type of join is known as pure natural join. Entering one column can recognize all other columns and will give results.

Here is the SQL statement:

SELECT {enter columns here } FROM { Source table} JOIN { target table} AND { Linked columns}

Scenario 3:

Retrieve columns by USING clause

Explanation:

If there are two columns and you need only one column you can use the USING column to retrieve the column you are wishing for.

Here is the SQL statement:

SELECT {enter columns here } FROM { Source table} JOIN { target table} USING { Required columns}

With this, we have given a thorough and complete introduction to inner join and in the next part, we will discuss Left and Right joins using a few examples. But before discussing these joins let us discuss equijoins and non-equijoins for better understanding of these concepts. Although not solely responsible for Right and Left joins these concepts are important for an overall understanding of the subject. Follow along!

What is Equijoin?

Equijoin refers to comparing connected columns using an operator equal to "=" in the connection condition. The query result will list all columns in the connected table, including duplicate columns. The types of connection columns in connection conditions must be comparable, but not necessarily the same. For example, it can be both character type or both date type; It can also be an integer type and a real type because they are both numeric types.

SQL RIGHT & LEFT JOIN

SQL Right and Left join works on the concept of external join. The inner join compares each column of records FROM the table in the FROM clause and returns all records that satisfy the join condition.

However, sometimes it is necessary to display all records in the table, including those records that do not meet the connection conditions. In this case, the external connection is required. Using outer join can easily query other records in a table in the join result. The query result of the external connection is an extension of the query result of the internal connection.

An obvious feature of external connection is that some data that do not meet the connection conditions are also output in the connection results. External connection takes the specified data table as the main body and outputs the data in the main body table that do not meet the connection conditions. According to the different rows saved by external connections, external connections can be divided into the following 3 types of connections.

(1) Left outer join: indicates that the results include data in the left table that do not meet the conditions.

(2) right join: indicates that the results include data in the right table that do not meet the conditions.

(3) Total External Connection: Data that do not meet the conditions in the left table and the right table appear in the results.

In the JOIN statement, the left side of the join keyword represents the left table and the right side represents the right table.

SQL Self-connection

Self-connection refers to the connection between the same table and itself. All databases process only one row in a table at a time. Users can access all columns in one row, but only in one row. If information of two different rows in a table is needed at the same time, the table needs to be connected with itself.

To better understand self-joining, one table can be thought of as two independent tables. In the FROM clause, the tables are listed twice. To distinguish, each table must be given an alias to distinguish the two copies.

SQL UNION

In SQL Server, combined queries are completed through the UNION operator. The UNION operator can be displayed by combining data FROM multiple tables, but unlike joins, UNION is not implemented by adding multiple tables in the from clause and specifying join conditions, but by combining the results of multiple queries.

The following points should be noted when using the UNION operator:

(1) The number of columns in the two query statements is required to be compatible with the data type of the columns.

(2) The column name in the final result set comes from the column name of the first SELECT statement.

(3) In combination query, duplicate rows will be deleted from the final result set by default unless the ALL keyword is used.

(4) The query results will automatically sort the columns in the SELECT list from left to right, regardless of the position of the query relative to the UNION operator.

Here is the syntax:

SELECT {UNION}

Merging multiple result sets through UNION is explained below by using a server management studio.

The operation steps are as follows:

(1) Select Start → All Programs → SQL Server Management Studio in turn. In the pop-up connection dialog box, select "SQL Server Authentication", login name is "Your choice" and password is empty.

(2) In the "Microsoft SQL Server Management Studio" window, click the "New Query" button, then enter the corresponding code in the code editing area, and click the Run button on the toolbar. The results will be displayed in the window.

SQL UNION {Enter parameters} Merge {Enter column names here}

SQL UNION ALL

When the UNION statement is used to merge the result sets in the query statement, the UNION statement will automatically delete duplicate rows and automatically sort the result sets. The UNION ALL statement does not delete duplicate rows in the result set and does not automatically sort. In most cases, UNION statements are used for merging, and UNION ALL statements are only used in some special cases.

For example:

(1) Know that there are duplicate lines and want to keep the duplicate lines.

(2) Know that there can be no repetition.

(3) I don't care if there are duplicate lines.

The UNION ALL statement will only be used in the above cases, and the UNION statement is better for other cases.

Use UNION ALL to Preserve Duplicate Rows

The operation steps are as follows:

(1) Select Start → All Programs → SQL Server Management Studio in turn. In the pop-up connection dialog box, select "SQL Server Authentication", login name is "your choice " and password is empty.

(2) In the "Microsoft SQL Server Management Studio" window, click the "New Query" button, then enter the corresponding code in the code editing area, and click the Run button on the toolbar. The results will be displayed in the window.

SQL UNION {Enter parameters} Duplicate {Enter column names here}

Improving the Readability of Query Results through UNION Statements

UNION statement can not only merge the query results of the SELECT statement but also increase the readability of query results. That is, by creating aliases for the column names in the results, the meaning of the query results can be better reflected.

Determine the Source of Data by Text in UNION

In UNION, the source of data is determined by the text, mainly by adding a new column to the result set and determining the source of data in the table through the new column. This method can ensure that duplicate rows in two tables are not deleted, and can show that duplicate rows come from different tables.

Chapter 9 *Using Functions*

I n regard to SQL, a built-in function can be defined as a portion of programming that accepts zero or any other input and returns an answer. There are different roles of built-in functions. These include the performance of calculations, obtaining of the system value, and application in textual data manipulation. This part aims at examining the various SQL built-in functions, categories of functions, pros and cons of functions and types of built-in functions.

Types of SQL Functions

The SQL functions are grouped into two groups: aggregate and scalar function. Working on Group by, the aggregate functions run on different records and deliver a summary. Scalar functions, on the other hand, run on different records independently.

These are as follows:

1.   Single Row Functions-They provide a one-row return for any queried table. They are found in select lists, START WIH, WHERE CLAUSE and others. Examples of single-row functions include numeric_, data_mining, Datetime_, conversion_ and XML_functions.

2.   Aggregate Function-When you apply this kind of function, you see a single row returns based on different rows. The aggregate function exists in Select lists, ORDER BY and HAVING CLAUSE. They go hand in hand with Group by Clause and SELECT statements. Many of them do not take attention to null values. Those that are usually used include AVG, EANK, MIN, SUM and others.

3.   Analytic Function-They are used to compute an aggregate value that are found on specific groups of rows. When you run this function, it delivers many rows for every group. The analytic functions are the last one to be run in a query. Examples of analytic functions include analytic-_clause and Order-by-Clause.

4. Model Functions-These are found in SELECT statements. Examples of model functions include CV, present and previous.

5. User-Defined Function-They are used in PL/SQL to offer functions that are not found in SQL. They are mostly used in sections where expressions occur. For instance, you can find them in select list of Select statement.

6. SQL COUNT Function-It is used to provide the number of rows in a table.

Categories of Functions

Functions are classified according to the role they play on the SQL database. The following are some of the function categories available:

1. Aggregate Functions-They do a calculation on a specific set of values and deliver a single value. The aggregate values are used in the SELECT LIST and HAVING clause. The aggregate functions are referred to as being deterministic. This means that they return the same value when running on the same input value.

2. Analytic Function-They calculate an aggregate value according to a group of rows. They return many rows for different groups. The analytic functions can be used to perform different computations like running totals, percentages and others.

3. Ranking Functions-They provide a ranking value for each portioned row. These kinds of functions are regarded as nondeterministic.

4. Rowset Functions- They're used to return an object that can be applied.

5. Scalar Functions-They work on a single value to return the same. There are various kinds of scalar values. These include configuration function, conversion function and others.

a) Configuration Functions-They offer information about the present configuration.

b) Conversion Functions-They support data changing.

c) Cursor Functions-They provide information concerning cursors.

d) Date and Time Data Type-They are concerned with operations as regards date and time.

6. Function Determinism-Functions that are found in SQL servers are either deterministic or nondeterministic. Deterministic functions provide the same answers when they are used. Nondeterministic functions, on the other hand, offer different results when they are applied.

SQL Calculations

There are various mathematical functions build-in the SQL server. The functions can be classified into 4 main groups, including Scientific and Trig Functions, rounding functions, signs and random numbers. Although there are numerous mathematical functions within each class, not all of them are used regularly. The various classes are highlighted and explained below:

1. Scientific and Trig Functions-Under this category, there are various subclasses found under it. These include P1, SQRT, and SQUARE. P1 function is used to compute the circumference and area in circles. How it works: SELECT 2 *10. SQRT connotes square root. This function is used most of the time. The function recognizes any number that can be changed to float datatype. Example: SELECT SQET (36) Returns 6.SQUARE means that you multiply any number by itself. The concept of Pythagoras theorem is useful here. This means that Asquared+Bsquared=Csquared. This can be performed as SELECT SQRT (SQUARE (A) + SQUARE(B)) as C.

2. Rounding Functions- Under this class, there are various subcategories which include the CEILING and FLOOR. The ceiling function is helpful when dealing with a float or decimal number. Your interest is to find out the highest or lowest integer. Whereas the CEILING is the best highest integer, the floor represents the lowest integer. The ROUND function is applied when you want to round a number to the nearest specific decimal place. This is expressed as ROUND (value, number of decimal places).

3. Signs- There are occasions that require that you obtain an absolute figure of a number. For instance, the absolute value of -7 is 7. The absolute number doesn't contain any sign. To assist you with this task, it's essential to utilize the ABS function.

4. COS (X)-This function recognizes an angle expressed as radian as the parameter. After an operation, you get a cosine value.

5.   SIN (X)-This function notices a radian angle. After computation, it gives back a sine value.

6.   Sign-You can use a sign function when you want a negative, positive, or zero value.

The Importance of SQL Built-In Functions and Mathematical Applications

The build-in functions are sub-programs that help users to achieve different results when handling SQL database. These applications are used several times when you want to manipulate or process data. The SQL functions provide tools that are applied when creating, processing, and manipulating data. The benefits of SQL in-build and maths functions are as follows:

1. Manipulation of Data-The in-built tools and maths functions play a significant role in data manipulation. Manipulating massive data may be difficult if you do it manually. This is especially when the data is massive. Therefore, these functions play a significant role in ensuring that your data is manipulated fast as per your demands.

2. Assist in The Processing of Data-To benefit from data; you must process it. You may never have the ability to process big data manually. Therefore, the built-in SQL functions and maths applications assist you in processing your database.

3. Simplifies Tasks-In case you're a programmers, you can attest to the fact that these functions and formulas make your work ease. You can work fast when you apply these in-build functions and formulas. Due to these tools, you'll accomplish many projects within a short time.

4. Increase Your Productivity-Using the in-built functions enhance your productivity as a programmers. This is because the functions enable you to work quickly on different projects. In case you were to handle data manually, you may take much time before you accomplish a task which ultimately injures your productivity. However, the built-in functions and calculations allow quick execution of tasks.

5. Time Saving-Because functions are written once and used several times, and they save much time. Besides timesaving, the functions offer support to modular programming.

6. They Enhance Performance- When you apply functions; you enhance the performance of your database. This is because the functions are prepared and inserted prior to usage.

7. Enhances Understanding of Complicated Logic-Handling of SQL database is a complex tax. Therefore, functions enable you to decompose data into smooth and manageable functions. In this way, you find it easy to maintain your database.

8. Cost Effective-Because the functions are in-build in the SQL database; you can use them many times without the need to invest in new ones. In this connection, therefore, they reduce the cost of operating and maintaining your SQL database.

Downsides of In-Built Functions

The SQL in-built functions have various limitations, including:

1. Testability- When using the in-built functions, it's challenging to test their business philosophy. This is a big challenge, especially when you want the functions to support your business philosophy. You may never understand whether the functions are in line with your business vision and mission.

2. Versioning-It's challenging to establish the kind of version that is used in the SQL build-functions. You need to understand whether there're any new versions that can probably provide the best service.

3. Errors-In case there are errors within the in-build functions which you don't know, they may disrupt the program. This may prove costly and time-wasting.

4. Fear of Change-In case there is change; you may not understand how it will affect your SQL built-in functions. The world of technology keeps changes, and this change may affect the in-built functions.

The SQL in-built functions and calculations are essential as they enable a programmer to execute a task fast with minimal errors. The calculations in the in-built database makes it possible to process and manipulate data.

Chapter 10   *Subqueries*

Definition

I n SQL, subqueries are queries within queries. The subqueries usually use the WHERE clause. Also called nested query or internal query, subqueries can also restrict the data being retrieved.

Creating subqueries are more complex than creating simple queries. You have to use essential key words such as, SELECT, DELETE, UPDATE, INSERT and the operators such as, BETWEEN (used only WITHIN a subquery and not WITH a subquery), IN, =, < =, > =, >, <, < >, and similar symbols.

In composing a subquery, you have to remember these pointers.

- It must be enclosed with an open and close parenthesis.

- It can be used in several ways.

- It is recommended that a subquery can run on its own.

- It can ascribe column values for files.

- It can be found anywhere in the main query. You can identify it because it is enclosed in parentheses.

- If it displays more than one row in response to an SQL command, this can only be accepted when there are multiple value operators. Example is the IN operator.

- In a subquery, the GROUP BY is used instead of the ORDER BY, which is used in the main statement or query.

- When creating subqueries, do not enclose it immediately in a set function.

- To create subqueries, it is easier to start with a FROM statement.

- Subqueries should also have names for easy identification.

- When using the SELECT key word, only one column should be included in your subquery. The exception is when the main query has selected many columns for comparison.

- Values that refer to a National Character Large Object (NCLOB), Binary Large Object (BLOB), Character Large Object (CLOB) and an Array, which is part of a collection data in variable sizes, should NOT be included in your SELECT list.

Working with the Queries

When you do set up the query that you would like to use, you will find that you are basically sending out an inquiry to the database that you already set up. You will find that there are a few methods to do this, but the SELECT command is going to be one of the best options to make this happen, and can instantly bring back the information that we need from there, based on our search.

For example, if you are working with a table that is going to hold onto all of the products that you offer for sale, then you would be able to use the command of SELECT in order to find the best selling products or ones that will meet another criterion that you have at that time. The request is going to be good on any of the information on the product that is stored in the database, and you will see that this is done pretty normally when we are talking about work in a relational database.

Working with the SELECT Command

Any time that you have a plan to go through and query your database, you will find that the command of SELECT is going to be the best option to make this happen. This command is important because it is going to be in charge of starting and then executing the queries that you would like to send out. In many cases, you will have to add something to the statement as just sending out SELECT is not going to help us to get some of the results that you want. You can choose the product that you would like to find along with the command, or even work with some of the features that show up as well.

Whenever you work with the SELECT command on one of your databases inside of the SQL language, you will find that there are four main keywords that we are able to focus on. These are going to be known as the four classes that we need to have present in order to make sure that we are able to complete the command that we want and see some good results. These four commands are going to include:

- SELECT—this command will be combined with the FROM command in order to obtain the necessary data in a format that is readable and organized. You will use this to help determine the data that is going to show up. The SELECT clause is going to introduce the columns that you would like to see out of the search results and then you can use the FROM in order to find the exact point that you need.

- FROM—the SELECT and the FROM commands often go together. It is mandatory because it takes your search from everything in the database, down to just the things that you would like. You will need to have at least one FROM clause for this to work. A good syntax that would use both the SELECT and the FROM properly includes:

- WHERE—this is what you will use when there are multiple conditions within the clause. For example, it is the element in the query that will display the selective data after the user puts in the information that they want to find. If you are using this feature, the right conditions to have along with it are the AND OR operators. The syntax that you should use for the WHERE command includes:

SELEC [* | ALL | DISTINCT COLUMN1, COLUMN2]

FROM TABLE1 [, TABLE2];

WHERE [CONDITION1 | EXPRESSION 1]

[AND CONDITION2 | EXPRESSION 2]

- ORDER BY—you are able to use this clause in order to arrange the output of your query. The server will be able to decide the order and the format that the different information comes up for the user after they do their basic query. The default for this query is going to be organizing the output going from A to Z, but you can make changes that you would like. The syntax that you can use for this will be the same as the one above, but add in the following line at the end:

ORDER BY COLUMN 1 | INTEGER [ASC/DESC]

You will quickly see that all of these are helpful and you can easily use them instead of the SELECT command if you would like. They can sometimes pull out the information that you need from the database you are working in a more efficient manner than you will see with just the SELECT command. But there are going to be many times when you will find that the SELECT command will be plenty to help you get things done when it is time to search your database as well.

A Look at Case Sensitivity

Unlike some of the other coding languages that are out there and that you may be tempted to use on your database searches, you may find that the case sensitivity in SQL is not going to be as important as it is in some of those other ones. You are able to use uppercase or lowercase words as you would like, and you can use either typing of the word and still get the part that you need out of the database. It is even possible for us to go through and enter in some clauses and statements in uppercase or lowercase, without having to worry too much about how these commands are going to work for our needs.

However, there are a few exceptions to this, which means there are going to be times when we need to worry about the case sensitivity that is going to show up in this language a bit more than we may want to. One of the main times for this is when we are looking at the data objects. For the most part, the data that you are storing should be done with uppercase letters. This is going to be helpful because it ensures that there is some consistency in the work that you are doing and can make it easier for us to get the results that we want.

For example, you could run into some issues down the road if one of the users is going through the database and typing in JOHN, but then the next person is typing in John, and then the third person is going through and typing in john to get the results. If you make sure that there is some consistency present, you will find that it is easier for all of the users to get the information that they want, and then you can make sure that you are able to provide the relevant information back when it is all done.

In this case, working with letters in uppercase is often one of the easiest ways to work with this because it is going to make it easier and the user is going to see that this is the norm in order options as well. If you choose to not go with uppercase in this, then you should try to find some other method that is going to keep the consistency that you are looking for during the whole thing. This allows the user a chance to figure out what you are doing, and will help them to find what they need with what is inside of their queries.

Chapter 11 *SQL Views and Transactions*

A Database View in SQL is defined as a "virtual or logical table" described as the SELECT statements containing join function. As a Database View is like a table in the database consisting of rows and columns, you will be able to run queries on it easily. Many DBMSs, including MySQL, enable users to modify information in the existing tables using Database View by meeting certain prerequisites, as shown in the picture below.

A SQL database View can be deemed dynamic since there is no connection between the SQL View to the physical system. The database system will store SQL Views in the form on SELECT statements using JOIN clause. When the information in the table is modified, the SQL View will also reflect that modification.

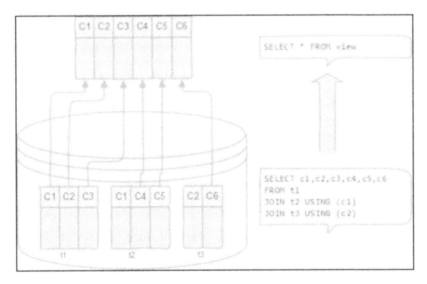

Pros of Using SQL View

- A SQL View enables simplification of complicated queries: a SQL View is characterized by a SQL statement which is associated with multiple tables. To conceal the complexity of the underlying tables from the end-users and external apps, SQL View is extremely helpful. You only need to use straightforward SQL statements instead of complicated ones with multiple JOIN clauses using the SQL View.

- A SQL View enables restricted access to information depending on the user requirements. Perhaps you would not like all users to be able to query a subset of confidential information. In such cases SQL View can be used to expose non-sensitive information to a targeted set of users selectively.

- The SQL View offers an additional layer of safety. Data security is a key component of every DBMS. It ensures additional security for the DBMS. It enables generation of a read only view to display read only information for targeted users. In read only view, users are able only to retrieve data and are not allowed to update any information.

- The SQL View is used to enable computed columns. The table in the database is not capable of containing computed columns but a SQL View can easily contain computed column. Assume in the OrderDetails table there is the quantity Order column for the amount of products ordered and priceEach column for the price of each item. But the OrderDetails table cannot contain a calculated column storing total sales for every product from the order. If it could, the database schema may have never been a good design. In such a situation, to display the calculated outcome, you could generate a computed column called total, which would be a product of quantityOrder and priceEach columns. When querying information from the SQL View, the calculated column information will be calculated on the fly.

- A SQL View allows for backward compatibility. Assume that we have a central database that is being used by multiple applications. Out of the blue you have been tasked to redesign the database accommodating the new business needs. As you delete some tables and create new ones, you would not want other applications to be affected by these modifications.

You could generate SQL Views in such situations, using the identical schematic of the legacy tables that you are planning to delete.

Cons of Using SQL View

In addition to the pros listed above, the use of SQL View may have certain disadvantages such as:

- Performance: Executing queries against SQL View could be slow, particularly if it is generated from another SQL View.

- Table dependencies: Since a SQL View is created from the underlying tables of the database. Anytime the tables structure connected with SQL View is modified, you also need to modify the SQL View.

Create SQL View with JOIN Clause

The MySQL database allows you to create SQL View using JOIN clause. For instance, the query below with the INNER JOIN clause can be used to create a view containing order no, client name, and totl sale per ordr:

CREATE VIEW clientOrdrs AS

SELECT

x.orderNo,

clientName,

SUM(qtyOrdrd * pricEch) total

FROM

orderDetail d

INNER JOIN

order r ON r.orderNo = x.orderNo

INNER JOIN

clients y ON y.clientNo = y.clientNo

GROUP BY x.orderNo

ORDER BY totl DESC;

By executing the syntax below, the desired data can be retrieved from the client order view:

SELECT *FROM

clientOrder;

The result set is displayed in the picture below:

orderNumber	customerName	total
10165	Dragon Souveniers, Ltd.	67392.84
10287	Vida Sport, Ltd	61402
10310	Toms Spezialitäten, Ltd	61234.66
10212	Euro+ Shopping Channel	59830.54
10207	Diecast Collectables	59265.14
10127	Muscle Machine Inc	58841.35
10204	Muscle Machine Inc	58793.53
10126	Comda Auto Replicas, Ltd	57131.92

Create SQL View with a Subquery

The query below can be used to generate a SQL View with a subquery, containing products with purchase prices greater than the average product prices.

CREATE VIEW abvAvgPdcts AS

SELECT

pdctCode, pdctName, buyPric

FROM

pdcts

WHERE

buyPric>

(SELECT

AVG(buyPric)

FROM

pdcts)

ORDER BY buyPric DESC;

The query to extract data from the aboveAvgPdcts view is even more straightforward, as shown in the picture below:

SELECT

    *

FROM

abvAvgPdcts;

The result set is displayed in the picture below:

	productCode	productName	buyPrice
▶	S10_4962	1962 LanciaA Delta 16V	103.42
	S18_2238	1998 Chrysler Plymouth Prowler	101.51
	S10_1949	1952 Alpine Renault 1300	98.58
	S24_3856	1956 Porsche 356A Coupe	98.3
	S12_1108	2001 Ferrari Enzo	95.59
	S12_1099	1968 Ford Mustang	95.34
	S18_1984	1995 Honda Civic	93.89
	S18_4027	1970 Triumph Spitfire	91.92

Check if an Existing View is Updatable

By running a query against the is_updtble column from the view in the info_schema database, you should verify whether a view in the database is updatable or not.

You can use the query below to display all the views from the classicmodeldb and check which for views that can be updated:

SELECT

tab_name,

is_updtble

FROM

info_schema.view

WHERE

tab_schema = 'classicmodel';

The result set is displayed in the picture below:

	table_name	is_updatable
▶	aboveavgproducts	YES
	customerorders	NO
	officeinfo	YES
	saleperorder	NO

Dropping Rows Using SQL View

To understand this concept, execute the syntax below first to create a table called itms, use the INSERT statements to add records into this table and then use the CREATE clause to generate a view containing items with prices higher than 701.

--- creating new tbl called itms

CREATE TABLE itms (

   identity INT AUTO_INCREMENT PRIMARY KEY,

nam VARCHAR (110) NOT NULL,

pric DECIMAL (10 , 1) NOT NULL

)

-- addingrecords into itmstbl

INSERT INTO itms (nam,pric)

VALUES ('Comp', 600.54), ('Laptop', 799.99),('Tablet', 699.50) ;

--- creating views based on itmstbl

CREATE VIEW LxryItms AS

SELECT

   *

FROM

itms

WHERE

pric> 899;

--- retrieve records from the LxryItms view

SELECT

   *

FROM

LxryItms;

The result set is displayed in the picture below:

id	name	price
1	Laptop	700.56
3	iPad	700.50

Now, using the DELETE clause record with identity value 3 can be dropped.

DELETE FROM LxryItms

WHERE

 id = 3;

After you run the query above, you will receive a message stating 1 row(s) affected.

Now, to verify the data with the view use the query below:

SELECT

   *

FROM

LxryItms;

The result set is displayed in the picture below:

id	name	price
▶ 1	Laptop	700.56

Finally, use the syntax below to retrieve desired records from the underlying table to confirm that the "DELETE" statement in fact removed the record:

SELECT

    *

FROM

itms;

The result set is displayed in the picture below, which confirms that the record with identity value 3 has been deleted from the items table:

id	name	price
▶ 1	Laptop	700.56
2	Desktop	699.99

Modification of SQL View

In MySQL, you can use ALTER VIEW and CREATE OR REPLACE VIEW statements to make changes to views that have already been created.

Using ALTER VIEWStatement

The syntax for ALTER VIEW works a lot like the CREATE VIEW statement that you learned earlier, the only difference being that the ALTER keyword is used instead of the CREATE keyword, as shown below:

ALTER

[ALGRTHM = {MERG | TEMPTBL | UNDEFND}]

VIEW [db_nam]. [vw_nam]

AS

[SELECT statemnt]

The query below will change the organization view by incorporating the email column in the table:

ALTER VIEW org

AS

SELECT CONCAT (x.lastname,x.firstname) AS Emplye,

x.emailAS emplyeEmail,

CONCAT(y.lstname, y.fstname) AS Mgr

FROM emplyes AS x

INNER JOIN emplyes AS y

ON y.emplyeNo = x.ReprtsTo

ORDER BY Mgr;

You may run the code below against the org view to verify the modification:

SELECT

*

FROM

Org;

The result set is displayed in the picture below:

Employee	employeeEmail	Manager
JonesBarry	bjones@classicmodelcars.com	BondurGerard
HernandezGerard	ghernande@classicmodelcars.com	BondurGerard
BottLarry	lbott@classicmodelcars.com	BondurGerard
GerardMartin	mgerard@classicmodelcars.com	BondurGerard
BondurLoui	lbondur@classicmodelcars.com	BondurGerard
CastilloPamela	pcastillo@classicmodelcars.com	BondurGerard
VanaufGeorge	gvanauf@classicmodelcars.com	BowAnthony

Using CREATE OR REPLACE VIEW Statement

These statements can be used to replace or generate a SQL View that already exists in the database. For all existing views, MySQL will easily modify the view but if the view is non-existent, it will create a new view based on the query.

The syntax below can be used to generate the contacts view on the basis of the employees table:

CREATE OR REPLACE VIEW cntcts AS

    SELECT

fstName, lstName, extnsn, eml

    FROM

emplyes;

The result set is displayed in the picture below:

firstName	lastName	extension	email
Diane	Murphy	x5800	dmurphy@classicmodelcars.com
Mary	Patterson	x4611	mpatterso@classicmodelcars.com
Jeff	Firrelli	x9273	jfirrelli@classicmodelcars.com
William	Patterson	x4871	wpatterson@classicmodelcars.com
Gerard	Bondur	x5408	gbondur@classicmodelcars.com
Anthony	Bow	x5428	abow@classicmodelcars.com
Leslie	Jennings	x3291	ljennings@classicmodelcars.com

Now, assume that you would like to insert the jobtitl column to the cntcts view. You can accomplish this with the syntax below:

CREATE OR REPLACE VIEW cntcts AS

   SELECT

fstName, lstName, extnsn, eml, jobtitl

   FROM

emplyes;

The result set is displayed in the picture below:

firstName	lastName	extension	email	jobtitle
Diane	Murphy	x5800	dmurphy@classicmodelcars.com	President
Mary	Patterson	x4611	mpatterso@classicmodelcars.com	VP Sales
Jeff	Firrelli	x9273	jfirrelli@classicmodelcars.com	VP Marketing
William	Patterson	x4871	wpatterson@classicmodelcars.com	Sales Manager (APAC)
Gerard	Bondur	x5408	gbondur@classicmodelcars.com	Sale Manager (EMEA)
Anthony	Bow	x5428	abow@classicmodelcars.com	Sales Manager (NA)
Leslie	Jennings	x3291	ljennings@classicmodelcars.com	Sales Rep

Dropping a SQL View

The DROP VIEW statement can be utilized to delete an existing view from the database, using the syntax below:

DROP VIEW [IF EXISTS] [db_name]. [vw_name]

The "IF EXISTS" clause is not mandatory in the statement above and is used to determine if the view already exists in the database. It prevents you from mistakenly removing a view that does not exists in the database.

You may, for instance, use the DROP VIEW statement as shown in the syntax below to delete the organization view:

DROP VIEW IF EXISTS org;

SQL TRANSACTIONS

Any actions that are executed on a database are called as transactions. These are actions that are executed logically, either manually by a user or automatically using by the database program.

Or simply put, they are the spread of one or more database modifications. For instance, every time you create a row, update a row, or delete a row a transaction is being executed on that table. To maintain data integrity and address database errors, it is essential to regulate these transactions.

Basically, to execute a transaction, you must group several SQL queries and run them at the same time.

Conclusion

S QL in full is the Structured Query Language and is a kind of ANSI computer language that has been specially designed to access, manipulate, and update database systems. SQL has different uses; the most significant of them is managing data in database systems that can store data in table forms. Additionally, SQL statements have been used regularly in updating and retrieving data from databases.

What we have thought since childhood is the best to learn a new concept is by practicing it. It is no exception; you have to do various equations related to SQL as a way of learning about them. I hope you can apply what you have learned from this book to be successful in your future projects.

Projects in SQL Programming

Below are random projects that you can encounter in SQL programming. They have been picked and randomly, and I believe if you practice them out, you will be better equipped in handling such situations. Before we list the projects, we first should get to understand the differences between exercises and projects. Well, logically, a task is more of a quick test you can do without a lot of complications: it is less complicated compared to projects. On the other hand, projects are a little more complicated and sophisticated. It requires advanced skills as well as data research to do it.

Having learned that, let's discuss the potential projects you can encounter in SQL programming.

i) Interviews

When making software for a particular company, you will need knowledge of an existing system that belongs to that company. For such purposes, you will have to carry out interviews for some individuals working in that company and collect critical information. You will have to do interviews on people that are aware of that software. Such people could be working as hostel wardens or trainers.

ii) Discussions (Groups)

They can be a kind of group discussion that has occurred between employees of the company you are working on. For a start, a good number of ideas might appear clustered together or filled by concepts that already exist. Such ideologies might be brought on board by programmers.

Additionally, it can be done through online observation. It is a procedure of obtaining more essential details about the existing software or web apps from the web. The primary purpose of this project is getting as close as possible to the system. SQL programming plays a critical role in ensuring the systems are up and running as recommended.

Application of SQL

The self-variable option lets you carry out the joining process on the same table, saving you the time you spend organizing the final table. There are, however, a few situations where this can be a good option. Imagine the chart you created earlier has the columns consisting of country and continent.

When faced with a task of listing countries located on the same continent, a clearly outlined set below should give you a glimpse of the results expected. SQL variable can further be subdivided into three different types: the left join, the right join as well as the full outer join. The outer join primary role is returning all the identified rows from a single table, and once the joining target is archived, it includes the columns from another table. Outer joins are different from inner joins in the essence that an inner join cannot involve the unmatched rows in the final set of results.

When using an order entry, for instance, you may be faced with situations where it is inevitable to list every employee regardless of the location, they put customer orders. In such a case, this kind of joins is beneficial. When you opt to use this kind of join, all employees, including those that have been given marching orders, will be included in the final result.

This is a kind of outer join that is responsible for returning each row from the first left side of the table and those row that match from the right side of the table. In case there are no matches on the right side, left join returns a null value for each of those columns. A type of outer join has the task of returning each row from the right side of the table and merging with the other side (left) of the table. Again, if there aren't any values for those digits in the column, the join returns null values for them.

It has the task of returning rows from their initial location in the inner join, and in case there is no match found, this join returns null results for those tables.

This is a kind of variable that is essentially a product of Cartesian elements that have been expressed in the SQL set up. Picture this; you require a whole set of combinations available between both tables or even in just one meal. You will have to use the cross join to achieve that technique. To help you understand this join better, you can go back to the two tables we created at the beginning of the article. Look at both the columns and try to compare the impact each one of them has to the final result. The cross join plays an essential in ensuring accuracy during merging. You ought to note that there are apparent differences between cross joins and outer joins despite the fact that the description makes them almost look similar.

Similarly, MySQL system has a slot that allows you to announce more than one set of variables that has a common type of data. Again, most of the technicians have had issues with how this command relays information to related databases. In the various methods of storing variances and variables, this one has proven to be more secure than others. Consequently, it has been known to be the most popular of them all.

Variables can be applied in mathematical expressions, for example, adding values altogether or combining and holding texts. This can be used as a section of the general information. For your information, variables are also applied in storing information so as one can participate in a kind of calculations. Additionally, variables can be part of the parameters and are used in procedural assessments. This is two in one method that not only lets you declare a variable but also setting it up with values that have a similar data type. Going back to the examples we gave earlier; we can affirm that varchar is a kind of data that lets you sustain more than one kind of character in just a single string.

Up to this point, you should be in a position to understand the kind of SQL Exercises and Programs as well as the various types in existence. This will not only let you be in an excellent place to tackle errors in case they occur and prevent them from happening as well. When Mark Suaman, a renown data scientist and a graduate of Havard University, first used varchar, he recommended it for being efficient and accurate. He rated it among the best types of data set in the market today. It does not have an allocation for potential occurrences of errors. It is hard to interfere with such a highly secure kind of data type.

Applications of SQL

Since its introduction in the computing world, SQL has played a significant role in revolutionizing data storage in a systematic manner as well as direct retrieval. As the digital world continues to grow steadily, the amount of data stored quickly escalates, making organizations and personal data piling up. Therefore, SQL acts as a platform where these data are stored while offering direct access without the emergence of limitations. As such, SQL is used in different sectors, including telecommunication, finance, trade, manufacturing, institutional, and transport. Its presence primarily deals with data but also accompanies other significant benefits on its application.

Data Integration

Across the sectors mentioned above, one of its main applications of SQL is the creation of data integration scripts commonly done by administrators and developers. SQL databases comprise of several tables which may contain different data. When these data are integrated, it creates a new experience essential for the provision of meaningful information, therefore, increasing productivity. Data integration scripts are crucial in any given organization, including the government, as it offers trusted data which can be utilized to promote the achievement of the set goals.

Analytical Queries

Data analysts regularly utilize Structured Query Language to smoothen their operations more so when establishing and executing queries. SQL comprises multiple tables that consist of different datasets. When these data are combined, it brings out more comprehensive information critical for any individual or organization. The same is also applicable for data analysts as they use a similar aspect. As they use an analytical query structure, queries, and tables from SQL are fed into the structure to deliver crucial results from varying sources. In this case, data analysts can readily acquire different queries and customize them to have a more comprehensive data to depend on as solutions.

Data Retrieval

This is another important application of SQL to retrieve data from different subsets within a database with big data. This is essential in financial sectors and analytics as to the use of numerical values typically consists of mixed statistical data. The most commonly used SQL elements are create, select, delete, and update, among others. The technique is made possible when the user quickly can search the database and acquire the needed data as SQL sieves the information to bring out the desired data. In some cases, the language may deliver similar or related data when the required data is missing. This is crucial as one can compare the results as well as make changes where the need arises.

CODING HTML:

Crash course to learn HTML & CSS language From Scratch. Discover The Art Of Computer Programming. Design And Code Your Own Project.

Ashton Miller

Introduction

H TML stands for Hypertext Markup Language. It's a special language that web browsers understand. It's basically a bunch of instructions about the structure of the document.

Hypertext is probably the most important part of HTML letters because it means that you can link one document to another one. Hypertext is a text file that contains links to other text files.

This is the foundation stone of web, which at the beginning wasn't much more than few pages interconnected with links. Today, the web is no longer just about text. Most of it is created by Hypermedia including video, photos and music. But if you strip down all the bells and whistles, you will still find this fundamental functionality of mutual linking between documents at the core of any modern web application including Twitter, Gmail and even the project we are about to build.

Markup means that HTML surrounds regular text with special code which tells the browser how to display the content of the document. It tells the browser what the structure of the document is.

Language means that HTML has some special syntax or the rules you need to follow to create the correct content. Just like with other languages where subjects and verbs have a special place in the sentence, HTML tags have a special structure you need to use. For instance, when you need to nest tags, you must place the closing part of the tag correctly.

When you build an HTML website, you actually need to learn different coding languages (even though it is called an HTML website). The structure or the core is provided by HTML, while CSS is about setting up the looks and the visual feel, in order to make your website appealing and pretty to look at. In order to make your website more dynamic and to add additional interaction with the user, you can use JavaScript. As you can see, in order to create a competitive website, you should at least learn the basics and how these languages work.

These days, people use many devices with different screen sizes and resolutions to browse the Internet, so it is very important to be able to change the visible content based on what kind of device the user is currently using. This is referred to as a responsive approach or responsiveness and we will dive into it when we talk about CSS.

CSS provides styling for the structure. Let's say you have a house with three rooms. One room is a kitchen, one room is a bedroom and one is a bathroom. Based on this description, you have a basic idea about the structure of the house, but you have no idea how big those rooms are and what are the colors of the walls. This is what CSS provides.

When it comes to real-world websites, the structure of the content is not enough. You probably experienced this yourself. When you search on the Internet for a restaurant, would you rather visit the one with a very nice, professional looking website or the one with just a simple blank page with general, unformatted text?

Regarding the content, they can both give you the same information as menu, opening hours, contact, and so on, but as you know, it's the package that sells the product.

That's why it's crucial to focus on the styling of your content in a way that's pleasing and useful for the visitor of your website.

CSS (cascading style sheets) is technologies that will allow you to make your page look anything you want without the need to change the structure of the HTML document.

CSS is immensely powerful in transforming the styling of the website without ever touching the content and its HTML structure.

Javascript provides the behavior. It gives HTML webpage event-driven functionality, like what will happen when the browser finishes loading the page or when the user clicks the Buy button on the web shop.

Javascript is the third language you are about to learn in this book. It is one of the three languages every web developer must know and understand.

As you already know, HTML defines the content of web pages, CSS specifies the layout and Javascript programs the behavior.

People usually don't appreciate the power of Javascript and this is probably caused by two main reasons.

First, they lack the proper understanding of the language fundamentals. Second, Javascript doesn't have a great reputation because in the early days of the web, the vendors of browsers implemented Javascript however they pleased. And this of course caused a lot of headaches to web developers, because they couldn't be sure how their code would run in different browsers, if at all.

Setting up frontend technologies is very easy. To get all three frontend technologies up and running, you need just one product, a web browser.

Also, you will need a good plaintext editor. Just make sure it doesn't add anything else to your code behind the scene. For this reason, you really shouldn't use document processors like Microsoft Word or Apple Pages. These are made for something entirely different and their built-in formatting features will ruin your code.

Chapter 1. *Fundamentals of HTML*

What Is HTML?

D ivisions were used for a long time in building a webpage structure. However, divisions have a problem in that they don't provide a semantic value, making it difficult to tell divisions intensions. However, new elements which are structurally based are introduced by HTML5. These elements include <header>, <nav>, <article>, <section>,

<aside>, and <footer>.

These elements give meaning to the way web pages are organized and improve the structural semantics. All of these are block-level elements and have no implied style or position. All of these elements can also be used severally in a web page provided each element has a proper reflection of its semantic meaning. Let us discuss this one by one.

Header

Just as the name suggests, the <header> elements help us to identify the top of a web page, section or article, or any other segment of a web page. The <header> element may have a heading, an introductory text, and navigation. It is created as follows:

<header>...</header>

Don't confuse this <header> element with the <head> element or headings <h1> through <h6>. They all have different meanings when it comes to semantics.

The <header> is a structural element that identifies the heading of a page segment. It should be added within the <body> element.

The <head> element isn't shown on a web page as it only provides the metadata for a web page. Examples of such metadata include the title of the web page and links to any external files. It should be added directly to the <html> element.

The headings <h1> through <h6> help us to designate the multiple levels of text headings throughout a web page.

Navigation

The <nav> element is used for identifying a section of the major navigational links on a web page. The <nav> element should be used for primary navigation sections only, like a table of contents, global navigation, previous/next links and other groups of navigational links. It is created as follows:

<nav>...</nav>

Article

We use the <article> element to identify a section of independent and self-contained content that can be used or distributed independently. Use the <article> element to markup newspaper articles, blog articles, user-submitted content, and other related content.

Before using the <article> element, you have to ask yourself whether it is possible for you to replicate the content elsewhere without introducing confusion. If you remove the contents of the <article> element and you place them somewhere else like in an email, the <article> element should still be able to make sense. It is created as follows:

<article>...</article>

Section

We use the <section> element to identify a group with same theme of content, which usually has a heading. The way the content is grouped within the <section> element can be general, but it will be good to ensure that the content is related.

Use the <section> element to separate and create a hierarchy within your web page. It is created as follows:

<section>...</section>

Sometimes, determining the element to be used based on the semantic meaning of the element might still be difficult for you to do. The trick is simple, consider the content. The trick is simple, consider the content.

The <section> and <article> elements play a significant contribution to the structure of a document and help in outlining documents. If styling is the purposes for grouping the content without adding value to the document structure, use the element <div>.

If the content has an impact on the outline of the document and can be redistributed independently, use the element <article>.

If the content has an impact on the outline of the document and is a representation of a group of content with a theme, use <section> element.

Aside

Use the <aside> element to hold contents such as inserts, sidebars and short explanations that are related to the surrounding content. When it is used with an <article> element, the <aside> element may be good for identifying the publisher of an article.

See the <aside> element as the element that is displayed off to the sides (left or right) of a page. Remember that all structural elements like the <aside> are elements on a block-level and they will appear in a new line, and they will occupy the entire width provided by the web page or cover the whole length of the element they are nested within the parent element.

It is created as follows:

<aside>...</aside>

Footer

The f<footer> element is used to identify the end or closing of a web page, or any other part of a web page. Usually, the footer is added to the bottom part of its parent. It is created as follows:

<footer>...</footer>

Practice

We need to put all the above into practice by creating a basic website. We will use hyperlinks to link together the various pages of the website.

Step 1) We will first link the "My Website" text inside an <h1> element within the <header> element to the index.html page. This is the page that is first loaded when the user opens the website, showing the home page. This means that when a user clicks My Website text, they will be taken to the home page of the website.

This is shown below:

<h1>

  <a href="index.html">My Website</a>

</h1>

Step 2) For us to be able to navigate through the different web pages, we will create the navigation menu using the <nav> element within the header element. This will be done within the <header> element. We will add the About Us, Services, Location and Contact Us pages to go together with the Home page. We have to create links for all of these. The navigation menu can be created as follows:

<header>

  ...

  <nav>

  <a href="index.html">Home</a>

  <a href="about.html">About Us</a>

  <a href="services.html">Services</a>

```
  <a href="location.html">Location</a>

  <a href="contact.html">Contact Us</a>

 </nav>

</header>
```

Step 3) For convenience purposes, let us add the same navigation to the footer section of the website. This can be done as follows:

```
<footer>

 ...

 <nav>

  <a href="index.html">Home</a>

  <a href="about.html">About Us</a>

  <a href="services.html">Services</a>

  <a href="location.html">Location</a>

  <a href="contact.html">Contact Us</a>

 </nav>

</footer>
```

Step 4) In the <section> element, that introduces our website, we need to add a link that will urge them to contact us now. It will be good for this link to be added below a paragraph:

```
<section>

 ...

 <a href="contact.html">Contact us Now</a>
```

```
</section>
```

Step 5) We need to add links to all sections that tease the other pages. Inside every section, we will wrap both <h3> and <h5> elements within an anchor element that links to the right page. This should be done for every section:

```
<section>

 <section>

  <a href="services.html">

   <h5>Services</h5>

   <h3>World-Class Services</h3>

  </a>

   <p>We served different customers from all over the world, and these are ready to share their testimonies.</p>

 </section>


 ...

</section>
```

After that, you should create the other pages and make sure that they are stored in the same folder as the index.html file. These pages are the about.html, services.html, location.html and contact.html.

For the purpose of ensuring that all pages look the same, use the same document structure for all pages and use the <header> and <footer> elements as the file index.html.

Your combined code should be as follows:

```
<!DOCTYPE html>
```

```
<html>

  <header>

<h1>

  <a href="index.html">My Website </a>

</h1>

  <nav>

    <a href="index.html">Home</a>

    <a href="about.html">About Us</a>

    <a href="services.html">Services</a>

    <a href="location.html">Location</a>

    <a href="contact.html">Contact Us</a>

  </nav>

  </header>

  <body>

    <section>

  <section>

   <a href="services.html">

    <h5>Services</h5>

    <h3>World-Class Services</h3>

   </a>
```

```
<p>We served different customers from all over the world, and these are ready to share their testimonies.</p>

...

</section>

<a href="contact.html">Contact us Now</a>

</section>

</body>

<footer>

<nav>

<a href="index.html">Home</a>

<a href="about.html">About Us</a>

<a href="services.html">Services</a>

<a href="location.html">Location</a>

<a href="contact.html">Contact Us</a>

</nav>

</footer>

</html>
```

It should return the following:

My Website

Home About Us Services Location Contact Us

Services

World-Class Services

We served different customers from all over the world, and these are ready to share their testimonies.

...
Contact us Now
Home About Us Services Location Contact Us

Chapter 2. HTML Styles

Text Style

T ext Style includes font-family, font-size, font-style, font-weight, font-variant.

Font	Value
font-family	Arial, Times New Roman, Courier New, Georgia, Verdana
font-size	9px, 10px......Large
font-style	normal, italic, oblique
font-weight	normal, bold, number
font-variant	normal, small-caps

Text Style can be specified by { property: value }.

Example 6.1

```
<html>

<style type = "text/css">

#f{ font-family: Times New Roman; font-size: 28px; font-style: italic; font-weight: bold; font-variant: normal }

</style>

<div id = "f">This is a text content using a different style.</div>

</html>
```

Output:

This is a text content using a different style.

Explanation:

"font-family, font-size, font-style, font-weight, font-variant." specifies the text style for the font.

Spacing

The line-height can specify line spacing.

The word-spacing can specify word spacing.

The letter-spacing can specify letter spacing.

Example 6.2

```html
<html>
<style type = "text/css">
#lineSpacing{ line-height:500% }
#wordSpacing{ word-spacing: 10px }
#letterSpacing{ letter-spacing: 5px }
</style>
<p id = "lineSpacing">Line Spacing Sample.</p>
<p id = "wordSpacing">Word Spacing Sample.</p>
<p id = "letterSpacing">Letter Spacing Sample.</p>
</html>
```

Output:

Line Spacing Sample.

Word   Spacing   Sample.

L e t t e r   S p a c i n g   S a m p l e .

Explanation:

"line-height:500%" specifies the line height as 500%.

"word-spacing: 10px" specifies the word spacing as 10px.

"letter-spacing: 5px" specifies the letter spacing as 5px.

Divided Style

The dividing <div></div> tags are used to group their content elements as blocks. <div> tags are useful for styling purposes.

```
<div class = "xxx"></div>

<div id = "xxx"></div>
```

The <div> tag can have id and class attribute in css style.

Example 6.3

<html>

<style type = "text/css">

```
.d1{font-style: italic; color: purple;}
```

```
#d2{font-family: arial black; color: blue;}
```

```
</style>
```

```
<body>
```

```
<div class = "d1"> <p>AAAAA</p> <p>BBBBB</p> <p>CCCCC</p>
```

```
</div>
```

```
<div id = "d2"> <p>EEEEE</p> <p>FFFFF</p> <p>GGGGG</p>
```

```
</div>
```

```
</body>
```

```
</html>
```

Output:

AAAAA

BBBBB

CCCCC

EEEEE

FFFFF

GGGGG

Explanation:

<div class = "d1"></div> is divided as the first group which contains three pairs of <p> tags. They use ".d1" style.

<div id = "d2"></div> is divided as the second group which contains other three pairs of <p> tags. They use "#d2" style.

Span Style

<span></span> can be used to group elements for styling purposes (using the class or id attributes).

<span class = "xxx"></span>

<span id = "xxx"></span>

The <span> tag can have id and class attribute in css style.

Example 6.4

<html>

<style type = "text/css">

div{background-color: yellow}

.d1{font-style: italic;color: purple;}

#d2{font-family: arial black;color: blue;}

</style>

<body>

<div><p>This is AAA text,

<span class = "d1">This is BBB text,</span>

This is CCC text,

<span id = "d2">This is DDD text,</span>

This is EEE text.</p></div>

```
</body>
```

```
</html>
```

Output:

This is AAA text, This is BBB text, This is CCC text, This is DDD text, This is EEE text.

Explanation:

The above uses <span></span> tags to set the css style of two pieces of text within a paragraph which is contained in a block.

<span> is very much like a <div> element, but <div> is a block-level element whereas a <span> is an inline element.

Border Style

```
border-style: value
```

"border-style: value" can set the border style by specifying different value. The "value" may be "solid, double, dashed, dotted, groove, ridge, inset, outset".

Example 6.5

```
<html>
```

```
<style type = "text/css">
```

```
#b1{border-style: solid; border-width: 10px;}
```

```
#b2{border-style: double; border-width: 10px;}
```

```
#b3{border-style: dashed; border-width: 10px;}
```

```
#b4{border-style: dotted; border-width: 10px;}
```

```
#b5{border-style: groove; border-width: 10px;}

#b6{border-style: ridge; border-width: 10px;}

#b7{border-style: inset; border-width: 10px;}

#b8{border-style: outset; border-width: 10px;}

</style>

<body>

<p id = "b1">This is solid border.</p><br>

<p id = "b2">This is double border.</p><br>

<p id = "b3">This is dashed border.</p><br>

<p id = "b4">This is dotted border.</p><br>

<p id = "b5">This is groove border.</p><br>

<p id = "b6">This is ridge border.</p><br>

<p id = "b7">This is inset border.</p><br>

<p id = "b8">This is outset border.</p><br>

</body>

</html>
```

Output:

This is solid border.

This is double border.

This is dashed border.

This is dotted border.

This is groove border.

This is ridge border.

This is inset border.

This is outset border.

Explanation:

The "border-style: value" may be "solid, double, dashed, dotted, groove, ridge, inset, outset".

The "border-width: 10px" specifies the border width as 10 px.

Border Color

border-color: value

"border-color: value" can set the bonder properties for color.

Example 6.6

<html>

<style type = "text/css">

#b5{border-style: groove;border-width: 20px; border-color:blue }

#b6{border-style: ridge;border-width: 20px; border-color:purple }

</style>

<p id = "b5">This is groove border.</p>

<p id = "b6">This is ridge border.</p>

</html>

Output:

This is groove border.

This is ridge border.

Explanation: "border-color: value" can set the bonder color.

Padding Style

The padding is the area around the text content in a content box. The padding width can be specified with a padding attribute.

```
padding: value
```

Example 6.7

<html>

<style type = "text/css">

#b1{border-style: solid; border-width: 5px; padding: 10px }

#b2{border-style: dotted; border-width: 5px; padding: 20px }

</style>

<p id = "b1">This padding is 10px.</p>

<p id = "b2">This padding is 20px.</p>

</html>

Output:

This padding is 10px.

This padding is 20px.

Explanation: "padding: value" can set the padding width.

Margin Style

The area around the border edges is called the margin..

The margin width can be specified with a margin attribute.

```
margin: value;
```

Example 6.8

<html>

<style type = "text/css">

#b1{border-style: solid; border-width: 5px; margin: 30px }

#b2{border-style: dotted; border-width: 5px; margin: 0px }

</style>

<p id = "b1">This margin is 30px.</p>

```
<p id = "b2">This margin is 0px.</p>
```

```
</html>
```

Output:

This margin is 30px.

This margin is 0px.

Explanation: "margin: value" can set the margin width.

Absolute Positioning

The content position can be specified by position attribute.

position: absolute; top: value; left: value;

"position: absolute" sets the precise location of the contents.

"top: value" sets the distance from the top edge of the window.

"left: value" sets the distance from the left edge of the window.

Example 6.9

```
<html>
```

```
<style type = "text/css">
```

```
#a1{ position:absolute; top: 0px; left: 30px }
```

```
#a2{ position:absolute; top: 30px; left: 60px }
```

`</style>`

`<p id = "a1">This is position1.</p>`

`<p id = "a2">This is position2.</p>`

`</html>`

Output:

This is position1.

This is position2.

Explanation: "position: absolute; top: value; left: value;" specifies the absolute distance from the browser window edge.

Relative Positioning

```
position: relative; top: percentage; left: percentage;
```

"position: relative" sets the relative location of the contents based on the browser window resolution or window size.

"top: percentage" sets the distance from the top edge of the window. "left: percentage" sets the distance from the left edge of the window.

Example 6.10

`<html>`

`<style type = "text/css">`

#r{ position:relative; top: 3%; left: 5% }

</style>

<p id = "r">This is the relative position.</p>

</html>

Output:

This is the relative position.

Explanation:

"position:relative; top: 3%; left: 5%" specifies the relative position based on the resolution or size of the browser window.

Html Symbols

In HTML documents, when you meet some special symbols such as &, <, >, and space, you need to use corresponding codes, & < >

Symbols	Source Codes
<	<
>	>
&	&
""	" "
©	©

®	&reg;
space	
!	&#33;
:	&#59;

Example 6.11

<html>

<body>

< Java in 8 Hours > & < Python in 8 Hours > are very books!

Copyright © 2016 by Ray Yao

All Rights Reserved!

</body>

</html>

Output:

< Java in 8 Hours > & < Python in 8 Hours > are very books!

Copyright © 2016 by Ray Yao   All Rights Reserved!

Explanation:

Symbols	Code
< >	< >

>	&gt;
&	&amp;
©	&copy;
space	
!	&#33;

Chapter 3. *Forms In HTML*

Web Forms Basics

Web pages are not just about reading documents and articles, but are also for social and business applications. You can hardly imagine any kind of web app without asking some data from users—just think about the most common functions, such as login and registration.

HTML forms are the part of the markup since the earliest versions, and now, after several twists—that are related to HTML-XHTML debates—we have a refined model of forms in HTML5, which still works with older browsers.

How Web Forms Work

This shows a web form in action, which contains user interface components—or, with another name, controls. Not only textboxes, checkboxes and radio buttons are controls in this form, but labels, and frames surrounding the sections, too, as well as the Register button.

A web form in action

To design and code web forms, you need to understand how they work. Here is a simplified overview:

When the browser displays a web form, it simply renders its controls just like any other element, such as text, menus, images, and so on. Users fill it out, and then click a button that submits the form. The submission of a form means that the browser collects the data entered by the user, puts it into an HTTP/HTTPS request, and sends it to the server. When the server side receives the request, the web server finds out the type of application or module to dispatch the request with the collected data. The entity receiving the request analyzes the information collected, and decides what to do next.

For example, if the request contains registration data, the web server may store it in the database and send back a message about the success of registration. Or, if the data is invalid, for example a mandatory field has not been filled out, the webserver might send back the original form with the data specified by the user, and with additional markup that summarizes the issues found by the server application.

So, this process contains these fundamental steps:

1. The browser collects the form data, and sends it to the web server.

2. The web server processes the data, and sends back the result to the browser.

3. The browser visualizes the result (which may be a web page, an error message, or some other kind of information, etc.)

Of course, the most difficult part of this process is step 2, which is carried out at the server side. There are many server technologies that can process web forms, but in this book we do not dive into them, we will only scratch the surface.

As the web evolved, and users expected fluent experience, new asynchronous technologies appeared, such as AJAX (Asynchronous JavaScript and XML). These do not expect the web server to retrieve a full web page, but only a part of the page—affected by the changes in regard to the information the users specified. This approach results in smaller network packages, and less flickering on the screen. The main virtue of the asynchronous technologies is that they can send data to—and retrieve data from—a server asynchronously in the background, without preventing user interaction.

In this chapter you will focus on building and using web forms at the client side.

Representing Web Forms in HTML

The key HTML element is <form> that defines a web form within a page. The simplest web form takes only a few lines of markup:

<form action="ProcessAtServer.html">

  <input type="submit" value="Do it!"/>

</form>

This <form> contains a single <input> tag that is decorated with the type="submit" attribute, and it represents a submit button. The action property of <form> is set to ProcessAtServer.htlm, so when the user clicks the submit button, the content of the form will be sent to that page. Of course, as shown in the figure below, this form does not have any other useful element, so actually there is no information to send to the action page.

A very simple and useless web form

So, let's create a form with a few real input fields:

<form action="#">

  <input name="fname" />

  <input name="lname" />

  <input type="submit" value="Do it!"/>

```
</form>
```

This markup contains two input fields, having the names fname (first name) and lname (last name), respectively. Their corresponding <input> tags are not decorated with the type attribute so that these fields will be rendered as text boxes. The action attribute of the form is set to #, which will send the form data to the page itself.

Let's assume, you've put this code into the form.html file. When you display it in the browser, you can type data into the text boxes, as shown in figure below.

A simple form with two input fields

When you click the submit button, the form sends the data to the form.html file through a web request. The page is displayed again, with empty input fields. Only the address bar of your browser tells you that the page is displayed as a result of web request from the form, its URL is something like this:

http://127.0.0.1:8080/?fname=John&lname=Smith#

In the URL you can see the form data as ?fname=John&lname=Smith, indicating that this information was passed through the URL.

Controls Overview

In these small markup snippets above you've already seen a few controls, such as the textbox and the submit button, but there are much more. You will learn to use them through exercises, but first you'll be given a short overview of them.

So, as you already know, <form> is the markup element that encapsulates all controls. Most controls can be rendered with the <input> element that has a type attribute. This attribute specifies the type of the control, it determines how the control is rendered in the browser, and how it behaves. If you do not specify type, the control will be a textbox (and this is the same as setting type to text). You can choose from several kind of buttons, such as button (clickable button mostly used with JavaScript), checkbox, radio (radio button), submit (submits the form), image (an image as the submit button), and reset (resets all form values to their defaults).

There are several predefined textual controls with some extra semantics, such as password (characters are masked), email (defines a field for an email address), url (field for entering an URL), tel (field for a telephone number), search (field for search text), and number (field for entering a number). The type file provides a file-select field with a Browse button for file uploads. You can place hidden fields in a form, used to set form values programmatically.

HTML5 adds a number of date and time related controls to the old markup through the type attribute of <input>: date (date control with year, month, day, and no time), datetime (date and time control with the precision of fraction of a second, based on UTC time zone), datetime-local (date and time control with no time zone), month (a month and year control), time (a control for entering time, no time zone), and week (a week and year control, not time zone).

NOTE: Using date and time related controls on your web pages means you're walking on thin ice. These controls are relatively new, and—as of this writing—in most browsers they are rendered only as text boxes, and not as nice date and time pickup controls.

HTML5 also adds two other types, color (color picker), and range (a kind of slider to choose a number in a specified range).

Beside <input> there are a few other HTML tags to allow specifying user data. With <select>, you can define a dropdown list with option values. To type in longer text, use the <textarea> element.

The <fieldset> element lets you group related controls into sections, the <legend> element adds a caption to a <fieldset> element.

Input fields do not tell anything about their role to users. You can use the <label> element to provide appellation to input controls. Besides adding a descriptive text, <label> element provides an improvement for people who uses mouse, because when the user clicks on the text within <label>, it allows it for control (for example a check box, or radio button), or moves the focus to the related input field.

Used with the button, submit or reset types, <input> elements are rendered as pushbuttons. With the <button> element you can create clickable buttons with the same behavior, but you can create compound button content instead of a simple text.

Chapter 4. *Frames, Colors, And Layout Of HTML*

HTML Frame

F rames used to decrease day by day. At the present time the frame is not useless, because it is quite hard to print finished pages using frames together. Apart from it, many dislike it. Instead, CSS is now used to divide a page into more than one section. But there is a need to have some idea about frames to enrich the knowledge base of HTML.

Example Programs

```
<html>

<head>

<title> www.lifeguruji.tk </title>

</head>

<body bgcolor ="#00cc99">

<frameset rows ="12%,88%">

<frame src = "style.html" scrolling ="no">

<frameset cols ="27%,74%">

<frame src ="link.html">

<frame src ="textfor.html">

</frameset>

</frameset>

</body>
```

```
</html>
```

Create a folder with any file name and put it in style.html, link.html and textfor.html three html files. Open a Notepad and enter the code above and click on Save as the File menu, save as file name: index.html, Save as type: All files, open the index.html file using Mozilla Firefox or Google Chrome, and check how it's look...

Discuss the program

First, frameset rows = "12%, 88%"> is divided into two parts along the row on the entire page.

Through the frameset cols = "27%, 74%"> the bottom row is divided into two sections along the column.

<frame src = "style.html" scrolling = "no"> The style.html page is displayed in the first frame.

<frame src = "link.html"> and <frame src = "textfor.html"> Arrangements are made to display links.html and textfor.html pages in the 1st and 2nd frame respectively.

Eye Frames

Eye frames are one of the main ways to display one or more web pages on a web page. It is important to publish a link to different web pages on topics relevant to the presentation, as well as it is not bad if it can be scrolled in the short space.

Example Programs

```
<html>

<head>

<title> www.lifeguruji.tk</title>

</head>

<body bgcolor=" #f00">

<center>
```

```
<h2 style="color:#f00">This is an example of iframe.</h2><br/>

<iframe src="http://www.lifeguruji.tk/bangla/html/" width="350" height="170">

<p>This browser does not support iframes.</p>

</iframe>

</center>

</body>

</html>
```

Open a Notepad and enter the code above and click on Save as from the File menu, save as file name: index.html, Save as type: All files, open the index.html file using Mozilla Firefox or Google Chrome, and check how it's look.

Sorry I don't have internet at the moment....

Program discussion

<Iframe> </iframe> tags are used to create eyebrows.

width = "350" height = "170" These two attributes indicate the size of the I frame.

If a browser does not support the I frame, then this page does not support iframes. <P> This browser does not support iframes. </P> The text will be displayed.

Colors And Codes

The use of colors on web pages is very important. A web page is composed of one or more paragraphs, titles, tables, borders, borders, etc. Each of these elements has to use some colors. To specify the background color of a particular page, after writing body in the <body> tag, bgcolor = "" should be written with a space followed by black, silver, gray, white, marrow, red, purple, fuchsia, green, lime, OLIVE, YELLOW, NAVY, BLUE, TEAL, and AQUA, any one of these sixteen colors will be visible in the page's background. Since case is not sensitive, there is no problem writing in lower case, as written, <body bgcolor = "green">.

Apart from the hexadecimal code, the background color can also be selected. For example, the above code can be written as: <body bgcolor = "# 00FF00">

The color piker can easily be collected for different color hexadecimal codes. Apart from the chart below, you can also do the job. The hexadecimal code has to start with a # symbol at the beginning of the code.

There is another interesting method to give a background color. These three colors are red, green and blue, and all the other colors are composed of these three colors. If you combine these three colors and create new colors, then it is not bad. To accomplish this task, the green background can be written as follows

<body bgcolor = "rgb (0,255,0)">.

Here rgb stands for red green blue (0, 255,0), meaning that the colors of red, green, blue, respectively, are 0%, 100%, 0% because of the pure green color here. And any color value can be up to 0-255. Since the value of g or green is 255 so that is 100%. By changing the color of the three colors to 0-255, you can create new colors as desired.

Example Programs

```
<html>

<head>

<title> www.lifeguruji.tk</title>

</head>

<body bgcolor="green">

<h2 style=" color:#ff0000" >

This is the body of your web site.

</h2>

<p style="color:#093">

This is a paragraph.<br/>

This is a paragraph. <br/>

This is a paragraph.<br/>

This is a paragraph.<br/>

</p>

</body>

</html>
```

Open a Notepad and enter the code above and click on Save as from the File menu, save as file name: index.html, Save as type: All files, open the index.html file using Mozilla Firefox or Google Chrome, and check how it's look...

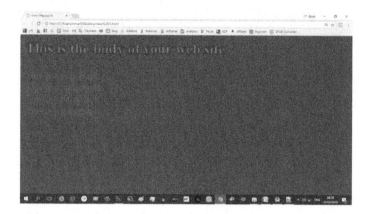

Layout

On the page layout, depending on how good a webpage should be. Previously all web site layouts were made using HTML only. Currently CSS is used with HTML. Rows and columns of <table> are used to create layouts using HTML only.

Example Programs

<html>

<head>

<title> www.lifeguruji.tk</title>

</head>

<body bgcolor="green">

<table width="400" border="0">

<tr>

<td colspan="3" style="background-color: #93C;">

<h1> Web Page header</h1>

```
</td>

</tr>

<tr valign="top">

<td style="background-color: #C99;width:100px;text-align:top;">

<p><b>Side bar</b><br />

<a href="#">PHP</a>

<br />

<a href="#">HTML</a>

<br />

<a href="#">CSS</a>

<a href="#">Wordpress</a>

</p></td>

<td      style="background-color:#EEEEEE;height:200px;width:400px;text-align:top;"><h2
style="color:#900">This is heading.</h2>

<p style="color: #006">This is a paragraph.This is a paragraph. This is a paragraph.<br />

This is a paragraph.This is a paragraph. This is a paragraph.<br />

This is a paragraph.This is a paragraph.This is a paragraph.<br />

This is a paragraph.This is a paragraph.This is a paragraph.</p></td>

</tr>

<tr>

<td colspan="2" style="background-color:#999;text-align:center;">
```

Copyright © 2018 by Omar Faruq</td>

</tr>

</table>

</body>

</html>

Open a Notepad and enter the code above and click on Save as from the File menu, save as file name: index.html, Save as type: All files, open the index.html file using Mozilla Firefox or Google Chrome, and check how it's look...

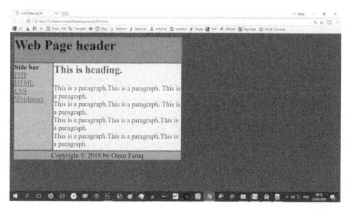

Chapter 5. *How to Put Images in HTML?*

There is a famous quotation that "picture says a thousand words". Quotation shows how powerful pictures are in terms of delivering a message. Web sites show pictures to make web pages more exciting, optical and lively.

How do we show image or picture on any web page?

Examples of Images

Let's see an example of picture on web page. Please go to the following page in Wikipedia https://en.wikipedia.org/wiki/Albert_Einstein . You see images as shown below:

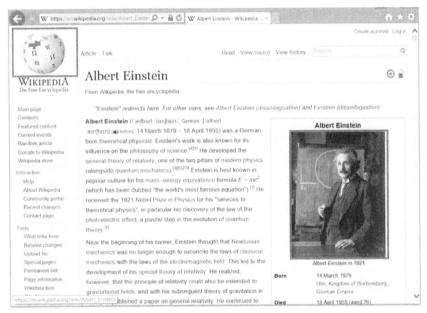

Images

Example

You can see that I have marked two images – one is of Albert Einstein and other is of Wikipedia Logo. Don't you agree that these images have made this page lively? Images on the web page can be used in two ways:

ü☐ One way is just show image. Just show; nothing else.

ü☐ Other way is to use image as hyperlink. It means when you click on the image, it will take you to some other page. How interesting!

Learning The Details

How do we show image on web page? We use <img> tag for this purpose. Please check the example below:

<img src="location of the image" alt="alternate text" width="width in pixel" height="height in pixel"></img>

We start <img> tag and then we close with </img> tag like we do for any HTML tag. But then we use various other attributes to make sure image is shown on the web page. Let's look into these attributes in the table below.

Table 6.1: Attributes of the <img> tag

<img> tag attribute   Purpose

src   src stands for source. Like hyperlink, you enter address of the image for this attribute. Address is the location where this image has been stored.

The address could be internet based image. It means image is stored at internet somewhere like any web page. Example is Albert Einstein image stored at Wikipedia. Address is:

https://upload.wikimedia.org/wikipedia/commons/thumb/3/3e/Einstein_19
21_by_F_Schmutzer_---_restoration.jpg/220px---

Einstein_1921_by_F_Schmutzer_---_restoration.jpg

Or it could an address from your computer/laptop hard disk. It means the image is stored somewhere in your local computer hard disk. You provide folder location of the image. Example is --- "file://C:/

Books\HTMLforKids/mybook.jpg"

You can use most types of images such as jpg, jpeg, png, gif and bmp.

alt alt stands for alternate text. This is the text shown on web page if image could not be shown on web page due to some reason. It is like a backup plan. You want to show some text in case image could not be shown due to some problem.

width This tells the width of the image. If you don't provide this value, then it will show image in its original width.

Width is measured in pixel. One pixel is like a dot on the screen. Just like you measure distance in meter or centimeter; in the same way you measure length of the image in pixel.

height Tells the height of the image. Similar to width, it is also measured in pixel.

If you don't provide this value, then it will show image in its original height.

Let me show you image in HTML. I am going to use Albert Einstein image address given in the table above and will show that in my HTML page. I will make height 200 pixel and width also 200 pixels; like square. The HTML looks like following:

<html>

<head>

<title></title>

</head>

<body>

<h2>Albert Einstein</h2>

<img

src="https://upload.wikimedia.org/wikipedia/commons/thumb/3/3e/Einstein_1921_
by_F_Schmu   tzer_-_restoration.jpg/220px-
Einstein_1921_by_F_Schmutzer__restoration.jpg"   alt="Albert   Einstein"   width="200"
height="200"></img>

</body> </html>

The HTML page will be displayed as shown below.

Albert Einstein

Web Page Display

You see it shows image in the square size (200 x 200) as I have mentioned in <img
> tag attribute.

What will happen if some problem comes with image? For example, you give wrong address
to image. I suggest you try it yourself.

You observed it right. It is showing Alternate Text as defined in <img> tag attribute in place of the image.

Let's move next! What about using image as hyperlink? Sounds great! Right? Following is the structure of hyperlink tag:

<a href="Address of web page"> text of hyperlink </a>

To make image as hyperlink, you will replace text of hyperlink with <img> tag. For example, if I want to make image of Albert Einstein hyperlink which will take me to Wikipedia page, then my HTML <a> tag will look like the following:

<a href=" https://en.wikipedia.org/wiki/Albert_Einstein"> <img

src="https://upload.wikimedia.org/wikipedia/commons/thumb/3/3e/Einstein_1921_by_F_Schmu

tzer_-_restoration.jpg/220px-Einstein_1921_by_F_Schmutzer_-_restoration.jpg"
alt="Albert Einstein" width="200" height="200"></img> </a>

Is this not simple and intuitive? I am sure you will agree with me.

Chapter 6. HTML Tables

T ables are very useful to represent the data in grid format. The data is divided into rows and columns. It helps us to understand the data on two axes. Each block in the table is called as table cell. Let's take a look at how table is created in the HTML.

Table Creation

<table> element is used to create a table. The contents of the table are written out row by row. <tr> element is used to represent a start of each row. <tr> means table row. Each cell of the table is represented using a <td> element. A table row can also be divided into table headings with the <the> tag. Let's take a closer look at table creation with an example

<!DOCTYPE html>

<html>

<body>

<table>

<tr>

<td>A</td>

<td>X</td>

<td>1</td>

</tr>

<tr>

<td>B</td>

<td>Y</td>

```
<td>2</td>

</tr>

<tr>

<td>C</td>

<td>Z</td>

<td>3</td>

</tr>

</table>

</body>

</html>
```

Table looks good with borders. We will learn how to draw borders around the tables using CSS.

Table Headings

The heading for either a row or column is represented using <th> element. <th> means table heading. Foe an empty cell you should use <td> or <th> element otherwise the table will not be created correctly. The scope attribute can be used on the <th> element to indicate whether it is row or column. It takes the values, row to indicate heading for a row or col to indicate heading for a column. The contents of <th> element is displayed in the bold and centered way. Table can also be given caption using <caption> tag.

<!DOCTYPE html>

<html>

```
<body>

<table>

<caption><b>Ticket Sales</b></caption>

<tr>

<th></th>

<th scope="col">Saturday</th>

<th scope="col">Sunday</th>

</tr>

<tr>

<th scope="row">Tickets Sold</th>

<td>50</td>

<td>20</td>

</tr>

<tr>

<th scope="row">Total Sale</th>

<td>100</td>

<td>150</td>

</tr>

</body>

</html>
```

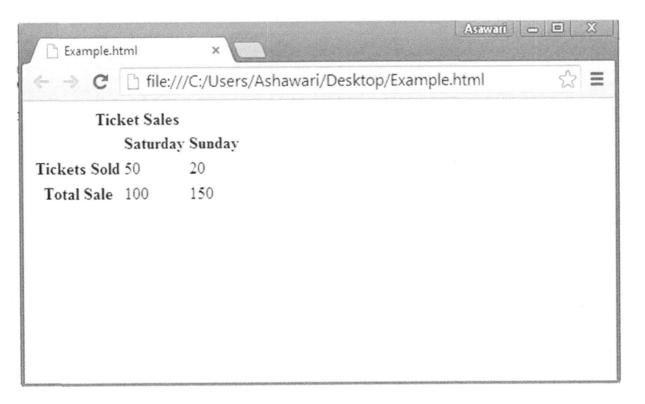

Spanning Columns

Sometimes you may need the entries in the table to stretch across many columns. For this purpose, colspan attribute is used. It indicates how many columns cell should run across.

<!DOCTYPE html>

<html>

<head>

<style>

table, th, td {

border: 1px solid black;

```
border-collapse: collapse;

}

th, td {

padding: 5px;

text-align: left;

}

</style>

</head>

<body>

<h2>Cell that spans two columns:</h2>

<table style="width:100%">

<tr>

<th>Name</th>

<th colspan="2">Telephone</th>

</tr>

<tr>

<td>Mr ABC</td>

<td>666 77 854</td>

<td>888 77 855</td>

</tr>

</table>
```

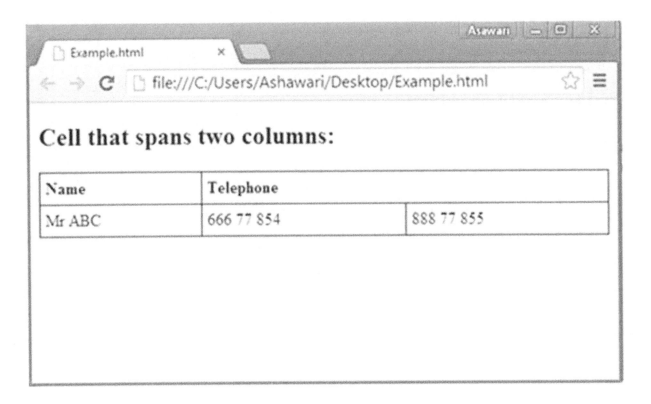

Spanning Rows

In order to span a cell more than one row, you can use the rowspan attribute. Check example below.

<html>

<head>

<style>

table, th, td {

border: 1px solid black;

border-collapse: collapse;

```
}

th, td {

padding: 5px;

text-align: left;

}

</style>

</head>

<body>

<h2>Cell that spans two rows:</h2>

<table style="width:100%">

<tr>

<th>Name:</th>

<td>Mr XYZ</td>

</tr>

<tr>

<th rowspan="2">Telephone:</th>

<td>222 77 854</td>

</tr>

<tr>

<td>888 77 855</td>

</tr>
```

</table>

</body>

</html>

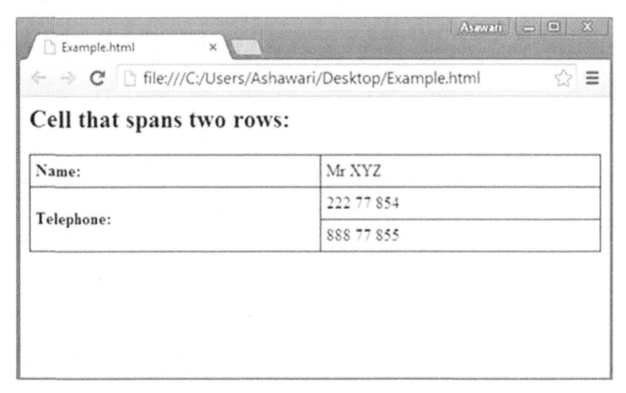

There is lot of code in HTML for formatting the table. But now we can use CSS for better formatting. Hence, details about table formatting in HTML have been omitted.

Chapter 7. Fundamentals Of CSS

W eb page development used to be relatively simple. Developers simply write a Web page in HTML that can be accessed by other similar computers. But times are changing in two ways. First, Web sites are becoming vastly more complex, often with hundreds if not thousands of Web pages, dynamic HTML that adjusts to different users, and greater demands from the customer base. Writing a page at a time can be a nightmare for developers, a problem for maintenance, and can cause inconsistencies across pages within a Web site that annoy the customers or viewer.

Second, Web pages used to be accessed by a computer with a monitor, or even a laptop with a reasonable viewing area. Now we access Web pages with tablets, small web books, phones, and even black and white eBook readers (like that Amazon Kindle, pre-Fire). Viewers using non-computer devices can get very frustrated as the viewing area exceeds the screen by several thousand percent, or keystrokes are required, or data entry exists with no easy way to enter the data. There is a wide diversity of browsers on the market now, but often, Web developers insist on developing for the 1024 x 768 pixel (or larger) computer monitor.

Web developer or managers should try to make their Web pages as universally accessible and available to their viewers or client base as possible, including those who want to view content on a smaller device. This can be done with newer technology, newer formatting, and newer Web page validation that have not been available for that long.

Previous versions of HTML (versions 3.2 and before) make use of the<font> tag and background tags for every HTML element, so that a table at the top of the page could (and often did) have different formatting than a table at the bottom of the page. The result was that many Web pages had vastly different appearances in HTML 3.2. Studies showed that this annoyed the users. A user who was used to one page would click on a link and be exposed to a whole new page, with new formatting, new form and table colors, and an overall new look. HTML 4.0 attempted to change this, by standardizing the look of every page, often through the use of a Cascading Style Sheet (also known as a CSS). The conceptual difference between HTML 3.2 (and before) and HTML 4.0 (and beyond).

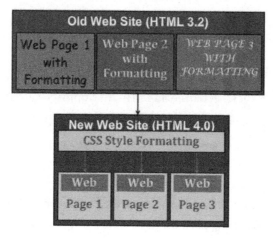

Conceptual Changes in Html 4.0

This shows how we can manage the formatting of a page from a single CSS. By using a single CSS linked to every page on your site, you not only streamline the look of your Web page across your site, but you also streamline maintenance and development costs by defining the formatting of page elements (like tables, text, and lists) only once.

Html Styles

The ways of formatting Web pages that were accepted in the 1990s and early 2000s have fallen out of favor.

Implementing styles requires some changes to your HTML. To make formatting consistent, you now use a style attribute to determine how something should look. This caused a change in the HTML language. Older tags, like the <font> tag, and older attributes, like bgcolor or border that used to control the appearance of HTML elements are now considered deprecated, or obsolete. The format for the style attribute is as follows:

```
<tagname style="          attribute1: value1;

                          attribute2: value2;

                          attribute3: value3;">
```

You can usually apply a style attribute to almost any HTML tag (like<li>,<td>,<p>, etc.). However, if you are just typing, and you want to change the font, color, etc., of the next paragraph or the rest of the sentence, you can use either a <div> or a <span> tag. A <div> tag returns to the next line before going any further. A <span> tag keeps you on the same line, and allows you to make a single line have different fonts, colors, etc. For example, the following <div> tag shows how to display text in red:

```
<div style="color: Red;">

    This text will be red

</div>
```

Fonts

Fonts are great for giving your page a crisp look that differs from the default font. The style attribute (or the <font> tag on older, pre-4.0 Web pages) is used to control the font displayed on your HTML page. Table 1 shows some things you can do with the style attribute and most tags, or use the <span> tag or the <div> tag (or the <font> tag, if you must).

	Current/Strict (New Way -- HTML 4.0)	Deprecated/Transitional (Old Way -- HTML 3.2)	Example
Change the Font (Font Family)	`<div style="font-family: Comic Sans MS, Arial, Helvetica;">` Browser will try Comic Sans MS first, then Arial, then Helvetica `</div>`	`<font face="Comic Sans MS, arial,helvetica">` Browser will try Comic Sans MS first, then Arial, then Helvetica `</font>`	Browser will try Comic Sans MS first, then Arial, then Helvetica
Set Font Size (Absolute)	`<span style="font-size: 18pt;">` define the font size `</span>`	`<font size="5">` define the font size `</font>`	define the font size
Increase Font Size (Relative)	`<td style="font-size: 2em;">` increase the size of the text `</td>`	`<font size="+3">` increase the size of the text `</font>`	increase the size of the text
Decrease Font Size (Relative)	`<span style="font-size: .6em;">` decrease the size of the text `</span>`	`<font size="-2">` decrease the size of the text `</font>`	decrease the size of the text

Table 1. Setting Fonts

pt vs. px vs. em

When you are specifying font size, you can specify the size in one of three ways:

- pt gives you the absolute point size which is defined by the user's client machine.

- px gives you the absolute pixel height, which is independent of machine (but can shrink with lower resolution and grow with higher resolution). This often used for setting borders and margins.

- em gives you the relative height, which is gives the height as the number of times the current height. This is a relative measure, depending on the current size.

You choose what you need.

Colors

Colors on computer monitors are defined by light, not pigment, so the primary colors are red, green, and blue. Also unlike pigments, combining all the colors of light results in a white light, whereas removing all the colors of light results in a black color. Figure below shows how the primary colors mix, and how that mixture looks, at a very high level.

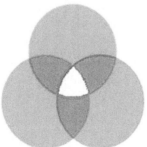

Figure2 – Red,Green,BlueColor

Colors are specified one of two ways. First, you can use an actual color (red, blue, purple, etc.) Second, you can use a RGB (red, green blue) representation of the color by providing the red component, the green component, and the blue component, each a number from 0 (hexadecimal #00 – black) to 255 (hexadecimal #ff – bright). For example, to get this color of purple, you specify <span style="color: #880088">. You can also use decimal with an RGB function, like <span style="color: rgb(133, 0, 133)">.

As with fonts, colors can be controlled using the <font> tag, but newer standards suggest using a style attribute, possibly in conjunction with a <span> or <div> tag. Table 6 shows the HTML for some color manipulation.

	Current/Strict (New Way -- HTML 4.0)	Deprecated/Transitional (Old Way -- HTML 3.2)	Example
Set the Color	<span style="color: red"> Change text color to red </span>	<font color="red"> Change text color to red </font>	Change text color to red
Set the Background	<td style="background: rgb(221, 153, 221)"> Change background to whatever color this is using RGB </td>	<td bgcolor="#dd99dd"> Change background to whatever color this is using Hex </td>	Change background to whatever color this is using RGB

Table 2. *Using Colors*

Alignment and Borders

You can use styles to control borders or to align images or text. The use of the float attribute can also make text float to the left or right with other text wrapping around the floating object. Table 7 shows some use of alignment.

	Current/Strict (New Way -- HTML 4.0)	Deprecated/Transitional (Old Way -- HTML 3.2)	Example

Align Text to the Right	`<td style="text-align: right">` 929 `<div style="text-decoration: underline">` + 84 `</div>` 1013 `</td>`	`<td align="right">` 929 ` <u>+ 84</u>` ` 1013` `</td>`	929 + 84 1013
Center Text	`<div style="text-align: center">` Centered ` ` Text `</div>`	`<center>` Centered ` ` Text `</center>`	Centered Text

Vertically Align Text (Top, Middle, Bottom)	`<td style="vertical-align: top">`
	
	vertical top
	
	`</td>`
		`<td valign="top"">`
		
		vertical top
		
		`</td>`
			Vertical top

Center a Table	`<table style="margin-left:auto; margin-right:auto">`
	
	`<tr>`
	
	`<th>head 1</th>`
	
	`<th>head 2</th>`
	
	`</tr>`
	
	`<tr>`
	
	`<td>cell 1</td>`
	
	`<td>cell 2</td>`
	
	`</tr>`
	
	`</table>`
		`<table align="center">`
		
		`<tr>`
		
		`<th>head 1</th>`
		
		`<th>head 2</th>`
		
		`</tr>`
		
		`<tr>`
		
		`<td>cell 1</td>`
		
		`<td>cell 2</td>`
		
		`</tr>`
		
		`</table>`
			head 1 head 2 / cell 1 cell 2

Place Border on Text (or anything else)	`<div`
	
	`style="border-width: 5px;`
	
	`border-style: outset;`
	
	`border-color: blue;`
	
	`text-align: center">`
	
	`Text with border`
	
	`</div>`
		{Cannot be done without a single-cell table}	Text with border

Table 3a. Alignment and Borders

(continued …)

	Current/Strict (New Way -- HTML 4.0)	Deprecated/Transitional (Old Way -- HTML 3.2)	Example

Place Border on Table	`<table`
	
	`style="border-width: 1px;`
	
	`border-style: outset;">`
	
	`<tr>`
	
	`<td`
	
	`style="border-width: 1px;`
	
	`border-style: inset;">`
	
	`cell 1`
	
	`</td>`
	
	`<td`
	
	`style="border-width: 1px;`
	
	`border-style: inset;">`
	
	`cell 2`
	
	`</td>`
	
	`</tr>`
	
	`<tr>`
	
	`<td`
	
	`style="border-width: 1px;`
	
	`border-style: inset;">`
	
	`cell 3`
		`<table border="1">`
		
		`<tr>`
		
		`<td>cell 1</td>`
		
		`<td>cell 2</td>`
		
		`</tr>`
		
		`<tr>`
		
		`<td>cell 3</td>`
		
		`<td>cell 4</td>`
		
		`</tr>`
		
		`</table>`
			
			<table><tr><td>cell 1</td><td>cell 2</td></tr><tr><td>cell 3</td><td>cell 4</td></tr></table>

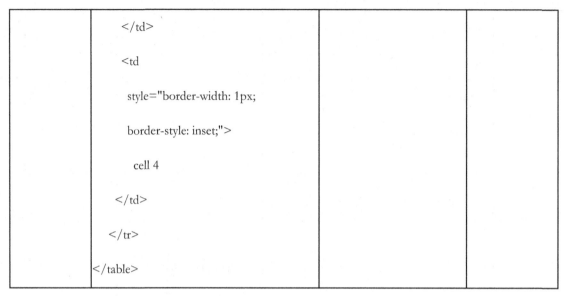

```
        </td>

        <td

          style="border-width: 1px;

          border-style: inset;">

          cell 4

        </td>

      </tr>

</table>
```

Table 3b. *Alignment and Borders (continued)*

Chapter 8. <u>CSS</u>

A style sheet is a type of document that contains formatting rules. A Web browser will simply read these rules and apply the formatting to your page. Using style sheets allows you to control page elements such as borders, colors, and margins, and even to embed fonts that aren't available locally on your computer.

Style sheets are officially known as CSS (for Cascading Style Sheets). CSS is a separate language with its own syntax, but don't let that frighten you. This language was specifically developed for formatting Web pages. It's so powerful that with a single command you can alter the appearance of a Web page.

You should always put your CSS rules into a separate file instead of embedding them directly into your Web page. The reason we do this is that it separates HTML code from your CSS rules and makes updating code much easier in the long run.

Before the introduction of CSS, Web designers looked for other ways to change the layouts on their Web pages. One such way was using table tags--a separate set of HTML tags that are used to make tables, table headers, table row, and so forth. But table tags were often misused. Instead of adding structure to a page, they were often being used to layout Web pages. And back before CSS, making changes to a large Web site with table tags or other formats was just difficult, time consuming and expensive, because you had to edit each page of a site individually.

CSS was specifically developed to eliminate the difficulties, expense, and time involved in using table tags. Just by editing a single CSS file you can instantly make changes to a large and complex Web site. For example, you can create a CSS rule to format font sizes, and every page on your Web site will then be updated to reflect those specific changes.

Your First Style Sheet

Now we should put all of the things we've learned together and create your first CSS (Cascading Style Sheet).

If you're familiar with Web and have visited many Web sites, you'll know that your browser displays text links in blue and with an underline. (This is the browser's default (automatic) format display for text links.) But what if the blue links are at odds with the general look and feel of your own Web page?

You can build a style sheet rule that will change the text color of the link on your Web page. To do this, you simply have to use a CSS style attribute and declare it within an HTML element. Here is an example:

```
<a href="#" style:"color: red;"> Click Here </a>
```

A style attribute is made up of two parts: a property name and a value. Here is the format every attribute follows and how it looks as code:

```
<style: property; name: value;>
```

In this example, the property specifies the type of formatting that is applied to your HTML element. Here "color" is the property, which sets the color of the anchor link. The value is the actual name of the color – "red. In another example of a CSS style attribute, the property name might be "font" and the value could be the "size" of font.

This CSS rule is commonly known as a statement. A statement is simply a piece of code; here, all it does is specifying the style property as color and make the anchor link ("Click Here") red (the color "value").

Create a new document in Sublime Text 2 by selecting File | New. Now type this code exactly as you see here:

```
<!doctype html>

 <html>

<head>

 <title> My First Style Sheet </title>
```

```
<meta charset="UTF-8" />

</head>

<body>

<p> <a href="#" style="color:red; text-decoration:none;">

Click Here </a> </p>

</body>

</html>
```

Once you've done this, save your file with the name colors.html in your HTML folder on your desktop. Now preview your file in your Web browser to check your work.

To remove the standard underlined text from your anchor link, use the text-decoration attribute and the value none (see example above, after color: red). The text-decoration is used to set the appearance of text – you can remove underlines, underline standard text, add a line above or through the middle of text and make the text blink.

The text-decoration attribute has the following possible values: underline, line-through, over line, none and blink. Here is an example of code for text decoration that makes the text blink:

text-decoration: blink;

Open up the Web page we've just been working on called colors.html and add the other values to the text-decoration attribute. Preview the file in your Web browser to see how your work is displayed.

```
<p> <a href="#" style="color:red; text-decoration:blink;">

Click Here </a> </p>
```

Try experimenting yourself by adding the values: underline, line-through and over line to the text-decoration attribute and see what happens.

Inline Styles

Inline styles allow you to insert a property name and value of a style sheet right into an HTML tag. But you should try to avoid using this approach if you can. As Inline styles mix formatting with HTML markup, and it becomes difficult to make changes to your Web page: every style on a page must be hunted down in the source code – as you'll soon see.

So here is our earlier example used to format an anchored link:

<a href="#" style="color:red; text-decoration:none;"> Click Here </a>

The rule above removes the default underline of the anchored link and makes the text color red. Inline style may seem much easier to use – it's straightforward, and you can apply it wherever you want on a page. But if you format a page like this it can get quite messy and confusing. You'll soon realize why Web designers tend not to use this technique. Adding inline style to each and every HTML tag on your Web page not only makes the code difficult to read, but it is almost impossible to separate the presentation formatting (style sheets) from the actual HTML. For example, let's consider our earlier example but with several inline style rules added to the tag:

<a href="#" style="color:red; text-decoration:none; border-style: solid; border-color:blue; text-align: left; font-size: 16"> Click Here </a>

See how the anchor tag is already becoming a bit disorderly and chaotic. It's quite difficult to separate content ("Click Here") from the presentation formatting in the example above. So as good practice, HTML markup should always be in a separate, presentation-free document. If you can, try to avoid using inline styles entirely.

The Anatomy of A CSS Rule

A style sheet is made up of rules. A rule is a formatting instruction that tells the Web browser to apply specific styles to your Web page.

Here is an example of a CSS rule that sets the color of a <p> paragraph element to red:

p { color:red;}

The CSS rule is then applied to our <p> paragraph element in the HTML document like this:

</p>

This shows an example of this paragraph style in action in a standard Web browser.

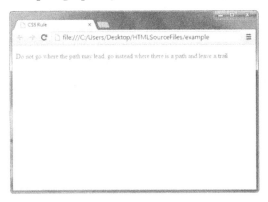

A css rule applied to the paragraph element

If you open up a style sheet to view the code in your browser, you'll see that CSS rules don't have any resemblance to HTML markup. Every CSS rule is basically made up of three things: selectors, properties and values. Ordinarily the property and value is always terminated by a semicolon(;).

Here is the format every CSS rule follows:

Selector {property: value;}

And here is what each part of the CSS rule actually means:

- The selector is an HTML element that you want to apply formatting to. For example, the (<p>) paragraph tag can be used as a selector. A Web browser will then look for all the common elements in your Web page that match the selector and apply the code within the curly braces to your elements.

- The property simply identifies the type of formatting you want to apply to your HTML element. So here you can choose from colors, fonts, sizes and so forth.
- The value sets a value for the property. For example, if the property is color, then the value could be green or light blue.

Selectors, properties and values are essentially the basic building blocks of CSS rules. Once you begin to understand these, you're well on your way to becoming a style sheet guru.

Creating an External Style Sheet

a {

color:red; text-decoration: none;

}

h1 {

font-family: arial, sans-serif

}

Before you go any farther, save your file with the name style.css in your main HTML folder on your desktop. A style sheet can have whatever name you want but must always use the file name extension .css. Remember, always save the style sheet in the same folder as your HTML pages, otherwise your page will not display the formatting.

Instead of embedding a style sheet directly into an HTML tag, you will be adding a link to the external .css style sheet from within the <head> portion of your document.

In the colors.html file, simply remove the inline style that was added to the anchor link previously. For comparison purposes, below are the old colors.html file with inline style and new colors.html file without inline style:

COLORS.HTML FILE WITH INLINE STYLE –

<!doctype html>

```html
<html>
<head>
<title> My First Style Sheet </title>
<meta charset="UTF-8" />
</head>
<body>
<h1> My First Style Sheet </h1>
<p> <a href="#" style="color:red; text-decoration:none;">
Click Here </a> </p>
</body>
</html>
```

COLORS.HTML FILE WITHOUT INLINE STYLE –

```html
<!doctype html>
<html>
<head>
<title> My First Style Sheet </title>
<meta charset="UTF-8" />
</head>
<body>
<h1> My First Style Sheet </h1>
<p> <a href="#"> Click Here </a> </p>
```

```
</body>

</html>
```

View the file in your web browser after you save it to check your work. You will see that the formatting rules in the style sheet has not yet been applied to your Web page. This is because we haven't told the browser to point (link) to the style sheet.

You have to add the <link> element to the <head> portion in your HTML document in order to do this. The <link> element simply points the browser to the external style sheet and the browser will then apply the style sheet's formatting rules to your page.

Here is the <link> element added to the <head> portion of our page:

```
<!doctype html>

<html>

<head>

<title> My First Style Sheet </title>

<link rel="stylesheet" href="style.css" />

<meta charset="UTF-8" />

</head>

<body>

<h1> My First Style Sheet </h1>

<p> <a href="#"> Click Here </a> </p>

</body>

</html>
```

The <link> element has two parts to it. The rel attribute simply defines the relationship between the current page and the linked document. In actual fact, you are telling the Web browser it's a style sheet.

The href attribute (href stands for hypertext reference) points to the actual location of the external style sheet. When you're linking to a style sheet the rel attribute should always be a style sheet.

Save the file and then open it in your Web browser to see your work. Congratulations! You've just created your first external style sheet.

Chapter 9. *CSS Links, Tables, And Forms*

Y ou can use a lot of other CSS properties to work with links and tables. You will learn how you can add color to each column of the chart to make it stands but of the rest. Similarly, you will also learn how to beautify the forms such as submissions forms, survey forms and any other form that you have created in HTML.

You will be able to create beautiful buttons that can be integrated into the forms. Each code example also contains the displayed results of the code. You can take up the code, recreate it, modify or run it to see how it works. Even simply reading it will give you a general idea of how you have to proceed.

```
<html>

<head>

<style>

a {

color: green;

}

</style>

</head>

<body>

<h1> Let me tell you a story.</h1>

<h2><b><a href="default.asp" target="_blank">Watch the video story here.</a></b></h2>
```

```
<p> Once, there was an eagle that flew high in the skies,

<br> touching upon the tip of the mountains.

<br> One day she found a ring, stuck in the branch of an apple tree. </p>

<p>She took it and flew to her nest. While playing with it, she got her head stuck in it.

<br>She didn't panic or hit her head on the stump of a tree to get rid of it.

<br>One day she drenched her head in oil and the ring came off of her neck.</p>

</body>

</html>
```

The result of the above style is as under. You can see the second line of code which has got a link hidden inside.

Let me tell you a story.

Watch the video story here.

Once, there was an eagle that flew high in the skies,

touching upon the tip of the mountains.

One day she found a ring stuck in the branch of an apple tree.

She took it and flew to her nest. While playing with it, she got her head stuck in it.

She didn't panic or hit her head on the stump of a tree to get rid of it.

Then, one day she drenched her head in oil and the ring came off of her neck.

CSS links are critical because many a time you have to connect your webpage to another website to offer your users an amazing and fruitful experience. There are four kinds of links that you can use for different purposes. They are named as a: link, a: hover, a: active, a: visited. Each link has a specific purpose. For example, a: hover is used to allow users to hover over the mouse on the link and make it open. Let's try to create links by all the four methods.

```
<html>

<head>

<style>

/* This is an unvisited link */

a:link {

color: green;

}

/* This is a visited link. */

a:visited {

color: blue;

}

/* This is a hover link. */

a:hover {

color: violet;

}

/* This is a selected link. */

a:active {

color: red;

}
```

```
</style>

</head>

<body>

<h1> Let me tell you a story.</h1>

<h2><b><a href="default.asp" target="_blank">Watch the video story here.</a></b></h2>

<p> Once, there was an eagle that flew high in the skies,

<br> touching upon the tip of the mountains.

<br> One day she found a ring, stuck in the branch of an apple tree.</p>

<p>She took it and flew to her nest. While playing with it, she got her head stuck in it.

<br>She didn't panic or hit her head on the stump of a tree to get rid of it.

<br>One day she drenched her head in oil and the ring came off of her neck.</p>

</body>

</html>
```

You might be thinking that I had entered four links, but just one color can be seen in the results if you have already tested the code. Links change their status. In the start, they are unvisited. Then you hover your mouse over them. Then you click them open and leave them visited. So, technically, you can add four different colors according to the status of your link. Let's see what other things we can do to the links. Also, we can decorate the text of links and also add color to the background. Let's see how to do that.

```
<html>

<head>
```

```
<style>
/* This is an unvisited link */
a:link {
color: green;
text-decoration: none;
background-color: yellow
}
/* This is a visited link. */
a:visited {
color: blue;
text-decoration: none;
background-color: gray
}
/* This is a hover link. */
a:hover {
color: violet;
text-decoration: underline;
background-color: pink
}
/* This is a selected link. */
a:active {
```

```
color: red;

text-decoration: underline;

background-color: hotpink

}

</style>

</head>

<body>

<h1> Let me tell you a story.</h1>

<h2><b><a href="default.asp" target="_blank">Watch the video story here.</a></b></h2>

<p> Once, there was an eagle that flew high in the skies,

<br> touching upon the tip of the mountains.

<br> One day she found a ring, stuck in the branch of an apple tree.</p>

<p>  She took it and flew to her nest. While playing with it, she got her head stuck into it.

<br> She didn't panic and hit her head into the stump of the tree to get rid of it.

<br> One day she drenched her head in oil and the ring moved out of her neck. </p>

</body>

</html>
```

CSS Tables

CSS allows you to transform the way your tables look in HTML. You can add colors to the headings and to the columns. The font style and font size of the text inside the tables can also be changed. Let's create one.

```html
<!DOCTYPE html>

<html>

<head>

<style>

#countries {

    font-family: "Courier New", Gerogia, Helvetica, sans-serif;

    border-collapse: collapse;

    width: 80%;

}

#countries td, #countries th {

    border: 2px solid green;

    padding: 6px;

}

#countries tr:nth-child(even) {background-color: violet;}

#countries tr:hover {background-color: #ddd;}

#countries th {

    padding-top: 15px;
```

```
      padding-bottom: 15px;

      text-align: left;

      background-color: #ffAc2b;

      color: gray;

   }

   </style>

   </head>

   <body>

   <table id="countries">

    <tr>

      <th>Country</th>

      <th>Capital</th>

      <th>Reasons for fame</th>

    </tr>

    <tr>

      <td>Germany</td>

      <td>Berlin</td>

      <td>BMW</td>

    </tr>

    <tr>

      <td>United States of America</td>
```

```
    <td>Washington DC</td>

    <td>Marvel</td>

  </tr>

  <tr>

    <td>China</td>

    <td>Beijing</td>

    <td>cheap products</td>

  </tr>

  <tr>

    <td>Pakistan</td>

    <td>Islamabad</td>

    <td>Footballs</td>

  </tr>

  <tr>

    <td>Japan</td>

    <td>Tokyo</td>

    <td>Robotics</td>

  </tr>

  <tr>

    <td>United Kingdom</td>

    <td>London</td>
```

```
    <td>Thames</td>
  </tr>
  <tr>
    <td>Egypt</td>
    <td>Cairo</td>
    <td>Pyramids</td>
  </tr>
  <tr>
    <td>India</td>
    <td>New Delhi</td>
    <td>Taj Mehal</td>
  </tr>
  <tr>
    <td>Brazil</td>
    <td>Sao Paulo</td>
    <td>Statue of Jesus</td>
  </tr>
  <tr>
    <td>Kingdom of Saudi Arabia</td>
    <td>Riyadh</td>
    <td>Pilgrimage</td>
```

```
  </tr>

</table>

</body>

</html>
```

The results of the above code example can be seen below. You can change the values and yield out a different output in the internet browser. Tables are an essential element for a web page. You need them if you are running a website that displays information about the rise and fall in the prices of stock market shares. If you don't style them properly with CSS, your visitors are not going to like their dull and boring look. Appropriately colored tables appear well on the website and keep visitors engaged for a while.

Country	Capital	Reasons for fame
Germany	Berlin	BMW
United States of America	Washington DC	Marvel
China	Beijing	cheap products
Pakistan	Islamabad	Footballs

Japan	Tokyo	Robotics
United Kingdom	London	Thames
Egypt	Cairo	Pyramids
India	New Delhi	Taj Mehal
Brazil	Sao Paulo	Statue of Jesus
Kingdom of Saudi Arabia	Riyadh	Pilgrimage

You can alter the colors, the border, and padding by making slight changes in the HTML document. Adding more columns or rows to suit your specific requirement is also being done. In the above example, I have added background colors, padding, border colors and have also adjusted the width of the columns. You can take the example document and customize for learning practice.

CSS Forms

HTML provides us with an easy way to create different types of forms that we can use to collect user information like their usernames, passwords, and email addresses. Some are subscription forms while others are survey forms. When we create an HTML form, its look is rigid and dull. Thanks to CSS, we can change that. We can make it look exceptionally well. Let's create a form and then transform its look by adding some simple CSS properties.

```
<!DOCTYPE html>

<html>

<style>

input[type=text], select {

  width: 100%;

  padding: 15px 25px;

  margin: 10px 0;

  display: inline-block;

  border: 2px solid green;

  border-radius: 6px;

  box-sizing: border-box;

}
input[type=submit] {

  width: 50%;

  background-color: pink;

  color: black;

  padding: 12px 18px;
```

```
    margin: 10px 0;

    border: 2px solid green;

    border-radius: 2px;

    cursor: pointer;

    font-size: 25px

}

input[type=submit]:hover {

    background-color: #45b049;

}

div {

    border-radius: 4px;

    background-color: #f1f1f1;

    padding: 15px;

}

</style>

<body>

<h1>I will be using CSS to style this raw HTML Form</h1>

<div>

  <form action="/action_page.php">

    <label for="name">Please enter your first Name</label>

    <input type="text" id="name" name="firstname" placeholder="Plese enter here..">
```

```
<label for="lname">Please enter your last Name</label>

<input type="text" id="lname" name="lastname" placeholder="Please enter here..">

<label for="country">Where do you live?</label>

<select id="country" name="country">

  <option value="USA">USA</option>

  <option value="canada">Canada</option>

<option value="UK">UK</option>

  <option value="china">China</option>

<option value="pakistan">Pakistan</option>

<option value="france">France</option>

 </select>

 <input type="submit" value="Submit">

 </form>

</div>

</body>

</html>
```

The result is as under:

I will be using CSS to style this raw HTML Form

Please enter your first Name

Please enter here.

Please enter your last Name

Please enter here.

Where do you live?

USA

Submit

I have styled the border, the input fields, the submit button and a lot more. Let's learn more about designing the buttons, as they are an essential part of forms on your web page.

<!DOCTYPE html>

<html>

<head>

<style>

input[type=refresh], input[type=submit], input[type=process] {

  background-color: #4CAFBB;

  border: 2px solid green;

  color: white;

```
    padding: 19px 34px;

    text-decoration: none;

    margin: 6px 4px;

    cursor: pointer;

}

</style>

</head>

<body>

<h1>You are seeing styled input buttons.</h1>

<input type="refresh" value="Refresh It">

<input type="process" value="Process">

<input type="submit" value="Submit">

</body>

</html>
```

The result is as under:

You are seeing styled input buttons.

| Refresh it | Preview | Submit |

In the end let's see an example of a complete form.

<!DOCTYPE html>

<html>

<head>

<style>

* {

  box-sizing: border-box;

}

input[type=text], select, textarea {

```css
  width: 50%;

  padding: 8px;

  border: 1px solid #bbb;

  border-radius: 2px;

  resize: vertical;

}

label {

  padding: 10px 0;

  display: inline-block;

}

input[type=submit] {

  background-color: #4CAF50;

  color: white;

  padding: 10px 18px;

  border: none;

  border-radius: 4px;

  cursor: pointer;

  float: right;

}

input[type=submit]:hover {

  background-color: #45a049;
```

```css
}
.container {
  border-radius: 7px;
  background-color: #f2f2f2;
  padding: 15px;
}
.col-25 {
  float: left;
  width: 50%;
  margin-top: 4px;
}
.col-75 {
  float: left;
  width: 50%;
  margin-top: 4px;
}
/* Clear floats */
.row:after {
  content: "";
  display: table;
  clear: both;
```

```css
}
/* Responsive layout */
@media screen and (max-width: 400px) {
  .col-25, .col-75, input[type=submit] {
    width: 50%;
    margin-top: 0;
  }
}
```

```html
</style>
</head>
<body>
<h2>This is an example of a responsive Form</h2>
<p>You will have to resize the browser window to see the effect.</p>
<div class="container">
  <form action="/action_page.php">
  <div class="row">
    <div class="col-25">
      <label for="nname">Please enter your First Name</label>
    </div>
    <div class="col-75">
      <input type="text" id="fname" name="firstname" placeholder="Please enter here..">
```

```html
    </div>

  </div>

  <div class="row">

    <div class="col-25">

      <label for="lname">Please enter your Last Name</label>

    </div>

    <div class="col-75">

      <input type="text" id="lname" name="lastname" placeholder="Please enter here..">

    </div>

  </div>

  <div class="row">

    <div class="col-25">

      <label for="country">Please choose your country</label>

    </div>

    <div class="col-75">

      <select id="country" name="country">

        <option value="usa">USA</option>

        <option value="canada">Canada</option>

        <option value="uk">UK</option>

      </select>

    </div>
```

```
</div>

<div class="row">

 <div class="col-25">

  <label for="bio">Please enter your bio here.</label>

 </div>

 <div class="col-75">

     <textarea     id="bio"     name="bio"     placeholder="Write     here.."
style="height:200px"></textarea>

 </div>

</div>

<div class="row">

 <input type="submit" value="Submit">

</div>

</form>

</div>

</body>

</html>
```

Your form will look like this:

This is an example of a responsive Form

You will have to resize the browser window to see the effect.

Please enter your First Name	Please enter here
Please enter your Last Name	Please enter here
Please choose your country	USA ▼
Please enter your bio here	Write here...

Submit

Chapter 10.   *Image Manipulation in CSS*

Y ou can add images to your documents using the img tag, or you can add a background image to the entire document.

Setting an image as background for a website.

You can use body tag's background-image property to set a background image for the entire page.

body { background-image: url('draft.gif'); }

Background

text text text text text text text text text text text text text text text text text text text text text text text text text text text text text text text text text text text text text text text text text text text text text text text text text text text text text text text text text text text text text text text text text text text text text

Positioning the background Image

Use the background-position property to specify where your background image will appear.

body {

   background-image: url('draft.gif');

   background-position: bottom right;

   background-repeat: no-repeat;

}

Background

text text text text text text text text text text text text text text text text text text text text text text text text text text text text text text text text text text text text text text text text text text text text text text text text text text text text text text text text text text text text text text text text text text text text text text text text text text text text text

DRAFT

You can use the following keyword combinations with the background-position property:

Keywords		
top left	center left	bottom left
top center	center center	bottom center
top right	center right	bottom right

These keywords can be written in either order. For example, "top left" and "left top" will both work correctly. The other value will default to center if you only specify a single value.

You can also use percentages to set the position.

background-position: 30% 80%;

If you want to position the image in the top left 0% 0% is the value, and 100% 100% would place it in the bottom right. Setting the background-position to 50% 50% would center the image, as would center center.

The following list shows how keyword settings match percentage settings:

Keywords	Percentages

left top	0% 0%
center top	50% 0%
right top	100% 0%
left center	0% 50%
center center	50% 50%
right center	100% 50%
left bottom	0% 100%
center bottom	50% 100%
right bottom	100% 100%

If you use keywords or percentages, your background image's position will adjust to the size of the window. You can also use pixels to set a non-adjusting position:

background-position: 20px 20px;

Adjusting background color or image position.

You can use the background-clip property to specify whether the background includes the border, padding, or only the content.

div {

   padding:10px;

   border: 5px dotted #000;

   background-color: #f00;

```
    background-clip:border-box;

}

div {
```

```
    padding:10px;

    border: 5px dotted #000;

    background-color: #f00;

    background-clip:padding-box;

}

div {
```

```
    padding:10px;

    border: 5px dotted #000;

    background-color: #f00;

    background-clip:content-box;

}
```

Adding more than one image to the background

With CSS3, you can specify multiple background images. If you are supporting old browser versions, you can specify one background image with the html tag and another with the body tag.

CSS approach

```
body {

    background-image: url('logo.gif'), url('draft.gif');
```

background-position: bottom right, 50% 50%;

background-repeat: no-repeat;

}

Older browser version approach

html {

    background-image: url('logo.gif');

    background-position: bottom right;

background-repeat: no-repeat;

}

body {

    background-attachment: fixed;

    background-image: url('draft.gif');

    background-position: 50% 50%;

    background-repeat: no-repeat;

}

Fixing a background image to avoid scrolling

You can use the background-attachment property to fix an image in place and prevent it from scrolling with rest of the page's content.

body {

    background-attachment: fixed;

    background-image: url('draft.gif');

background-position: 50% 50%;

background-repeat: no-repeat;

}

Value	Description
repeat	The background repeats horizontally and vertically.
	This is the default setting.
repeat-x	The background repeats horizontally but not vertically.
repeat-y	The background repeats vertically bit not horizontally.
no-repeat	The background does not repeat horizontally or vertically.

How do I resize a background image to fit an element?

You can use the background-size property to resize a background image to fit a larger or smaller element automatically.

Value	Description
contain	Scales the image so the height and width fit in the element
cover	Scales the image so the height or width fits (whichever is smaller)
length	Sets the height and width
	If you only specify one value, the image is sized proportionally.
percentage	Sets the height and width as a percentage of the parent element
	If you only specify one value, the image is sized proportionally.

Adding a shadow to the image

You can use the box-shadow property to add a shadow to images.

img { box-shadow: 5px 5px 10px 10px #f00; }

You can specify the following options for the shadow:

Value	Description
blur	Amount (in pixels) of blurring around the shadow's edge
color	The shadow's color
offset-x	Horizontal offset (in pixels) of the shadow
offset-y	Vertical offset (in pixels) of the shadow
inset	Specifies an inner shadow
spread	Size (in pixels) of the shadow
	0 – shadow is the same size as the element

Using an image as a border

You can use the border-image property to use an image as an element's border.

border-image:url(diamond.png) 20 20 round;

The following properties can be used to specify border images for different sides of the element:

border-top-image

border-right-image

border-bottom-image

border-left-image

Value	Description
border-image-source	Path to the image
border-image-slice	The image's height and width offset
border-image-width	The image's width
border-image-outset	The image's height
border-image-repeat	Whether the image should be repeat or stretch

Wrapping text to an image

You can use the float property to wrap text around an image.

CSS rule

.caution {

  float: left;

  margin-right: 10px;

}

Usage

<p><img class="caution" src="caution.jpg" />

caution caution caution</p>

The margin-left property can be used to add space between the image and the text.

Programming for Beginners

Placing of text on top of image

You can assign negative values to the position, top, and left properties to position text on top of an image. If the version is below the picture, setting its top property to a negative value will move the text on top of the film.

CSS rule

.overlap {

  position: relative;

  top: -200px;

  left: 180px;

  color: #ffffff;

}

Usage

<img src="sample.jpg" />

<p class="overlap">floating text</p>

Adding a border around the image

Borders are most often used with tables, but you can also add borders around images using the border properties.

```
img {

  border-width: 3px;

  border-style: solid;

  border-color: #000000;

}
```

Click**Start**

You can also use CSS shorthand to specify borders:

img { border: 1px solid #000000; }

The examples above will add a border to all images. You can create a class if you want to apply borders only to specified images.

.imgBorder { border: 1px solid #000000; }

<img class="imgBorder" src="sampleImage.jpg" />

Or, you can apply a border to all images inside a div tag:

CSS rule

#menuBar img { border: 1px solid #000000; }

Usage

<div id="menuBar"><img src="sampleImage.jpg" /></div>

Adding a drop shadow to an image

You can use Internet Explorer's filter property to add a drop shadow to an image.

img {

filter: progid:DXImageTransform.Microsoft.dropShadow   (offX='3',   offY='5',
color='#c0c0c0', positive='true');

}

The filter property was created by Microsoft and is not a part of the CSS recommendation. It is only supported by Internet Explorer.

For more information about Internet Explorer filters, see "How do I use Internet Explorer's filters?"

For other browsers, you can use the box-shadow property can be used to add a drop shadow around an image. However, it will not add the drop shadow inside transparent images.

Another option is to use HTML5's canvas element. See the following website for an example: philip.html5.org/demos/canvas/shadows/various.html

Making an image transparent

Using the opacity property to make an image transparent can also be done. For Internet Explorer, you can use the IE-specific alpha filter.

```
img {

  filter:alpha(opacity=50);

  opacity:.50;

}
```

Removing link borders from an image

You can set an image's border property to "0" to remove the border that appears around image links by default.

img { border: 0; }

How do I zoom images when the user hovers over them?

You can use the hover pseudo class to change an image's width and height.

First, wrap a link around the image:

```
<a href="javascript:void(0);">

  <img src="clickstart.jpg" />

</a>
```

Then, specify the image's width and height when the user hovers over the image's link:

a:hover img { width: 800px; height: 400px; }

In this example, the image will expand to 800x400 when the user hovers over the image, and when the mouse moves from the image it will return to its original size.

Making image expand on hover

You can use the transition property to make an image expand when the user hovers over it and shrink when it loses focus. For example, you could provide a "thumbnail" of an image that expands to full-size when the user hovers over it.

CSS rule

```
.thumbTrans {

  width: 50px;

  height: 50px;

  -moz-transition-property: width,height;

  -moz-transition-duration: 4s;

  -moz-transition-delay: 1s;

  -webkit-transition-property: width,height;

  -webkit-transition-duration: 4s;

  -webkit-transition-delay: 1s;

  -o-transition-property: width,height;

  -o-transition-duration: 4s;

  -o-transition-delay: 1s;

  transition-property: width,height;

  transition-duration: 4s;

  transition-delay: 1s;

}

.thumbTrans:hover {

  width: 100%;

  height: 100%;

  -moz-transition-property: width,height;
```

```
    -moz-transition-duration: 4s;

    -moz-transition-delay: 1s;

    -webkit-transition-property: width,height;

    -webkit-transition-duration: 4s;

    -webkit-transition-delay: 1s;

    -o-transition-property: width,height;

    -o-transition-duration: 4s;

    -o-transition-delay: 1s;

    transition-property: width,height;

    transition-duration: 4s;

    transition-delay: 1s;

}
```

Making an image 'pop-out' on hover

You can use the hover pseudo class to rotate images and add a shadow.

```
img:hover {

    box-shadow:1px 2px 5px #666666;

    -moz-transform:rotate(5deg) scale(1.5);

    -webkit-transform:rotate(5deg) scale(1.5);

    transform:rotate(5deg) scale(1.5);

}
```

Inserting content using CSS

Using the content property to insert content before or after an element can also be done.

To insert content at the top or bottom of the page:

body:before {

  content: "Confidential";

  font-weight: bold;

}

body:after {

  content: "\000A Copyright 2012";

}

To insert content before an element:

h1:before {

  content: ">> ";

  color: silver;

}

To add quotes before and after an element:

p.quotes:before { content: open-quote; }

p.quotes:after { content: close-quote; }

To add curly quotes:

p.boldCurlyQuotes { quotes: "\201C" "\201D"; }

p.boldCurlyQuotes:before { content: open-quote; }

p.boldCurlyQuotes:after { content: close-quote; }

The following table provides the Unicode values for commonly-used characters that can be inserted using the content property.

Symbol	Description	Unicode value
"	double quotation	0022
'	single quotation (apostrophe)	0027
"	double left curly quotation	201C
"	double right curly quotation	201D
<	single left angle quotation	003C
>	single right angle quotation	003E
«	double left angle quotation	00AB
»	double right angle quotation	00BB
`	grave accent	0060
´	acute accent	00B4

Chapter 11. <u>*Length Units*</u>

A s you have followed this tutorial, you may have noticed that when you change the size of text using CSS, there are a number of options.

You can see this for yourself in TopStyle.

Create a new style sheet, and click the "New Selector" button. Select the "Simple" tab and select h1 from the HTML elements list. Next click the "Add" button, followed by "OK".

In the style inspector, scroll down to the font category and click on the font-size property. Click the downward arrow on the right of this row to view the options available:

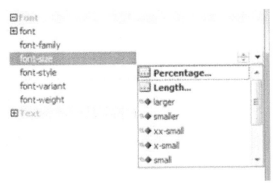

In this book, we will concentrate on the first two items in this list – Percentage and Length.

Percentage is a relative measurement (i.e., it defines a size that is relative to another one).

Length is an absolute measurement, since it defines an exact analysis. However, with precise measurements come units.

What are the units for an absolute measurement?

Well, let's find out. Click on the font-size dropdown arrow, and select length.

Another dialogue box opens up, with another dropdown box (set to the default 'px').

Click on the down arrow of that dropdown box, and you'll see several more options:

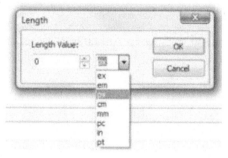

WOW! That's a lot of different units.

These units can be divided into two groups:

1. relative units (size is comparable to something)

2. absolute units (size is an exact measurement)

The 'relative' units are:

-   ex

-   em

-   px

(The percentage unit is also relative).

The 'absolute' units are:

-   cm

-   mm

-   pc

-   in

-   pt

The main reason for using absolute units is to freeze the design of the web page so that it always looks the same, no matter how it's viewed.

When relative measurements are used, the web design may look different, depending on the users Web browser settings.

Let's look at an example.

This header uses an RELATIVE measurement to define its size.

This header uses a ABSOLUTE measurement to define its size.

There are two headers, one defined in absolute terms, and the other in relative terms.

Older web browsers use to allow users to change the size of the fonts in their browsers to:

- Largest

- Larger

- Medium

- Smaller

- Smallest

The problem was that any font size defined in absolute terms would not increase in size because it was set in total measurements, and therefore would always appear the same size on the screen. The font size defined in relative terms would increase in size.

If you increased the font size to "Largest", you'd see the relative header increase in size while the absolute header would stay at the same size.

To some extent, web browsers have taken away the functionality of absolute measurements because they introduced a zoom feature instead of a font size feature. This then magnified all text, absolute or relative, to the same extent, throwing out some web designer's carefully designed layouts.

OK, let's consider the units for measurements, and what they represent.

The five absolute measurements are as follows:

1. cm - centimeters

2. mm - millimeters

3. in - inches

4. pc - picas (1/6 inch or 12 points)

5. pt - points (1/72 inch)

It should be noted that even if absolute measurements did work properly in browsers with the new zoom features, they would only ever work as desired if the browser knew the size of the screen, and the number of pixels the screen displayed. In many cases, the browser would have to guess! This, together with the more recent addition of zoom features, means that absolute measurements aren't the best units to use when designing your pages so that we won't be looking into these.

It was important to mention absolute measurements in this book though, because I am sure you will come across them when you are exploring the CSS of your own (and other people's) web pages.

So relative measurements provide us with the best solution, especially when we don't know what device the end user will be viewing the site on. For example, nowadays they could be browsing on a computer, a tablet, a Smartphone, or even some e-readers. With relative measurements, the font sizes will be comparable to the size of the screen, and therefore give the user the very best viewing experience.

Here are the relative measurements in some detail:

EX

The 'ex' is a measurement relative to the size of the font's lowercase 'x'. I never use this measurement so that we won't be looking at it in this book.

PX

The px is a relative measurement in screen pixels.

Pixels offer the designer the best control over layouts. You will see them used a lot for things like borders, margins, padding, plus height and width of screen regions when creating CSS layouts without tables.

What pixels are not recommended for is text size. Most modern browser won't have a problem, but some of the older ones won't resize pixel-based text.

Percentage

Percentage measurements are always relative to another value. For example, if we want to increase the spacing between lines of a paragraph, you can define the line-height as a percentage (it will be a percentage of the font size).

Say for example we have: line-height: 150%. This will create a space between the lines that is 150% of the font size. Therefore, if the font size is 10px, then the space between lines will be 15px. It is wise to define the font-size in your CSS file if using percentages, otherwise results can be unpredictable in the different browsers. This is because the font-size will be taken from the web browsers default CSS file.

Here is an example showing line spacing using percentages:

A normal Paragraph:

px- relative measurement in screen pixels. Pixels offer the designer the best control
borders, margins, padding, plus height and width of screen regions when creating C
this series). What pixels are not recommended for is text size. Some browser wont
friend Internet Explorer wont resize pixel based text. Therefore, to give the best exp
pixels.

A paragraph where lines are spaced at 150% (line-height:150%):

px- relative measurement in screen pixels. Pixels offer the designer the best control
borders, margins, padding, plus height and width of screen regions when creating C
this series). What pixels are not recommended for is text size. Some browser wont
friend Internet Explorer wont resize pixel based text. Therefore, to give the best exp
pixels.

A paragraph where lines are spaced at 200% (line-height:200%):

px- relative measurement in screen pixels. Pixels offer the designer the best control

borders, margins, padding, plus height and width of screen regions when creating C

this series). What pixels are not recommended for is text size. Some browser wont

friend Internet Explorer wont resize pixel based text. Therefore, to give the best exp

pixels.

(9.1.html and 9.1.css)

EM

The "em" is a relative measurement for the font size. Think of it as being the size of a capital "M" to help you remember it, though that isn't entirely accurate, but it is an excellent way to memorize it.

This is my preferred unit for defining text size. Because it's a measurement relative to the font size, if we set a font-size of say 10px, then one em is equal to 10px. 2 em would be similar to 20px, and 1.5 em would be 15 px.

To make this as easy as possible, it's a good idea to define the font size in the style sheet as follows:

Create a new style sheet.

Click on the "New Selector" button, and then go to the "Simple" tab.

Select body from the HTML Element list, and then click the "Add" button followed by "OK".

You'll see the following in your style sheet:

body {

}

Whatever properties you enter will be the default properties for all elements on the page that appear between the <body></body> tags, i.e., everything.

I can define a default font-size like this:

body { font-size: 11px; }

This would make the default font size 11px. Here is a web page where I have defined the default text size in this manner:

This is a normal paragraph - Since I have not defined a size for <p> tags in the style sheet, it appears as 1em.

H1 header defined as 2.5 em

H2 header defined as 2 em

H3 header defined as 1.5 em

(9.2.html and 9.2.css)

In some older browsers, if you choose a larger font size, these sizes will remain the same because we defined the default font as 20 px – an absolute measurement. However, since most browsers now use the zoom feature, this is less of a problem that it used to be. Nevertheless, just to be safe, we are probably better off defining the default font-size this way:

body {   font-size: 0.7em; }

This would make the default text size 70% of the default text size. So just what is the default text size?

Well, every browser has its own default CSS that it uses to display web pages. If you want to see what that size looks like in different browsers, create a style sheet that sets the body text size to 1em.

body {   font-size: 1.0em; }

Then create a web page with some text on it that uses the style sheet, and view it in a few different browsers, or just look at 9.3.html and 9.3.css, as I have done this for you.

Here is an excellent article on using em for sizing text. Richard Rutter uses percentages instead of em to define the default font-size:

http://clagnut.com/blog/348

Chapter 12. <u>*CSS IDs and Classes*</u>

I D selectors can only (or should only), be used **ONCE** on a web page, and identify **ONE** item on the page.

By using an ID selector to reference two images on the page, I was breaking a CSS rule. I should have used a CLASS instead.

ID Selectors and classes do mostly the same thing, BUT, an ID can only be used once on the page, **whereas** types can be used multiple times.

Before we look at classes, let me give you an easy way to remember this:

Your ID refers to YOU and you alone. No one else can have your ID.

A class is a group of people so that a level can refer to multiple individuals.

Therefore, an ID is only used once, and a class can be used multiple times.

For this reason, we will use IDs for page elements that only occur once, e.g., when we come to look at page layouts using CSS, we'll define IDs for the page header area, the right and left margins, the main content section, and the footer. These are obvious choices, since each of those sections only occurs once per page.

We will use classes whenever we want to reuse a style on a page more than once, for example, the alignment of images, font styling, and bullet points, etc.

OK, we know that IDs and Classes can be used to override default display properties, but we still haven't looked at how to create or use them yet. Let's look at that now, so that you can start using them in your page designs.

ID Selectors

Start TopStyle and click on the "New Selector" button.

Switch to the "advanced" tab, and you will see a pair of radio buttons (aka option buttons), labeled Class and ID.

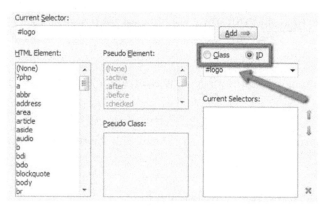

Select ID, and then in the box underneath the radio buttons, type in a name for your ID. I typed in "logo" for mine, since I am going to create the ID to be applied to the logo on the page (it only appears once).

You will notice that as you type, TopStyle adds a '#' to the start of your ID. Click the "Add" button (located above the radio buttons), and then click the "OK" button on the bottom right. This will add this selector to your style sheet.

In style sheets, the '#' symbol specifies that what follows is an ID. Here's how mind looks:

#logo {

}

You can now add some styles to the ID in exactly the same way we have done in other examples. I've added a few to mine, and here the finished logo ID:

#logo {

      font-size: 3em;

      font-variant: small-caps;

      font-weight: bolder;

      background-color: Silver;

      font-family: Verdana, Geneva, Arial, Helvetica, sans-serif;

}

The idea of this ID is to change the text properties in the logo area of my page so that it is more extensive ("em" is a unit of measurement). My sample here uses small caps, bold, has a silver background, and is the Verdana, Geneva… font family. You probably knew this from seeing the style sheet though, didn't you?

You can see the effects of what this does to the page here:

(8.1.html and 8.1.css)

To use the ID in a web page, you simply modify the HTML tag to include:

ID = "logo"

Here is the HTML code before modifying:

<p>Mylogo.com</p>

Just before the first single right-pointing angle quotation mark ">", is where you insert your ID code:

<p ID="logo">Mylogo.com</p>

Now, anything inside the <p></p> tags will be formatted according to the properties of the ID "logo".

You will notice that in the raw HTML, the text is lowercase apart from the first letter "M". In the web page preview (above), the book is small capitals, or small caps. That is what happens when we add the property: font-variant: small-caps;

Classes are used in a very similar way, so let's now take a look at that:

Class Selectors

Create a new style sheet, and click on the "New Selector" button. Go to the "Advanced" tab again and click on the "Class" radio button. Enter a name for your class underneath the radio button. I am using "yellowhighlight" for mine, as that is what my class will do. i.e., highlight some text in yellow.

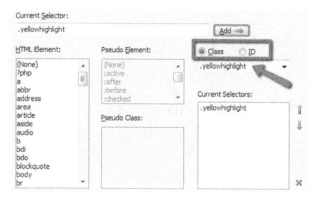

You'll notice that as you type, TopStyle adds a "." in front of the text you are typing. In CSS, that "." specifies that whatever follows is a class.

OK, once done, click the "Add" button and then click "OK" to save the changes to your style sheet.

```
<body>
<p ID = "logo">Mylogo.com</p>
<h1>This page demonstrates the use of an ID.</h1>
<p>Start Topstyle Lite, and click on the &quot;New Selector&quot;
<p class = "yellowhighlight">You'll see a pair of radio buttons la
<p>You will notice that as you type, Topstyle adds a '#' to the st
<p>In style sheets, the '#' denotes that what follows is an ID.</p
<p>OK, name typed in? </p>
<p>Click OK, and your style sheet will be updated as follows:</p>
<p>#logo {<br>
   }<br>
</p>
```

This is what mine looks like:

.yellowhighlight {

}

I will make just one style change to the background color:

.yellowhighlight { background-color: Yellow; }

Now I can simply highlight a paragraph in yellow by adding the following code to the HTML tag for the paragraph I want to change:

class="yellowhighlight"

We add it in the exact same way that we added the ID earlier. Insert it right after the first ">" of the <p> tag.

Here is the html code:

<p class="yellowhighlight">the paragraph goes here</p>

Now look at this page:

MYLOGO.COM

This page demonstrates the use of an ID.

Start Topstyle Lite, and click on the "New Selector" button.

You'll see a pair of radio buttons labelled Class and ID. Select ID, and then, in the box underneath the radio buttons, type in a name for your ID. I am going to type in "logo" for mine, since I am going to create the ID to be applied to the logo on the page (it only appears once).

You will notice that as you type, Topstyle adds a '#' to the start of your ID.

In style sheets, the '#' denotes that what follows is an ID.

OK, name typed in?

(8.2.html and 8.2.css)

The second paragraph is now highlighted in yellow. Note how the <p> tag has been modified from <p> to <p class = "yellowhighlight">:

Here is the HTML.

Because I used a class to define the highlighting, I can happily use it on multiple paragraphs if I want to:

MYLOGO.COM

This page demonstrates the use of an ID.

Start Topstyle Lite, and click on the "New Selector" button.

You'll see a pair of radio buttons labelled Class and ID. Select ID, and then, in the box underneath the radio buttons, type in a name for your ID. I am going to type in "logo" for mine, since I am going to create the ID to be applied to the logo on the page (it only appears once).

You will notice that as you type, Topstyle adds a '#' to the start of your ID.

In style sheets, the '#' denotes that what follows is an ID.

OK, name typed in?

Click OK, and your style sheet will be updated as follows:

#logo {
}

(8.3.html and 8.3.css)

That's how easy it is to identify and use classes.

Before we leave this though, I can hear you asking: "But what if we only want to highlight certain text in a paragraph, and not the whole section?"

Well, the problem here is that the way we have used the class so far is to modify a complete HTML tag (the whole paragraph), because we declared the course within the <p> tag.

However, there is another option. You can use a "span" tag, to surround a selection of text, and apply a class only to the "spanned" text. To do this, you have to surround the text you want to highlight with a <span></span> tag. Let's look at an example:

<p>I only want to highlight <span>this text</span>here.</p>

We can now add the class within the opening <span> tag, right before the ">", in much the same way as you saw previously with the other tags:

<p>I only want to highlight <span class="yellowhighlight">this text </span>here.</p>

Here it is in action on a web page:

Start Topstyle Lite, and click on the "New Selector" button.

You'll see a pair of radio buttons labelled Class and ID. Select ID, and then, in the box underneath the radio buttons, type in a name for your ID. I am going to type in "logo" for mine, since I am going to create the ID to be applied to the logo on the page (it only appears once).

You will notice that as you type, Topstyle adds a '#' to the start of your ID.

(8.4.html and 8.4.css)

This is an integral part of the CSS course, with some big lessons to learn. We learnt how to use IDs and Classes to modify the elements of our web pages, and although there's still more to cover on classes, we'll take a break for now.

Chapter 13. __*The Box Model In CSS*__

T he basis of the CSS layout is the box model since it directs the way in which elements are shown and the way in which they associate with one another. Imagine every element on the page as a rectangular box. Every box is made of particular dimensions and takes up a particular measure of space. The space the box occupies depends on the content in it, as well as the margins and the padding borders around the content:

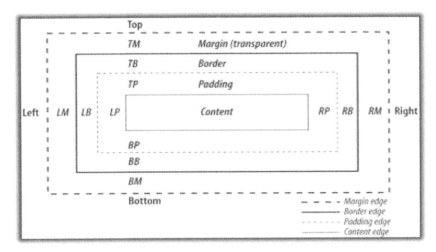

So, the box model is what dictates the amount of space each element has on the page. Now, let's dive somewhat deeper into this idea by revising the main components that constitute the CSS box model. Start thinking of each HTML component on the page as a box. In fact, you can apply a global style rule that will add a red outline to all the elements on the page. To do this, simply add the following style rule to the top of the stylesheet:

```
* {

  outline: 2px solid red;

}
```

This will add an outline to all the elements on the page and it will let us easily visualize each of the items on the page as a box:

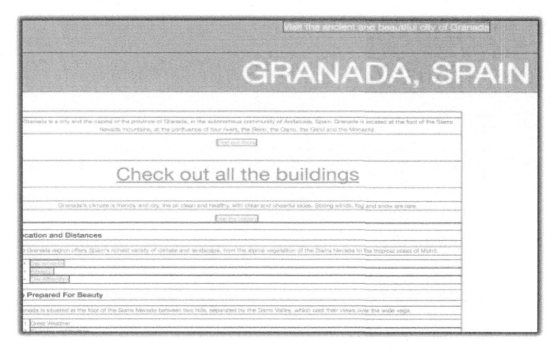

Each element is designed with a box or rectangle. Now, to effectively understand the concept of the CSS box model, it is essential that we know the two ways in which elements can be displayed. Every detail has a display property, depending on the kind of item it is. The default of most items is inline or block. Now, block elements are composed of a separate block that has to take up the full width that is available. A few examples of block elements include, list items, paragraphs, divs and any heading tag.

You can observe how the block-level divs on our page, and also the lists and headings are taking up a whole line of content. They're additionally forcing another new line of text before and after the next element. Also, inline elements only take up as much width as they have to. They don't constrain any lines, and they remain in line with whatever remains of the rest of the text. A few examples of inline elements are images, anchor elements, and span tags.

In the title span element, observe how its width consumes the space of its text, and the reason it's shown on its line is because a block-level h1 part exists beneath it. The block-level h1 forces the new line. So now, let's examine how the margins, borders, and padding interact with one another to form a box since it's essential to understand. The box model is designed with four distinct parts.

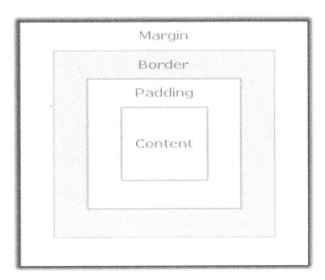

The core component and innermost area of the box is the content area. This is the area in which the actual content, such as image or text of the element is contained. Surrounding the area of the text is the padding area. Padding is used to give elements some breathing space. The next outermost part of the box is known as the border area of the box. Think of it as an outline to the box model. There are a range of styles for borders such as thickness and color. Finally, the margin area is positioned outside of the box. This is the space around an element that isolates it from different components.

The padding area makes space inside of the box, and the margin area makes space outside of and around the box. Imagine you have a cardboard box that you have filled with fragile items, but you have surrounded it with bubble wrap to cushion any impact. The padding in the box model is similar to the bubble wrap, in that it is added inside the box. The Google Chrome dev tool provides a really clear view of the box model for each element on the page. If you click on View > Developer > Developer Tools:

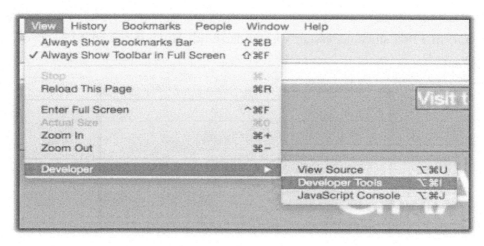

It will display the chrome developer tool panel at the bottom of the page:

Once you have the dev tools panel open, in the elements tab on the left, open up the header element and click on the h1 element. This will be the element selected in the chrome dev tool and you will see the h1 highlighted on the page:

Once the h1 element is selected, you can increase the width of the styles tab on the right and scroll down until you see the box model for the h1:

As you can see from the above screenshot, the h1 element's box model can be seen clearly. We have a default margin applied to the top and bottom, and it has no border or padding. Hopefully, this will give you a better understanding of how each element on the page is represented, and how they interact with each other based on their display type.

Chapter 14. <u>*Step By Step Addition Of CSS To HTML Document*</u>

The Three Ways To Add CSS To An HTML Document

Y ou may recall from your HTML knowledge that there are three ways to add CSS to an HTML document: as inline style, as an internal style, and as a link to an external stylesheet. In this the book internal style method will be used because it more easily demonstrates, for learning purposes, how CSS relates to HTML in a single screen window and when using short economical code snippets. However, normally you will want to be using CSS script in external style sheets, since that is the generally preferred method. Also for visual clarity, many redundant elements will be omitted, such as <!DOCTYPE html>, <html> and <body>. Just assume that, if these examples were used on real web pages, you would have all the requisite elements in place.

For review, let's just remind ourselves of the syntax and method for each manner of adding CSS to an HTML document.

Inline Style

Inline CSS is presented within the opening HTML tag, where style is a Global Attribute that can be used by any HTML element. The value of any applied style attribute is a property:value pairing declared inside of quotation marks, attached to the attribute through the assignment operator equal sign, = . Every property:value pairing should end in a semi-colon, and similarly when combining more than one inline style, each property: a semicolon should separate value pairing.

Before Cascading Style Sheets, a vast amount of work was entailed by having to style every HTML element individually. Any change of a style decided later on meant that each element that had the style had to be manually adjusted. Here's an example of inline CSS as part of an HTML text file:

<h1 style="color:red; font-style:italic; font-weight:100;">Red Heading Typography</h1>

Red Heading Typography

Above three styles have been applied, making the font color red, its style italic, and the font weight 100 (on a 9-item scale 100 to 900– note that not all fonts support all nine available CSS weights).

Internal Style

With internal CSS, the style is placed inside the <head> section of the HTML document, which is always above the <body> section, you will recall. This method is internal to the HTML document, i.e. a single web page, as a whole, rather than specific to a single element, which is why it is called internal. The CSS is applied within the <style> HTML opening and closing tags instead of a style attribute declaration and is declared in the standard CSS format. The basic CSS syntax is:

s {

property : value;

property: value;

}

The "s" above stands for "selector", which is any HTML element (in this context, "s" is not the HTML tag for "strikethrough!"). With internal CSS, the property:value pairs are declared within curly braces, {   }, instead of quotation marks. The property:value pairs taken together with the curly braces make up a declaration in CSS. At a high level, the syntactical construct can be understood as:

Selector {Declaration} {Declaration} {Declaration}

Selector {Declaration} {Declaration}

And each declaration in turn is made up of:

{property:value; property:value; property:value;}

{property:value; property:value;}

etc.

A selector and its declaration(s) together make up a rule set:

rule set = selector {declaration(s)}

To ground this syntax in a typical example, let's look at the use of multiple declarations applied to a single selector. Note that sometimes the order of declarations has no effect on the visual result, but in other cases the order does have an effect.

<style>

h2 {

text-align: center;

font-family: cursive;

color: orange;

}

</style>

<h2>

Hi, I've been styled.

</h2>

Hi, I've been styled.

Multiple declarations on the <h2> selector.

Instead of declaring styles one after the another on the same line as with inline CSS, with internal CSS each style declaration starts a new line and is completed with a semicolon. You must always complete a declaration with a semicolon even with the final one, since it's possible that later on you or another designer may add new styles and not realize that there are missing semicolons above in the code that can cause a bug when rendering the style.

The code below is the internal CSS version of the same style we applied above in the inline example. The CSS is now located inside of curly braces, which are inside of the <style> tags which are inside of the <head> section. The CSS is applied in the head first (before the body) since a browser linearly parses the code. In this way, the browser does not first load an unstyled version of a page and then get to work restyling it all, which is what would happen if internal CSS was placed at the bottom of the .html file. Rather, the browser obtains the needed style information first in the <head>, then all subsequent HTML content is rendered in the style that was first parsed from the internal style declarations.

<head>

<style>

h1 {

color: red;

font-style: italic;

font-weight: 100;

}

```
</style>
```

```
</head>
```

```
<h1>Red Heading Typography</h1>
```

Red Heading Typography

External Stylesheet

Well-developed styles are made up of many lines of code, and for this reason it is usually impractical to create too many style statements as internal CSS within the <head> area of an .html document. Instead, CSS code is usually placed in its own text file(s) that have the file extension .css. This external style is then linked to in the <head> of an .html document via a <link> element. This link to the external .css file will instruct the browser to obtain the styling information from the external file first before continuing to load, and style, the subsequent HTML content. When using code editors to write CSS les, make sure you set the file's syntax to CSS, though many editors will automatically detect the language you are writing in. When you save the file, make sure it has the .css file extension so that it is usable as a style sheet for a browser.

```
<html>
```

```
<head>
```

```
<link rel="stylesheet" href="css.css" type="text/css">
```

```
</head>
```

```
<body>
```

```
</body>
```

```
</html>
```

Above, we define the relationship (the rel attribute in <link>) between the .html document and the external resource as a stylesheet relationship. The URL to locate the external style sheet is a relative URL path– in this example, the CSS file is in the same directory as the index.html document. As your websites become more complex, you will eventually want to have your CSS source code files in their directories or folders, in which case the URL in the href might instead be "CSS/css.css" or "scripts/css.css" and so on. These forward slashes indicate that the .css file is to be found inside of a directory called "CSS" or "scripts," and that these directories are in the same directory as the .html file. Finally, the Media Type of the stylesheet is declared with the type attribute. CSS, like all source code, is always just a text file, but instead of the usual .txt file extension used for text files, .css is used so that the browser knows to parse the code as containing styling information.

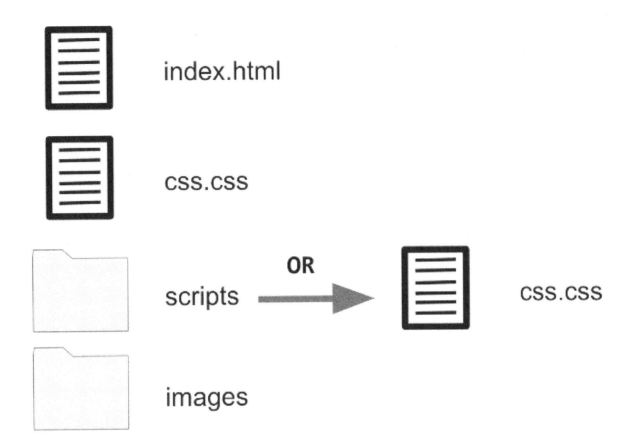

Placing the .css file in the same directory as the .html file, OR alternately, in a scripts directory. The value of the href attribute has to specify the path needed to find the external style document.

Chapter 15. <u>*Introduction To JavaScript*</u>

H TML is used to develop web pages, and web pages can become complex documents that define the content of a page. Materials produced using HTML can get CSS added to it, and done in different ways like attaching a background color, changing font sizes, image size, typeface, shadow, colour intensity, and so on. HTML and CSS can be used to attain a static beauty of a web page. With JavaScript, you can inject life into web pages using JavaScript effects such as form validation, modal, slider, pop up, and so on. The practice of developing web pages or applications with HTML, CSS, and JavaScript is called Frontend development, and it enhances the user's interaction with web pages. JavaScript is a well-built client-side scripting language. JavaScript is also generally used for mobile and game application development.

A Brief History of JavaScript

·   1995: While working at Netscape, "LiveScript" was created by Brendan Eich and later renamed to "JavaScript."

·   1996: Javascript released by Microsoft, a port, for IE3.

·   1997: JavaScript became standardized in the "ECMAScript" spec.

·   2005: "AJAX" was coined, and the web 2.0 age began.

·   2006: jQuery 1.0 was released.

·   2010: node.JS was released.

·   2010: angular.JS was released.

·   2012: ECMAScript Harmony spec nearly finalised.

Several programmers tend to believe that JavaScript and Java belong to the same category, and this opinion is false because Java and JavaScript are different from each other. Java is a sophisticated programming language, while JavaScript is a scripting language only. The C programming language influences the JavaScript Syntax.

What does the future hold for JavaScript?

The technologies of HTML5 and JavaScript can be used to create extensions for Windows 8 desktop widgets, browsers, Chrome OS, and Firefox OS applications. A large number of non-web related applications also adopt the scripting language of JavaScript, and it can be used to create HTML templates (Mustache), attach activities to PDF documents, database interaction (MongoDB), and also control (Cylon.js). JavaScript has a bright future because web platforms continue to mature and advance its usage beyond only browsers. This scripting language will remain an integral part of future developments.

How to Run JavaScript?

JavaScript is a scripting language that cannot run on its own. The browser does the code running of JavaScript. When a user requests an HTML page that contains JavaScript, the browser receives the script, and then the browser gets to decide its execution. All modern browsers support JavaScript, which is a massive advantage for the scripting language. JavaScript also runs on operating systems like Linux, Mac, and Windows.

Requirements to Learning JavaScript

- Basic knowledge of HTML and CSS

- A text editor

- A browser

- Logical thinking and tenacity

Programming

Computer programming is the act of implementing and creating a different set of rules to allow a computer to perform a specific task. It is the process of speaking the computer language, which involves picking an algorithm and encoding it into a notation so that the computer can get it executed.

Types of Programming Languages

1. Low-level language

• Machine code

• Assembly language

2. High-level language

Inscribed in different languages such as Java, PHP, C, C++, JavaScript, C#, Python, etc. Computer programs can be either interpreted or compiled language, although JavaScript is an excellent example of Interpretation.

Keeping Them Separate

HTML: It defines the page content.

CSS: It determines the content's presentation.

JavaScript: It controls content characters.

When these technologies are used in developing a web page, they must be stored differently.

1. Create a separate .html file for HTML

2. Create a separate .css for CSS

3. Create a separate .js for JavaScript

The Wrong Approach

<p>

Whatever you do, <a href="666.html" style="color: red;" onclick="alert('I said dont

click')">don't click this link</a>!

</p>

The Right Approach

<p>

Whatever you do, <a href="666.html" id="warning">don't click this link</a>! </p>

<style>

#warning{

color:red;

}

</style>

<script>

var warningLink=document.getElementById("warning");

warningLink.addEventListener('click',alerter, false);

function alerter(){

alert("I said don't click");

}

</script>

The best approach is to save the style and script into a separate .css file and .js file and unite them via link tag and script tag in the HTML document. This approach is utilized in this manual.

<link rel="stylesheet" href="warning.css" /> <p>

Whatever you do, <a href ="666.html" id="warning">don't click this link</a>!

</p>

```
<script src="warning.js"></script>
```

JavaScript Basics

Statements

The JavaScript syntax is also known as a C-style syntax which is related to the syntax used by PHP. A JavaScript program consists of JavaScript language construct, command, and keyword. This manual will teach you how to develop amazing things with the use of JavaScript language constructs, command and keyword. Every statement must end with a semicolon or a new line. By popular convention a JavaScript programmer should write one statement per line and with a semicolon at the end.

```
document.write('Hello World') document.write('Here comes the JS Engineer')
```

```
document.write('Hello World'); document.write('Here comes the JS Engineer');
```

```
document.write('Hello World');
```

```
document.write('Here comes the JS Engineer');
```

Comments

These are human-readable texts which the computer disregards. JavaScript consists of two types of comments:

```
//This is a single line comment
```

```
/*
```

This is a multiple line comment on line one

This is a multiple line comment on line two

This is a multiple line comment on line three

```
*/
```

Variable

To declare a variable, Use the "var" keyword.

A variable is used to store data and references the memory location in computer memory (RAM.) A variable can perform 3 actions, and they are:

1. Declaring the variable

2. Inserting data inside the variable

3. Getting the data into the variable

It is important to name a variable to enable easy differentiation. Few rules guide naming variables.

Variable naming rules

- They consist of the following character; numbers, letters, dollar signs or underscores but a number cannot be the first character

- Variables are case sensitive, therefore 'number-one' differs from 'NumberOne.'

- Variables cannot be JavaScript reserved words

- Variables select meaning and clarity

- Variables do not hold space variable that creates more than a word, therefore 'number one' is written   as 'numberone' but for easy readability 'numberone' is often written as 'number_one' or 'numberOne.'

- Select a naming convention and become accustomed to it.

var 2numberOne; //invalid variable name because it started with number

var numberOne!; //invalid variable name because it contains a non-permitted character!

var x; //valid variable name but not descriptive

```
var numberOne; //variable declaration

var numberTwo; //variable declaration

numberOne=5; //assigning data to variable

numberTwo=10; //assigning data to variable

document.write(numberOne); //calling data inside a variable

document.write(numberTwo); //calling data inside a variable

var numberOne=3; //variable declaration and assignment

var numberOne, numberTwo, numberTwo; //multiple variable declaration

var numberOne=2, numberTwo=4, numberTwo=6; //multiple variable declaration and
assignment
```

Chapter 16.   *JavaScript Syntax*

W e finally start to see JavaScript source code! So far everything we have seen in this manual may have seemed very theoretical, but from now on we hope you find it more enjoyable to start seeing more practical and directly related to programming.

The JavaScript language has a syntax very similar to Java because it is based on it. It is also very similar to that of the C language, so if the reader knows any of these two languages it will be easy to handle with the code

Comments in The Code

A comment is a part of code that is not interpreted by the browser and whose utility lies in making it easier for the programmer to read. The programmer, as he develops the script, leaves individual phrases or words, called comments, which help him or anyone else to read the script more easily when modifying or debugging it.

Some JavaScript comments have been seen previously, but now we are going to count them again. The language has two types of comments. One of them, the double bar, is used to comment on a line of code. The other comment can be used to comment on several lines and is indicated with the signs / * to start the comment and * / to end it. Let's see some examples.

<SCRIPT>

// This is a one-line comment

/ * This comment can be extended

along several lines.

The ones you want * /

</SCRIPT>

Upper Case and Lower Case

In JavaScript uppercase and lowercase letters must be respected. If we make a mistake when using them, the browser will respond with an error message, either syntax or indefinite reference.

For example, the alert () function is not the same as the Alert () function. The first displays text in a dialog box, and the second (with the first capital A) simply does not exist, unless we define it ourselves. As you can see, for the function to recognize JavaScript, you have to write all lowercase. We will see another clear example when we deal with variables, since the names we give to the variables are also case sensitive.

As a general rule, the names of things in JavaScript are always written in lowercase, unless a name with more than one word is used, since in this case the initials of the words following the first will be capitalized. For example, document.bgColor (which is a place where the background color of the web page is saved), it is written with the capital "C", as it is the first letter of the second word. You can also use capital letters in the initials of the first words in some cases, such as the names of the classes.

Separation of Instructions

The different instructions that our scripts contain must be conveniently separated so that the browser does not indicate the corresponding syntax errors. JavaScript has two ways of separating instructions. The first is through the semicolon (;) character and the second is through a line break.

For this reason, JavaScript statements do not need to end with a semicolon unless we put two instructions on the same line.

It is not a bad idea, anyway, to get used to using the semicolon after each instruction because other languages such as Java or C force them to be used and we will be getting used to making a syntax more similar to the usual one in advanced programming environments.

Variables in JavaScript

This is the first of the articles that we are going to dedicate to variables in JavaScript within the JavaScript Manual. We will see, if we do not already know, that variables are one of the fundamental elements when making programs, in JavaScript as well as in most of the existing programming languages.

So let's start by getting to know the concept of a variable and we'll learn how to declare them in JavaScript, along with detailed explanations of their use in the language.

Variable Concept

A variable is a space in memory where data is stored, an area where we can store any type of information that we need to carry out the actions of our programs. We can think of it as a box, where we store data. That box has a name, so that later we can refer to the variable, retrieve the data as well as assign a value to the variable whenever we want.

For example, if our program performs sums, it will be very normal for us to store in variables the different addends that participate in the operation and the result of the sum. The effect would be something like this.

adding1 = 23

adding2 = 33

sum = adding1 + adding2

In this example we have three variables, adding1, adding2 and sum, where we save the result. We see that their use for us is as if we had a section where to save a data and that they can be accessed just by putting their name.

Rules for Variable Naming in JavaScript

Variable names must be constructed with alphanumeric characters (numbers and letters), the underscore or underscore (_), and the dollar character $. Apart from this, there are a number of additional rules for constructing names for variables. The most important is that they cannot start with a numeric character. We cannot use rare styles such as the + sign, a space, or a - sign. Supported names for variables could be:

Age

country of birth

_Name

$ element

Other $ _Names

We must also avoid using reserved names as variables, for example we will not be able to call our variable words like return or for, which we will see that they are used for structures of the language itself. Let's now look at some variable names that you are not allowed to use:

12 months

your name

return

for

more or less

pe% pe

Variable Names in JavaScript Are Case Sensitive

Remember that JavaScript is a case-sensitive language, so variables are also affected by that distinction. Therefore, the variable named "myname" is not the same as the variable "myName". "Age" is not the same as "age".

Keep this detail in mind, as it is a common source of code problems that are sometimes difficult to detect. This is because sometimes you think you are using a variable, which should have a specific data, but if you make a mistake when writing it and put upper or lower case where it should not, then it will be another different variable, which will not have the expected data. Since JavaScript does not force you to declare variables, the program will run without producing an error, however, the execution will not provide the desired effects.

Declaration of Variables in JavaScript

Declaring variables consists of defining, and incidentally informing the system, that you are going to use a variable. It is a common custom in programming languages to explicitly specify the variables to be used in programs. In many programming languages there are some strict rules when it comes to declaring variables, but the truth is that JavaScript is quite permissive.

JavaScript skips many rules for being a somewhat free language when programming and one of the cases in which it gives a little freedom is when declaring the variables, since we are not obliged to do so, contrary to what happens in other programming languages like Java, C, C # and many others.

Variable Declaration with Var

JavaScript has the word "var" that we will use when we want to declare one or more variables. Not surprisingly, that word is used to define the variable before using it.

Note: Although JavaScript does not force us to declare variables explicitly, it is advisable to declare them before using them and we will see from now on that it is also a good habit. In addition, in successive articles we will see that in some special cases, a script in which we have declared a variable and another in which we have not, will not produce exactly the same results, since the declaration does not affect the scope of the variables.

var operand1

var operand2

You can also assign a value to the variable when it is being declared

var operand1 = 23

var operand2 = 33

It is also allowed to declare several variables on the same line, provided they are separated by commas.

var operand1, operand2

Declaration of JavaScript Variables with Let and Const

From Javascript in modern versions (remember that JavaScript is a standard and that as it evolves over time), specifically in Javascript in its ES6 version, there are other ways to declare variables:

Let declaration: This new way of declaring variables affects their scope, since they are local to the block where they are being declared.

Const Declaration: Actually "const" does not declare a variable but a constant, which cannot change its value during the execution of a program.

Perhaps at this point in the Javascript manual it is not necessary to delve too deeply into these declaration models and for those who are learning we recommend focusing on the use of declarations with "var". However, if you want to have more information about these new types of variables, we explain them in the article Let and const: variables in ECMAScript 2015. If you want to see other news about the Javascript standard that came in 2015, we recommend reading the ES6 Manual.

Chapter 17.   *Definition of Arrays in JavaScript*

A nother thing we need to take a look at when we work in this language is what an array is all about. To keep it simple, an array is just going to be a structure of data that can contain our group of elements. In most coding languages including JavaScript, we will find that the items inside an array are usually the same type of data, such as a string or an integer. Collections are going to be used in order to help a computer program, or your coding language, organize and sort your data so that a set of values that are related can be sorted through or searched through well.

No matter what kind of coding language you decide to work with, you will find that keeping the data and the objects organized will be necessary. If you don't take care of these objects and types of data, they are going to float around the work you are doing, and you will run into some troubles in the code. The part of the system you are in will not be able to find the objects and classes they need and your order won't work.

But when you are working with many of the modern types of coding languages out there, including JavaScript and a few others, you are going to rely on a bit more organization than what we are going to find in some of the older languages. You need to make sure things are organized, and the set of values that are related are going to be easy to search through and sort through as much as you would like.

While the program is able to create a new variable, if it wanted, for all of the results that are found in it, this can really take up a lot of time and space in some of the codings you are doing, and it is definitely not going to be the most efficient method you can use here. Instead, you will find that storing all of the results (while we are still on the search engine example) in an array will be a more efficient method to use to pull up the results you want, while also managing your memory.

Now, there are going to be a few different parameters and properties that can come with the array you would like to create. Being able to make this come together and work the way you want is essential, and understanding what each of these properties is all about will be a great way to get a better understanding of what you can do with them. Some of the features that come along with your array object, along with information on what all of these means, includes:

1. Constructor: This will help us get back a reference to our array function, the one that was able to create the object.

2. Index: This will be the property in our array that will represent the zero-based index that will match up to that part inside of our string.

3. Input: This will be a property we are only going to see in specific arrays. When a range has been created by a regular expression and it all matches, then we are going to have this input.

4. Length: This will show us the number of elements we are going to be able to see in our array.

5. Prototype: We will discuss this one more in this guidebook, but this particular property will allow us a way to add methods and features to our object.

This may not make a lot of sense right now, but we are going to expand upon it a bit and see more about what we will be able to do with these arrays and the different parts that come with it. Before we move into this though, we need to take some time to talk about some of the array methods that are important to our code. There are a lot of different ways that happen with our object of an array, so let's take a look at what all of these mean.

1. Concat: This one will return to us a new array that will be comprised of not only this array but with the other values or ranges that we need.

2. Every(): This one will return true if we find that each and every element that falls in our array will satisfy the testing function that we provided.

3. Filter(): This one is responsible for creating a new array with all of the elements that fall into the current range for which the provided filtering function will give us honestly as the result.

4. forEach(): This one is responsible for calling up a function for each of the elements that are inside of our array.

5. indexOf(): This one will return the first (or the least) index that comes with the element that is inside of our array, as long as it is equal to the value that we specify. Or it will work with -1 if nothing is found to match in it.

6. Join(): This one will join together all of the elements of an array and can help turn these into a string.

7. lastIndexOf(): This one will return the previous, or the greatest, index of your element in the array as long as that element is equal to the value that we are trying to specify, or we will work with -1 if we can't find a match in the array.

8. Map(): This one is responsible for helping us to create a brand new array with the results of calling up a provided function of all the elements that fall into this array.

9. Pop(): This one will help us remove the last element out of our array and then will return the item that we want.

10. Push(): This one is nice because it is able to add in at least one, but sometimes more, elements to the end of your array and then will return to you the new length that this makes your array.

11. Reduce: This will apply the function that you want at the same time against two values of the array, going from the left side over to the right side, in order to reduce it by one amount.

12. reduceRight(): This will be the same idea, but instead of going from the left side to the right side, we are going to reverse this and go from the right side to the left side.

13. Reverse: This will be responsible for reversing the order that your array elements are going to be in. The first element in the array will become the last element, and then the part that was the last one will go to the beginning of the collection.

14. Shift(): This one will remove the first element out of your array and then will give you a return of that element.

15. Slice: This one will extract a section of your array and will give you a return that has a brand new collection in it.

16. Some(): This one will return true as long as you have one or more elements in the array that is able to satisfy the testing function that you provided.

17. toSource(): This one will help us to represent the source code that comes with our object.

18. Sort(): This one can be useful because it will help us to sort through all of the elements that come with our array.

19. Splice: This one will be there to help us to either add or remove the elements of the array.

20. toString(): This one will return a string that will represent the array and all of the elements that happen in it.

21. Unshift: This final one will take some time to add in one or more elements to the beginning of our array and then will let us know what the new length of this array will be when it is done.

As we can see here, there are a lot of possibilities that we can work with when it comes to handling the arrays that show up in our codes. These arrays are going to help us to hold onto some of the data that we have more efficiently and will ensure that we can put it all together and pull out the elements that we need and want without a lot of struggle along the way. Make sure to take a look at some of the methods and functions available with these arrays, especially with JavaScript, so you know how to use them for some of your own needs as well.

Chapter 18. <u>*What to Do Next?*</u>

H opefully by now, you have a somewhat solid understanding of how HTML and CSS work together. It's important to understand that we've only scratched the surface of HTML and CSS.

What's important to take away from this book is not to memorize all the different elements in HTML and properties in CSS. It's to be able to understand the two and how they work hand-in-hand.

There's no need to learn every single element and property. It will do more harm than good and chances are, you're not going to absorb all that information. That's precisely why I didn't want this book to be a 500-page manual of all the HTML elements and CSS properties. When you learn English, you don't just open up a dictionary and start reading. Coding is no different.

The critical skill that hopefully you have by now is to be able to look at new HTML elements and CSS properties and deduce and understand their functionalities from the code.

Debugging

By far the most powerful tool in all of HTML and CSS is the ability to identify and fix errors. If you master this skill, it doesn't really matter how much you know and it doesn't matter if your initial code is filled with mistakes because it's the ability to spot and fix errors that brings you to your end result. It's also going through this process that allows you to absorb and understand concepts truly.

When it comes to debugging, your best friend is a browser developer tool. All of the main browsers have developer tools for you to look at the HTML and CSS of any given page you load. Safari has web inspector, Firefox has firebug, and Chrome has inspected element. We're going to showcase Chrome's inspect element.

So you're coding away and you open up your web page in your browser and something's not right. It looks off but you have no idea where you've made an error. Open up inspect element (right click -> click on inspect element).

Inspect element will show you exactly why the code is displayed in the way it is. As the mouse hover over the elements in the HTML on the left side, it will highlight the corresponding area in your window. Clicking on an HTML element, will show the CSS rule that corresponds to it on the right hand side. If you drag down the 'compound style' tab, it shows exactly the property values that are given and where they're coming from. A lot of the times, CSS rules are passed down from parent elements, and with this, you can see which parent rule is resulting in the given value.

Apart from the occasional careless mistake that takes a second to fix once you have realized it, the more trivial errors are always related to the CSS properties display and position. Things like font-size, colors, borders, etc. are all one-step fixes. Display and position can get way more complicated. It's by far the hardest concept to grasp for HTML and CSS. If you know display and position inside out, you're a HTML/CSS master.

The reason display and positioning can get complicated is because of the number of variables in play. Your output is not only indicative of the value of one property, but a combination of many. The display, position, and float properties of sister elements all work hand-in-hand. Not only that, but they also correlate to the properties of the parent element. Debugging this is not as simple as looking at one element. You must look at the bigger picture.

Here's how you should debug display and positioning errors.

Isolate your error. Figure out which element is resulting in the wrong display or position. Look at your declarations of not only this element, but also the sister and parent elements. When you debug display and position, it's important to realize that you have to look beyond just the specific element.

If you have an idea why the error is present, try and fix it in your browser. Remember, you can change and update values in your inspect element and the changes will be reflected live. If you're right and the changes correct the error, go to your code and make the same changes.

If you're completely clueless and have no clue why your position or display is wrong, do some research. Turn to Google and search for your problem. Simple searches like 'absolute position center issue' or 'can't see fixed position element' will render plenty of results. Literally every question that you can think of related to HTML and CSS has been asked and answered online. Tutorials and forums are great places to find answers. Use them hand-in-hand.

As for forums, the place for everything and anything coding related is stackoverflow.com. Chances are your answers will be there, but if not, there are plenty of more resources out there.

Learning More

You're in a position now where you understand the language of HTML and CSS. What separates you from someone who's a master of HTML and CSS is simply experience. The way to learn and be good at coding is to code. Reading books or online manuals on all the specific rules is pointless. What you should do is set out to create a product. Even if you're not completely sure how to complete it, just get the ball rolling. Your generic questions will turn into specific questions, which you'll be able to find the answers to.

One last thing to keep in mind:

You can look for any code on any website, that's the beauty of the HTML and CSS language. Your browser is the most powerful tool for learning. When you come across a website that has a spectacular design or something you want to implement, you can look at how it's done right in your browser. Take advantage of the power of your browser.

You can also use this for debugging. If you're drawing a blank for a display and position error, resort to reputable websites and see how they do it. The top technology websites spend a lot of money to hire the best of the best to code their website. Take advantage of this. Go to their websites and see how they style things. If there's something that Google or Facebook or

Amazon or Twitter does that intrigues you, you can't go wrong learning from how they do it. There are no more hidden secrets and techniques when it comes to HTML & CSS. Everything is out there.

Chapter 19. <u>**Art of Computer Programming**</u>

B ecoming the best programmers depends on many factors besides learning programming techniques in classes or over the internet. In simple terms, it is not about programming as most beginners think. From my experience, your level of impacts plays a lot in determining the level of your success or how best you are as a programmer. Truly, people will not measure your experience from how happy you look when doing programing projects but how your programming projects are impacting the lives of many people in society. For example, there are some people who always feel happy after spending the whole day without doing any programming tasks while others feel unhappy if they do not handle any projects. Also, drinking alcohol everyday can make a person feel happy. Therefore, you level of experience and knowledge does not on how happy you are but how you use the learned skills.

Several studies have proved that slacking off in computer programming not only makes person's programming logic weaker but also destroys his/her tempo. Normally, we miss many things when we don't attend the classes just like drinking coke every day ruins both our teeth and internal organs. Just like alcohol has impacts in our bodies, your success in programming is measured through its impacts. We will see you as a weaker programmer if you do not use the learned programming skills to create positive impact to you or to the society.

Levels of Impacts Resulting from Programming

Ideally, there are different levels of impacts we can use to determine how perfect you are with programming. Yes, most programmers do not know that their programming knowledge is judged on how it impacts them or the society. The following are levels of the impacts:

First Level of Impact: You/ a person

One of the step to determine how you can measure the impact is by looking at the effects of programming has made on an individual. It is not only the simplest way but also very important since all programmers have goals in their mind before starting programming. Usually, you engage in various activities or jobs because you want a result not nothing. For example, we take our children to schools with two reasons; (1) get job in their future lives to live better life, and (2) obtain knowledge that will help them associate with other people in the society. It is important to know that doing something without a purpose makes you to experience an unexpected result on your way. Therefore, the impacts of programming on you show how best and successful you are as a programmer.

Relationships in Life

Do you know that programming can cause certain impacts on your relationship? In order to determine the effects of programming on your relationship, we always look at how close you are to your love, friends, and other people in the society. Some people chose to be software programmers because it is their passion while others chose it because of peer pressure or their parents forced them.

Another main reason why people chose programming is getting jobs. In most cases, we work in projects, deliver them, and earn income once users use them. As programmers, we are only required to maintain the projects if there are crashes or bugs. This gives us more time for our relationships. Truly, human life is all about relationship but not how much we earn per day. You may be earning five or six digits but you are not happy at all because you lack freedom to associate with people, particularly your love ones and relatives. Let me tell you, people get more fulfillments out of life when there are some people whom they love and care for. You should spend your earnings with the people you love. As such, work is supposed to improve your relationship with love and relatives.

Impacts On Your Health and Life

In this modern life, your mind and body are the two main assets you must value most. Both body and mind are irreplaceable in our life. Therefore, you must take care of our mind and bodies to avoid them deteriorating over the time. Surely, every person wants to have a longer life, and as such, it is important to consider health when measuring how best you are as a programmer. You career as a programmer would not be either good if you are not healthy.

Money is worthless when compared to our mind and health. I tell you, money will always come on your way when you develop a good mind, which include practicing daily to solve problems, looking for answers, and thinking deep and creatively. You should not only get enough sleep but also build a habit that will train your mind just like writing and reading books. Make coding to be a favorite way to train you. The best programmers always spend at least thirty to forty minutes per day on programming. This is very important to their health. We can say health is your life and you should take care of it in order to live longer.

Having Full Enjoyment

We have seen previously that happy is not the measurement of the success of a person; it is only a part of it, though we need it. You can increase your productivity in programming by engaging in things that you enjoy. What do I mean? I mean that a person can be more productivity in his/her programming work if he/she gives himself/herself a chance to enjoy life. Being more productivity in programming has more impact too. In addition, you should know that there is a great difference between passion and hobbies. While hobby refers to doing something you enjoy, passion refers to thing you like doing throughout the life. For example, my passion is coding and my hobby is learning Japanese language. I always study Japanese when I am a little bit frustrated with some complex coding. This gives enough time to refresh my mind before diving back into the world of coding.

Giving yourself enough time to relax or take a break to make your brain work on the problem subconsciously is always the right thing to do. But what do you do if you find it hard to solve the problem even after relaxing? It is easy. Just give your brain enough time to solve the problem in the background. In fact, this is one of the main reasons why most ideas come in our minds when we are eating, showering, or drinking tea.

The Second Level of Impact

Now let us discuss how we can measure you programming level using the second level of impact.

Impact On Others

Before you consider yourself as the best programmers, it is important to ask yourself about the impact you cause to other people when you are coding. Okay, you may be like that you know how to code because it is the most useful tool available for impacting the lives of many people positively. You can impact people by either enabling them to get data easily, improve their websites, or increase sales. One of the goals in programming is helping other people achieve their objectives. You will be recognized as the best programmers when you help others and organizations to succeed and at the same time meeting your goals. I know it is sometimes difficult for most programmers, but you can become the best programmers if you do this.

Giving Purpose to Other People

Every person has their own purpose (known or unknown) in life, and this is seen when an individual dedicates his/her life to doing certain thing. For programmers, their purpose is revealed when they engage in building projects and software. Now, let us ask ourselves where this sense of purpose comes from. In normal cases, our purpose comes from the surrounding, society, friends, and internet. For example, we develop an interest in programming after we encounter those who do programming and have achieved a lot in their lives. To be precise, they are the main people who can inspire you to engage in programming. But what will you do in case those people fail to give us ideas? There is a higher chance that you will not have a right purpose. We all have different purpose in our lives and that is the main reason why we all do different work. We were not born to do the same job. While some people are born to be developers, others are born to be doctors, teachers, or politicians.

According to Mark Zuckerberg during his Harvard Commencement Speech, people must have a generational challenge for our society to continue moving forward. We should not only create new jobs for the youth or our people but promote a sense of purpose. However, it is not easy to have a purpose for yourself. You should also create a sense of purpose to other people in the society. Let us take the following example. You need to hire workers if you build a company. These workers play a significant role to the growth of your company. It is, however, your responsibility, as an employer, not only to give them a sense of purpose but also help them to grow in society.

Conclusion

C reating a web page is something that has been wreathed in mysticism and cyber mumbo jumbo for years, but I hope that I've shown you that it's not as scary as you might think. In fact, HTML is actually fairly straight forward. If you're looking for a hobby that can really accomplish something and is easy to explain, then you've come to the right place. These are the foundations for you to build your web page and push on to greater things like CSS, Java, JavaScript, C++, and the list goes on and on. Remember, that you can never really get in over your head if you master and truly understand what it is that you're working on in the moment.

If something doesn't make sense to you or is confusing, my best suggestion to you is to open up your TextEdit or Notepad and start working on it. Pull it up in your browser and have a look at what it does for your page. Taking everything step by step will inevitably lead you to the path of success. There is never a reason to jump ahead without fully understanding what it is that you've done.

All of these programming languages are quite vast in their own right. However, since they are also simple and easy, you should not have too much of a problem mastering them. With hard work and a bit of time, you will be able to create full-fledged websites in no time at all. The concepts will help you understand and apply the different scope of variables, invent types, loops and arrays, form structure, positioning, and so on.

Of course, this book should have given you enough to have a good base for all three languages. You should have already seen the hello world examples and noted how easy they are. As such, you should have no problems with the basic syntax for each language.

You will have come across the basic functions, statements, and tags that are commonly used in these languages. More importantly, you should no longer have any problem using them in a web page of your creation.

In HTML, you came to know how a simple web page can be written and filled with content. Then, with CSS, you will have been able to stylize that web page and make it look attractive.

Finally, JavaScript allowed you to make your web page more interactive. As such, your web page should now be looking and feeling a lot like the web pages you have previously admired.

As we get to the end, you have learned quite a lot about web development, and you learned the creation of functional and well-structured HTML documents as well as styling, color usage, layouts, and typography using tags. Practice what you have learned because practice is the best way to learn.

With everything that I have presented to you, you should be able to get the grasp on the beginnings of a web page and if you can get the beginning, it's just a matter of taking the next step piece by piece. So good luck and get out there and make an amazing web page.

I hope you have learned something!

Made in the USA
Las Vegas, NV
17 January 2025

16529656R00319